Praise for *Going to Seed*

'This is a fascinating, funny and moving record of an extraordinary life lived in extraordinary times.' **GEORGE MONBIOT**

'Simon Fairlie is one of a kind. *Going to Seed* is brilliant, bloody-minded, funny and full of hard-learned lessons that we would do well to heed.' **PAUL KINGSNORTH**

'Authentic counter-cultural voices, true to a set of consistent values and principles shaped over a lifetime, are few and far between. Simon Fairlie's voice is one of those, highlighting so much of what is wrong about our current model of progress.' **JONATHON PORRITT**, cofounder, Forum for the Future; author of *Hope in Hell*

'Pull up a chair by a rustic fireside, with a glass of local cider in hand, and allow master raconteur Simon Fairlie to regale you with tales from his extraordinary life. It is so important that the great modern activists capture their stories and the rarely-written histories of progressive social change. These are the shoulders on which we all stand, and there is much wisdom to be discovered here.' **ROB HOPKINS**, author of *From What Is to What If*; founder, Transition movement

'Beautifully written—both informative and entertaining, and I found myself laughing aloud on numerous occasions. This book is an essential read and a source of inspiration for anyone who ever has been, or ever hopes to be, involved in any kind of "alternative society".' **MIKE ABBOTT**, author and pioneer of the green woodwork revival in the UK

'Sooner or later anyone who gets involved in low-impact housing or agriculture in Britain, and perhaps beyond, will find a path through the weeds already mown for them by the well-honed scythe of the pioneering Simon Fairlie. In his wonderful new book, Simon takes us behind the scenes with a warts-and-all personal memoir about an unconventional life lived with gusto. At the same time, and without seeming to try, he sketches a social history of postwar England of surprising thoroughness. Most importantly, while it's debatable how much tuning in resulted from the dropping out of many in his generation, in these pages Simon forges an acute and nuanced political analysis out of his counter-cultural experiences that's of urgent mainstream relevance today.' CHRIS SMAJE, author of *A Small Farm Future*

'An ideological romp through a life well lived, as irascible, rebellious and perspicacious as the man himself. Genuinely gripping.' MADDY HARLAND, editor and cofounder of *Permaculture* magazine

'A fascinating insight into the life of a true pioneer. This energetic memoir charts half a century of environmental resistance, from almost accidental activism to becoming one of the most powerful advocates for sustainable land use in my lifetime. Without his inspiration, I would never have been able to introduce One Planet Developments in Wales.' JANE DAVIDSON, author of *#futuregen: Lessons from a Small Country* and former Welsh minister

'A riveting memoir of a timeless English radicalism; a chronicle of insight, wit and wisdom of the land.' ALASTAIR McINTOSH, author of *Soil and Soul;* fellow, Centre for Human Ecology

GOING TO SEED

GOING TO SEED

A COUNTERCULTURE MEMOIR

Simon Fairlie

Chelsea Green Publishing
White River Junction, Vermont
London, UK

Excerpted from Shelter ©1973 by Lloyd Kahn. Shelter Publications, Bolinas, California.
Reprinted with permission.

Commissioning Editor: Jonathan Rae
Project Manager: Patricia Stone
Developmental Editor: Brianne Goodspeed
Copy Editor: Susan Pegg
Proofreader: Laura Booth
Designer: Melissa Jacobson

Printed in the United States of America.
First printing January 2022.
10 9 8 7 6 5 4 3 2 1   22 23 24 25 26

Library of Congress Cataloging-in-Publication Data
Names: Fairlie, Simon, author.
Title: Going to seed : a counterculture memoir / Simon Fairlie.
Description: White River Junction, Vermont : Chelsea Green Publishing, [2022]
Identifiers: LCCN 2021051827 | ISBN 9781645020615 (paperback) |
  ISBN 9781645020622 (ebook)
Subjects: LCSH: Fairlie, Simon. | Hippies—Great Britain—Biography. |
  Journalists—Great Britain—Biography. | Farmers—Great Britain—Biography. |
  Counterculture—Great Britain—History. | Environmentalism—Great Britain—
  History. | Great Britain—Social conditions—1945–
Classification: LCC HQ799.8.G7 F35 2022 | DDC 305.5/68092
  [B]—dc23/eng/20211206
LC record available at https://lccn.loc.gov/2021051827

Chelsea Green Publishing
85 North Main Street, Suite 120
White River Junction, Vermont USA

Somerset House
London, UK

www.chelseagreen.com

'What happened to the flower children? They went to seed.'

– Remark attributed to Timothy Leary

Contents

Introduction

In 1976 my father, Henry Fairlie, a Fleet Street journalist who had emigrated to the United States some ten years previously, wrote a book called *The Spoiled Child of the Western World*. Its subtitle is *The Miscarriage of the American Idea in Our Time*, and its purpose was to defend an agenda of democratic humanism, laid down by the founders of the republic, that he viewed as a beacon for oppressed humanity. It was critical of the solipsism and self-infatuation of the then trendy, leftist counterculture, but equally, and prophetically, of the elitism of the nascent neoconservative lobby.

It was not his best work, and it received little attention. It is over-written and obsessively punctuated by gratuitous quotations as if composed by a desperate A level student. He relies for evidence on what people have said, rather than what they have done. He was often a fine writer, but none of his books carried the punch of the best of his articles. The only book of his that still sells well is called *The Seven Deadly Sins Today*, and it is remembered, not by the political analysts for whom he normally wrote, but by small-town Christian pastors of a liberal persuasion.

I recently reread *The Spoiled Child of the Western World*, because some sections of the book seem to be addressed to me, at least obliquely. I felt so at the time, and still think so. When the book was published in 1976 I was twenty-five, and my father and I had not spoken for about five years. To his dismay I had dropped out of university and hitch-hiked to India; on

1

my return after a footloose two years, I settled on a commune in the South of France. It was another six years before we got in touch. It is inconceivable that when writing the passages critical of what he called 'the Movement' he did not have his disappointment with his only son in mind. Moreover, there are passages in the book that are repetitions of things he had said to me before in discussions and letters.

When I read the book a year or two after it was published I was not impressed. My reaction was incredulity that anyone could write in 1976 about the hippie movement and the 'American idea' without referring to the Vietnam War. There is just one passing mention of that conflict throughout the entire book, whereas Thomas Jefferson features on nineteen pages. His prescient warnings about the rise of the far right passed over me since I had never heard of Irving Kristol, Daniel Bell, or any of the early promoters of that tendency, and Ronald Reagan was yet to happen.

I am now twenty years older than my father was when he wrote that book, and in a better position to assess the accuracy of his thesis. With the benefit of hindsight, there is no doubt that he underestimated the change in consciousness that was at least partially triggered through the hippie movement, and failed to anticipate the benign influence it would have in a number of spheres. He focused too much on what the movement said, oblivious to what it did. Had he taken the *Whole Earth Catalog* as his main source of information, rather than Jerry Rubin, he would have had to reach very different conclusions. On the other hand he did pinpoint the hippie philosophy's primary weakness, a narcissistic obsession with the self, which is still in evidence today in what remains of the movement, but has also spread through mainstream culture.

My father's critique of 'the spoiled child' is a useful spring-board from which to launch this memoir. It proposes an intergenerational dialogue, to which I can respond both in the general, as participant in a historical movement, and in the particular, as a son that was spoilt.

My focus is on matters of politics (in the wider sense of the term), social relations and economics (i.e. work). It is a political memoir by someone who never entered politics (in the narrow sense of the term). As far as is consistent with the narrative, I have tried to keep personal relations out of it, especially my love life – the best bits of which are beyond my powers of description, and the worst bits too embarrassing to mention. Some people who were important in my personal life don't feature in the narrative at all.

People's memories of shared moments can diverge over time. I apologise to anyone whose memory of the events described differs markedly from my own. Where I suspect that certain people may see things very differently from me, I have changed their names.

A Note on Nomenclature

My father mostly referred to 'the Movement', which in his view spanned a relatively small spectrum in US history, stretching from Students for a Democratic Society to the Yippies. Other terms in use at the time included the Alternative Society, the Counterculture, the Underground, Flower Children, Freaks, and so on; but none of these, except possibly counterculture, are in current widespread use. I quite liked the French term *les Marginaux*, but that too seems to have died away. The one word that has stuck is Hippie. People talk about hippie kids, or ageing Hippies and we know what they mean. It is sometimes a term of ridicule or abuse – 'bloody hippie' – though there can be a hint of affection when used in this way (such as one might evince for Neil in the TV series *The Young Ones*).

It comes from Black and later beatnik slang 'hip' or 'hep', meaning 'in the know' (as in Blossom Dearie's line, 'When it was hip to be hep, I was hep'), but the addition of the suffix '-pie' or sometimes '-py' makes it sound juvenile and fey. And confusingly, the more robust sounding 'hipster' has (like that other jazz word 'cool') come back into use, signifying a fashionable urban bohemian. I prefer the more derisory French *bobo*, short for 'bourgeois bohemian', an expression I will use later. But 'hippie' is the word that has stuck, and I'm not going to try to coin another.

CHAPTER ONE

In Praise of the 1950s

Spoilt or not, I was born privileged: a middle-class, white, male baby-boomer in a prosperous country, at a peaceful period in European history. Not many people are so fortunate.

I also drew a good hand as far as my parents were concerned. My father Henry, who was intellectually brilliant, controversial, charming and a minor celebrity, was a great role model for a lad. Since he was also a heavy drinker, hopeless with money, inclined to go AWOL and an appalling husband, he might have been a disaster as a father, had it not been for my mother, Lisette. Described as 'long-suffering' by more than one contemporary, she was loving, dependable, good with money (when she had any) and held the family, which included my two younger sisters, together for seventeen years until it fell apart, more or less by mutual agreement.

Henry was born in 1924 into a Scottish family of six siblings of which he was the black sheep. The family had deep Presbyterian and farming roots, but Henry's father James also broke the mould. He became a journalist, originally for a Dundee paper, but then he moved to Fleet Street and worked for the *Daily Express*. He was a heavy drinker and died young, when my father was thirteen. After a dinner with Lord Beaverbrook, he was bundled into a cab to take him home to his wife; when the taxi arrived he was dead in the back.

Had he been born ten years earlier Henry's spirit of youthful rebellion might have taken him to revolutionary Spain. Had he been born twenty years later I suspect he might have been part of 'The Movement' that he critiqued in *Spoiled Child*. But the generation that came of age at about the end of the Second World War had no beacon of left-wing hope to follow, just revelations of the horrors of Stalin's Russia. There were bohemian tendencies amongst the Fleet Street set he moved in, a touch of the Angry Young Men, but the dominant flavour of their politics was Conservative.

Henry was already writing editorials for *The Times* in his early twenties. But he made his name with a piece written in 1955 for *The Spectator*, which analysed how the elite of the time had moved to protect the families of Guy Burgess and Donald Maclean, Foreign Office civil servants who had spied for the Soviet Union, and then fled there. His article made 'the Establishment' a household term for what he defined as 'the whole matrix of official and social relations within which power is exercised'. Yet it is an unexpectedly slight piece, which does little more than assign a name to the bleedin' obvious. Henry makes no attempt to examine what privileges the establishment might be trying to protect, let alone why two of its members should devote their lives to fighting against it.

These matters, of course, were of no concern to a young child. I was also only dimly aware of the domestic chaos my mother had to cope with. My father's policy towards letters in brown envelopes was to throw them into the bin unopened. Rent and bills were left unpaid so that rounds in El Vino's wine bar and late night taxi fares could be bought. We were more than once evicted from accommodation for non-payment of rent or mortgage: on one occasion, when I returned from boarding school at the end of term, I was met at Lewes station by my mother who told me that the house had been repossessed, along with most of my books and my clockwork train set, and we were to stay with friends in London. But Henry always managed eventually to find somewhere else, partly on the strength of being a well-known journalist, and partly by being charming.

Sometimes he would disappear completely leaving the family with little or no money. When I was about six he put my mother, my infant sister and me into a posh hotel off Fleet Street, and then failed to turn up for about four days. Since my mother had no money, we enjoyed splendid breakfasts on the hotel tab, then ate almost nothing for the rest of the day. On another occasion Henry was a panellist on *Any Questions?* I believe it was the occasion, still repeated by the BBC, when he talked obliquely about the Suez Crisis even though it was subject to some sort of legal blackout. Meanwhile Inland Revenue were seeking him for non-payment of bills, and at the end of the programme he was arrested, handcuffed and taken to prison. When my mother was questioned about the matter at the time, she remarked, 'At least I know where he is.'

At other moments of crisis I got farmed out. I stayed with an aunt and uncle in Barnet, North London, where I did a term at the local primary school; with George Gale of the *Daily Express* (allegedly and believably the model for *Private Eye*'s Lunchtime O'Booze) and his equally terrifying wife Pat; and with Kingsley and Hilly Amis in Swansea, where I also did a term at the local school, along with their sons Philip and Martin. This was just before Henry had an affair with Hilly. The main things I remember about Kingsley were that he had a 78 rpm record of 'Rock Around the Clock', and that he let us kids smoke cigarettes at weekends – the front cover of Martin's autobiography *Experience* has a photo of him about eight years old with a fag hanging out of his mouth.

By the time I was eight I had lived in ten homes and been to six schools, plus a period of 'home schooling'. This seemed normal, and not the least bit upsetting: I was astonished to be told that some kids never moved house at all. I had got pretty good at adapting to new schools, but this didn't prepare me for what was to follow.

———

As far as I can gather there was an arrangement between my parents that my father would have the final word about the education of his son, and my mother about her daughters. This meant that at the age of eight, against my mother's better judgement, I was sent to a 'preparatory' boarding school, whereas my sisters went to local day schools.

Boarding schools are gregarious. In the 1950s, Seaford, a small town on the South coast between Brighton and Eastbourne, was to boarding schools what Hay-on-Wye is to bookshops today. There were about eight boys' prep schools, plus a couple for girls, each with about one hundred pupils. You could see all of them in their institutional finery on Sunday mornings, when crocodile lines of uniformed children would converge on St Peter's church, where the vicar led a special school service, for which he was rewarded with a heap of bags full of threepenny bits in the collection tray.

The purpose of these prep schools was to 'prepare' their charges for public school, then Oxbridge (ideally) and a career in the upper strata of British society. This involved endowing them with a classical education and instilling them with moral fibre, through a regime founded on discipline and privation. Not that St Wilfrid's, my school, could rival the levels of brutality that George Orwell suffered in his pre-war prep school in Eastbourne. Corporal punishment was meted out with a measure of moderation, and little evident sadism: I held the respected position of most caned boy in the school in my last year, with just eleven beatings to my credit, though the previous incumbent had received more than thirty.

Instead, life at St Wilfrid's was characterised by relentless regimentation of a kind one might have expected at a borstal – the prisons I have since stayed in have all had regimes more relaxed than that of my boarding school. Everything, from the moment you woke up in the dormitory in the morning, to the moment lights went out in the evening was structured and monitored. Everything had to be inspected and 'passed'. Matron passed your back to see you had properly entered the cold shower, and then again to ensure that you had dried it; you bared your teeth before her and showed both sides of your hands to prove that they were clean; the dormitory monitor passed the bottom sheet of your bed as you made it, then the bed-making in its entirety, the brushing of your hair and the knotting of your tie.

At breakfast, masters sat at the end of each table, checking that you ate the food you were given. Then, during an institution called 'morning prep', the register was read out while pupils performed what might have been called homework were there a home to go to. When your name was read out you were given a 'ticket', a metal number from one to ten screwed to a piece of wood the size of a cigarette box. This was the number of the toilet where you were supposed to go and defecate. If you didn't want to perform, you had to pretend to, because the master-on-duty would be prowling around checking that every boy was doing his duty. So ingrained was this institution that the school euphemism for taking a shit was 'having a ticket'.

And so it went on throughout the day, everything timed to the minute, inspected and passed: assembly and morning service, drill, lessons, washing for lunch, finishing your food, changing for sport or Scouts, then washing and changing back again, more lessons, tea, evening prep, more washing and bathing, till lights out. And so it continued for twelve interminable weeks at a time.

Deviation from the prescribed routine was regarded as insubordination, if not rebellion. You could run, but only at allocated times in allocated spaces – i.e. at sports and drill; not down the corridors. If you learnt the piano you had to start with 'Dancing Round the Maypole' and graduate to 'Für Elise'; attempting to play pop songs or experimenting with boogie-woogie riffs would earn you a minus mark. The only comics allowed were the wholesome Hulton Press publications *Eagle* and *Swift*, and a dreary black and white throwback to the Edwardian era called *Arthur Mee's Children's Newspaper.* Sweets were rationed to four a day, while money was strictly forbidden, and not much use anyway, since the only time you were allowed out was on the detested crocodile-formation walks. Sweets were therefore the currency of the school's black economy, and could buy illicit comics, protective friendship, or a bet on a horse in the 'sweet-stake' on Derby Day. The ration of four sweets a day was doled out by 'sweet monitors', senior boys whose coveted position provided ample scope for bribery and corruption.

There was some relief from this on the three weekends in the middle of a term when your parents were allowed to visit and take you out for the afternoon. And of course there were the holidays. The difficulty here was meeting other kids, since for most children the main conduit for meeting friends is their day school. As for girls, I didn't meet any. Aside from my younger sisters, my world until the age of thirteen was a girl-free environment, not a great help in the years to come.

The other welcome form of escape was to fall ill and be consigned to the sickroom, a couple of small dormitories in the attic where none of the normal rules applied. Here, there were no lessons, no sports, no pressure to finish your meal, no cold showers, or regimented ablutions and defecations. Instead there was a radio and a huge pile of *Beano*, *Dandy*, *Beezer* and *Topper* comic annuals; even a few of the highly prized *War Picture Library*. And here, Matron revealed herself to be quite a nice person. It didn't matter how ill you felt, it was better than being at school.

But the best thing of all about the sickroom, was that you met boys of a different age. An intrinsic failing of many school systems is that they stream pupils according to age, so they rarely get the chance to socialise with older or younger kids (especially at a boarding school). In environments or countries where school is less dominant you find children of all ages running around together. The younger kids learn from the older ones, and the older kids look after the younger ones.

The sickroom was my only opportunity to socialise with older boys, who down below wouldn't be seen dead by their peers talking to a squirt like me, unless it was to exercise prefectorial authority. Here I learnt about crystal radios, and Airfix kits, and why Elvis Presley was cooler than Tommy Steele. Here I played 'Dare, Love, Kiss or Promise' for the first time. And here, if anywhere, was where I learnt the facts of life. It was, after all, in the sickroom during my first term at the school, that Susan, the freckled sixteen-year-old from town who worked as one of the maids, was discovered committing some unspeakable act with one of the older boys, and summarily dismissed. After that, the school employed only dumpy middle-aged Spanish women – and all further capers, of which there were many, were homosexual and tacitly tolerated by the housemaster.

Because of the paradise in the attic, I spent a lot of my time and energy trying to be ill, and got quite good at it. Never a term went by when I did not enjoy some time in the sickroom. I may even have benefited from it, as I now appear to have a strong immune system. But at the time it never occurred to me that there might be something perverse about an upbringing that made me want to be ill.

To maintain sanity in this somewhat grim world you needed something upon which to ground your self-respect. It might be academic achievement, or prowess at sports, or popularity with your mates. It might be something less publicly acknowledged, such as an ability to draw, or an interest in the workings of model steam engines.

But if you didn't have anything like that and were at a loss, there was no family to support you. There were boys who had been dumped there by parents living on the other side of the world and who saw them perhaps once a year. There were boys of eight or nine who were so disturbed they wet their bed at night – not a clever thing to do in a dormitory full of your peers. There were boys who masturbated obsessively, keeping others awake with the creaking of their bed. There were boys who were bullied and in the absence of parents had no one to turn to. A recurrent form of protest, that unhappy boys could carry out anonymously behind a locked door, was to smear shit all over the lavatory walls – a tactic later employed by IRA prisoners.

At one point there was a sudden spate of boys running away – three in one term. None of them came back. After the third escapee, the headmaster delivered the school a sermon on the matter in the school chapel, emphasising what a cowardly thing it is to run away. 'And I must warn you all,' he proclaimed in conclusion, 'that any boy attempting to run away will be immediately *expelled*.' The absurdity of invoking expulsion as a deterrent was not lost on us, and we knew that the real cowards were those who did not have the guts to run away.

————

I hated St Wilfrid's when I was there, and I detested it still more after I left and found that school and life could be different. However in 1998 I found myself by chance in Seaford, and decided to see what had happened to it. Unsurprisingly, it had shut down, and the main school building had been demolished. I was only able to recognise where it had stood because the building that had accommodated the older boys' dormitories had been spared and converted into flats. In place of the school were cul-de-sacs of detached houses each with its lawn, garage and TV aerial.

What did surprise me was that instead of exultation at the demise of this ghastly institution, I felt dismay at its loss. Once there had been an Edwardian mansion, with its annexes, gymnasium, chapel, workshops, lawns, playgrounds, cricket fields, vegetable gardens, hedges, Scout hut, fives court and model boating pond; now all this had been destroyed so that a handful of retired gentlefolk could live out their days in bungalows. What, I wondered, did the demolition men say to one another as they sledge-hammered the oak panelling in the dining room, emblazoned with the names of head boys and sports captains dating back to 1910 and threw the shards in the skip? Did the bulldozer driver, who in a matter of hours turned the cricket pitch into a building site, reflect that he was obliterating eighty years of conscientious grassland management?

What hit me was the realisation that a community had been destroyed; not a particularly nice one perhaps, but a community nonetheless, with a history, in stark contrast to the line of lace-curtained bungalows fenced off from one another in their fastidious gardens.

During term time St Wilfrid's had provided a home for some eighty-five boys and the majority of the members of staff. It provided employment for a wide range of people: Mr Darwall-Smith, a former Sussex County cricketer who owned the place; Mr Moon, the portly, puce-faced headmaster; his sister Mary who guarded the sweet cupboard; the wayward junior teachers fresh out of university; the matrons, groundsmen and gardeners; Russell, the long-suffering janitor who had to clean the toilets; and the rotund Spanish maids. Most of these people were fed by the school, which grew its own vegetables in immaculately hoed rows of a length and order that would put the raised beds in some modern communities to shame. The school repaired its own clothes in a room where matrons worked treadle sewing machines, and provided its own amusements in the form of a film show on the Sunday evenings when there was not evensong in the school chapel.

It was in these respects a self-sufficient community, and, by modern standards, a sustainable one. The ambient temperature maintained in winter was far from toasty, though adequate for kids in woollen sweaters and blazers, and teachers in tweeds. Given the number of boys in classrooms and dormitories, the heating bill per person must have been modest. As for cars, they were virtually non-existent. Darwall-Smith had a smart shooting wagon, which he kept at his home across the road; the maths master occasionally rocked up in his ageing Alvis; and sometimes one of the young masters living on site would try to wring a few months' life out of an ailing 'Baby Austin'. That was more or less it. Few if any of the staff who lived off site drove to work, and from one end of term to the other we kids never went anywhere except on foot.

All of which was unsurprising for the 1950s, which, arguably, was the decade that best matched a decent standard of living to a sustainable way of life. There is some nostalgia within green circles for the 1940s, mainly because the war and subsequent rationing imposed a healthy diet (by modern standards) and very low tolerance of waste. But the forties were austere, and many Europeans spent the first half of the decade trying to kill one another, and the second half hungry. The fifties, by contrast, maintained many of the environmentally benign habits of the previous decade while providing an altogether better standard of living, not for everybody perhaps, but for the bulk of the population. 'Most of our people have never had it so good,' Harold Macmillan proclaimed in 1957. This was hardly a radical achievement after twenty years of slump, war and rationing. Meanwhile social attitudes only shifted slowly over the decade and life could be more complicated if you were black, or gay, or female or a child born out of wedlock.

Like 80 per cent of British households in the 1950s, my parents did not own a car, nor did they aspire to. Neither of them learnt to drive. This was no handicap even when we lived some distance into the Sussex countryside. Southdown provided an hourly bus service along main rural roads. There were no bus stops; you could hail them anywhere except on a blind corner. They connected with a railway service that had not yet been eviscerated by Marples and Beeching. We could get from our rural home outside Lewes to London's Victoria Station in about an hour and a half, which is roughly how long it takes today. Most rural kids got to school by walking to the bus clutching a penny-halfpenny for the fare. There was no school bus because there was a regular omnibus; and there was no traffic congestion round the school gates at 9 am and 3 pm because the 'school run', which interrupts the day for so many modern parents, didn't exist.

Meanwhile bulky goods were supplied by delivery. The milkman came daily, the postman came twice a day, and the jolly baker came twice weekly. The grocer, greengrocer, butcher and coalman all delivered to order. A shopping expedition with my mother in Lewes included placing orders at the grocer and the greengrocer, which would be delivered later that day so she didn't have to lug it back on the bus.

In towns, where shops were closer, deliveries were unnecessary, apart from the daily milkman, and the horse-drawn coalmen, who loaded black hessian sacks of anthracite onto their back from their dray and lugged them up garden paths.

Sometimes they took a break at the end of the street, munching smutty sandwiches while the horse ate from a nosebag.

Another daily visitor was the paper boy who brought the news and comment that people now find online, and promptly enough. As a reporter, my father could cable in a story in the afternoon from somewhere like Addis Ababa, which would be recorded by shorthand typists, laid out in letterpress, printed in Fleet Street, sent out by night train, and delivered by lads on bicycles to millions of households the next morning.

The dustbin men came as well, though it is doubtful how much they had to take away beyond dust and ashes. There wasn't a great deal of packaging and none of it was plastic. Bubble packs, polystyrene fill, and other such pointless irritations didn't exist, nor did the plastic bags that society is now trying to ban; every housewife had her shopping bag. Dry items were normally sold in paper that could be used to light the fire. Biscuits were sold loose from large tin boxes on display at grocers, from which they were weighed into brown paper bags – a bonus for well-behaved children on shopping expeditions, who might be awarded a broken biscuit by the shopkeeper. Items such as fish and chips, and hardware were wrapped in yesterday's newspapers.

Glass milk bottles were washed and left out for the milkman. You could reclaim the deposit on beer and pop bottles and soda syphons, though this wasn't the case with lesser items such as ketchup bottles. Baked bean and sardine tins were much the same as they are now, but items such as coffee, milk powder, tobacco and posh sweets were sold in reusable tins and those that survive now command a good price in antique shops.

Dustmen in those days didn't do recycling, other than totting, the unofficial recuperation of items of value. In towns, large-scale recycling was performed by another horse-drawn character, the rag and bone man, who would announce his presence outside houses with his eponymous cry, 'Rag 'n' bone ... any old iron?' Bones were used for making glue, gelatine, fertilisers and a number of other commodities, while metals were recycled much as they are today. Rags went for rough materials such as blankets and carpet underlay, and also for making paper. The majority of jettisoned clothes were made from natural materials – wool, cotton, linen and silk – and so could easily be recycled, unlike synthetic materials such as nylon, polyester and acrylic, which were just beginning to hit the market. These now result in about three hundred thousand tonnes of landfill and incinerated waste a year in Britain and are responsible for the spread of plastic microfilaments throughout the oceans.

Clothes were also relatively expensive, compared to today, so made to last. There was a fashion industry, but nothing to compare with the neophiliac trends of the sixties and subsequent decades. It was still acceptable to patch clothes when they wore through. Boys wore shorts, because knees mend sooner than trouser legs, while adult men, unless they were footballers, wouldn't be seen dead in them.

In common with most households, we didn't have a fridge, yet the amount of food wasted was minimal. Like many women who came of age during the war, my mother couldn't bear to see food thrown away. Everything that wasn't eaten was served up again as bubble and squeak, or rissoles. Butter papers were meticulously folded and kept in a drawer for greasing the frying pan. Some molecules of fat in the chip pan were probably ten years old. My mother held that fresh bread, warm from the oven, was bad for you, whereas I reckoned it was an old wives' tale designed to ensure that we ate up all the old crusts first.

Other than cooked dishes, the only common foodstuff we used that derived any benefit from being kept in a fridge was fresh milk, and since the milkman came every day, there was no shortage of it. The problem was how to deal with any surplus before it went off: the answer was to make milk puddings. Semolina, rice pudding, custard, junket and flummeries were no accident of English cookery, but the easiest way to use up a perishable surplus, while other favourites such as bread and butter pudding, and eggy bread (*pain perdu* or 'lost bread' in France) incorporated stale loaves into the salvage exercise.

Food was simple and mostly indigenous, in the sense that it could be grown in Britain, though bananas and oranges were plentiful. Fresh peaches were unavailable outside places like the Savoy, green peppers were weird and kiwis and avocado pears were unheard of. Soft fruits such as strawberries, raspberries and blackcurrants were only available in season, making them a treat. Spaghetti was almost unknown outside Hampstead: a long blue packet of the stuff, adorned with medals and Italian script, lay unopened at the back of my mother's food cupboard for years, along with a dusty bottle of Mazola cooking oil. The fats she used were bacon grease, dripping, lard, suet, butter and Stork margarine.

Most meat was from pasture-fed livestock, because the price of wheat and barley was higher than it is today, so feeding it to animals was extravagant. Chicken was therefore very expensive and a treat that we would only have at Christmas and Easter. Eggs were reserved for Sundays. Pork was more affordable since pigs were partly fed on food waste. But the most common meats were beef and lamb, the reverse of the situation today.

In common with many families, our diet at home was structured on a weekly basis around a joint of beef, lamb or occasionally pork. Cooked and eaten with sacramental reverence for Sunday lunch, along with vegetables, Yorkshire pudding, potatoes and gravy, it would be reincarnated on Monday as cold cuts, on Tuesday as shepherd's pie, on Wednesday as rissoles and on Thursday as dripping sandwiches. Friday was often fish, and Saturday might be something like liver sausage.

Although most of the meat we ate was pasture-fed, and although a single cut of it was ingeniously eked out over four or five days, there was one respect in which the diet was unsustainable. There was no way in which Britain could produce enough beef and lamb to supply Sunday joints for all of its 50 million inhabitants. How many people in 1950s Britain couldn't afford a joint, I have no idea; but many who could were buying beef imported from the New World, notably Argentina, or lamb from New Zealand. There was no prospect of feeding burgeoning numbers of global consumers, avid for meat, on pasture-fed ruminants, and in subsequent decades the meat industry turned to the still more unsustainable strategy of feeding grains, fishmeal and soya beans to chickens, and worse still cows.

But the factor that really made the British way of life in the fifties unsustainable was a resource supplied entirely on British soil: coal. Nobody was concerned at the time, but coal emits much larger volumes of carbon dioxide per unit of energy generated than oil or gas, and hence causes more global warming. By abandoning coal in favour of gas, and through improvements in technological efficiency, today we only produce two-thirds as much greenhouse gas per person as we did in the 1950s.

Bravo! This is a cause for rejoicing – until you include the figures for UK consumption (i.e. all the goods we import, notably from China), in which case the figure bounces back more or less to where it was in the 1950s. In other words, despite relinquishing coal, and despite all the improvements in efficiency, and despite the fact that we now generate a fair amount of renewable energy, we are each still causing just as much global warming as we were in the 1950s. Maybe we should be looking at the 1950s way of life and seeing what aspects could be emulated. Perhaps we already are. Note, for example, the return of the shopping bag.

There is a feeling amongst some who can't remember the fifties that they were colourless and grim. It is true that buildings in cities such as London and Manchester were black with soot, and the programme of scrubbing them up in subsequent decades did a lot to brighten up the urban environment. Aside from London buses and phone boxes, primary colours were in short supply, because few things were made from plastic. High-vis jackets had not been invented and Day-Glo yellow was unimaginable. Flashing neon lights belonged in Piccadilly. The evocation of gloom is compounded by the fact that most photos from the fifties are black and white, whereas colour film arrived in people's cameras just in time to capture the swinging sixties.

But the sun shone then, as it does now, waves beat upon the white cliffs of Dover, flowers blossomed in spring, corn three-foot-high turned yellow in summer, apples ripened in autumn. Stars twinkled at night, brighter than they do now, and Christmas trees were aglow with real candles. Bells rang in church, juke boxes blared in chrome-lined milk bars and the BBC played *Music While You Work*. Girls jived in flared skirts with boys sporting loud ties, and choirboys had rosy cheeks and crisp white surplices. There were no punks with purple hair, but well-to-do widows painted their lips scarlet and draped dead foxes round their necks.

Colours shone brighter then precisely because they were not put in the shade by flashing lights, illuminated screens and crude plastic. There is a lot to be said for a restricted palette. To understand what was best about the fifties, compare the finely crafted illustrations and the urbane layout of *Radio Times* when it was a black and white letterpress publication, to the garish computer-generated image soup that appears under the same title today, and judge which represents the higher level of civilisation. Less is often more, and that is a lesson to draw from the 1950s.

CHAPTER TWO

Boy Scout to Anarchist

I got a first hint of what the sixties had in store in 1957, listening to *Saturday Skiffle Club*, a radio programme compèred by Brian Matthew and launched tentatively on the BBC with a weekly budget of £55. Skiffle was a curious musical tendency that adapted US country blues for English taste. Like doo-wop in the States, and subsequently punk, it promoted the idea that a bunch of musically motivated mates with the requisite equipment, in this case a guitar, a washboard and a tea chest bass, could perform something half decent. Lonnie Donegan was skiffles' most famous exponent, but my favourite track was 'Last Train to San Fernando' by Johnny Duncan and the Blue Grass Boys.

I clocked on to *Skiffle Club* at the age of seven because it was broadcast at 10 am on Saturday morning, immediately after Uncle Mac's *Children's Favourites*. Not a lot of the avuncular Derek McCulloch's selection was to my taste. To catch something good, such as 'I Am a Mole and I Live in a Hole' by the British Jamaican group the Southlanders, you had to sit through a disproportionate quantity of soppy stuff – for example a choir of shrill frauleins singing about tramping through the Alps with a knapsack on their back; and the programme invariably ended with either the 1812 Overture or the 'Dambusters March'.

After so much drivel and pomp, the sound of Donegan's 'Rock Island Line' or Bob Cort's 'Six-Five Special' was a breath of fresh air. The hot rhythm, the blues inflexions and guitar solos from the likes of Ken Sykora and Denny Wright left Danny Kaye and Max Bygraves far behind. What I didn't know at the time was that skiffle had its roots in black music.

Unfortunately *Skiffle Club* was a voice crying in the wilderness. After about a year the skiffle craze died down, and the BBC replaced the show with *Saturday Club*, still fronted by Brian Matthew, but focusing increasingly on pop music. There was plenty of good rock 'n' roll and doo-wop around in 1958 but most of it was American. Since the number of records the BBC could play was severely limited by 'needle time' agreements with the Musicians' Union much of the programme consisted of prerecorded 'live' performances by British artists. This was no problem with skiffle, which despite its American roots was a uniquely British phenomenon, but *Saturday Club* consisted substantially of cover versions of American hits, and even an eight-year-old could tell the difference. The situation improved after 1959 as restrictions on US performers visiting Britain were relaxed, but by then I was in boarding school, where radios were not allowed.

————

During my last few terms at prep school, the prospect of going to public school filled me with increasing foreboding. We were warned of the custom of 'fagging' where new boys served as servants to the seniors. Bullying was rife we were told; caning was severe. Old boys who returned spoke of initiation rituals – heads down toilets, that sort of thing. I had read *Tom Brown's School Days*, and there was nothing to reassure me that anything had changed.

To my relief, I had a stay of execution, because my father had failed to register me in time for attendance at Westminster, one of the top-notch fee-paying schools. I was dispatched for one term to Saint-Quentin, a nondescript town in the north of France where I attended the lycée. I lodged with a friendly family, consisting of M LeBrun, an astute and diminutive engineer, the voluminous and bosomy Mme LeBrun who spent most of the time cooking, seventeen-year-old Bernard who introduced me to Dave Brubeck and arty French cinema, and Colette, a lass of fifteen whose voluptuousness, though unattainable, was not lost on a lad turning fourteen. I consoled myself with pin-ups of Françoise Hardy. By the end of my stay I was almost fluent in French, and had picked up a taste for seven-course meals, and drinking beer at lunch and wine in the evening.

When I did get to Westminster, I found there was nothing to worry about. In the 1960s, it was by some distance the most liberal of public schools. With its premises in Little Dean's Yard, directly behind Westminster Abbey (which served as the school chapel), they could hardly keep their pupils shut in, and we were half a mile from Soho and Tin Pan Alley. The school was adept at turning out popular singers. Michael Flanders and Donald Swann met there, as did Peter and Gordon, who left just before I arrived, after shooting to fame with their recording of the Lennon-McCartney song 'A World Without Love'. A few years later Shane MacGowan, future lead singer of The Pogues, was expelled for using drugs. The first thing I learnt when I got there was that at the end of the previous term two boys had written out large sections of Allen Ginsberg's 'Howl' on the housemaster's door.

This environment was so different from that of St Wilfrid's that it was perhaps not surprising that I should embark on a trajectory that would take me from boy scout to anarchist within two years. One of the first things that happened was that the school decided whether you were of sporting calibre or not by getting a fast bowler to sling a few balls at you. Sportsmen were given cricket whites and coaching at the playing fields in nearby Vincent Square, while the rest were dispatched to Grove Park, at the far end of Lewisham some distance away. My performance was undistinguished, and I was consigned to the ignominy of Grove Park, without any prospect of promotion.

The trip to Grove Park on sports afternoons required a bus ride to Charing Cross, a twenty-five-minute train journey then a fifteen minute walk. By the time we got there it was almost time to come back. Since the athletic types had been creamed off, the Grove Park cohort included most of the boys with incipient bohemian or rebellious tendencies, the sort who looned around and smoked cigarettes and blew up condoms like balloons in the privacy of the train compartment. The masters who supervised the activity were those who didn't give a toss about sports either, so the whole exercise was a farce.

Back in Charing Cross, with a couple of hours to spare, the West End was there to explore. Charing Cross Road was packed with specialist bookshops: Solosy's for political tracts, Zwemmer's for art, Watkins for the esoteric, Better Books for beat poetry. It was at Better Books that I picked up a copy of *Howl and Other Poems* to find out what they had written on the housemaster's door:

> *'I saw the best minds of my generation destroyed by madness, starving hysterical naked,'... etc., etc.*

Gosh! This was a bit different from Walter de la Mare and Rudyard Kipling.

At the far end of Charing Cross Road was the HMV record shop, where we could shut ourselves in a sound-proofed cubicle and smoke fags while listening to the LPs of our choice. No one seemed to mind. Mostly we clocked into bluesmen like Howlin' Wolf and John Lee Hooker, whose names we had gleaned from The Animals and Manfred Mann LPs. In Tottenham Court Road and Oxford Street there were small cinemas where you could see films that weren't on general release (and where we could smoke). Most memorable was Peter Watkins' *The War Game*, depicting the effects of a nuclear war resulting from a Chinese invasion of Vietnam, which the BBC had commissioned but subsequently banned.

There were pubs where a fourteen-year-old could get served without question. Around Bond Street were posh art galleries where you could wander round exhibitions for free. And at the end of Oxford Street is Speakers' Corner where there were always performances worth watching, be it from nutcases, firebrands or geniuses. The heckling was often as accomplished as the speaking, and better natured than the current trolling on the internet. It was at Speakers' Corner that one day that I saw Ginsberg, munificently bearded, sitting on the ground cross-legged, intoning a mantra and attended by acolytes. I was less impressed by 'Om' than I had been by 'Howl'.

One day at Speakers' Corner, I fell upon a small anti-Vietnam War demonstration. Harold Wilson's Labour government, and its foreign secretary Michael Stewart, did not openly send troops to Vietnam, but the UK provided arms and supported the US position. I was handed leaflets inviting me to a 'teach in' at the Methodist Hall in Parliament Square, which was just across the road from my school. I attended and came back with a pile of pamphlets that convinced me that the US were on a futile and arrogant colonialist mission and should be made to go home.

None of this escaped the keen eye of my housemaster. After some mates and I went to a Billy Graham 'crusade' at Wembley, I arrived back at school late and was confronted by Mr Keeley. 'Where have you been?' he asked. 'I've been converted,' I answered more or less truthfully, but he wasn't taking this for an excuse. 'You will write three thousand words on the Vietnam War. I want it from you by Friday week.'

What a good punishment! I delivered it, and it was the first half-decently researched piece I had carried out. The subject was more interesting than schismatic popes, or the rise of the Capetian dynasty. In his report for that term the housemaster commented:

> *I particularly enjoyed S. Fairlie's piece on L.B. Johnson's policy towards Vietnam and the attitude of N.D. Diem and H.C. Minh. K. Marx might have admired and H.C. Keeley was much enlightened. E. Tudor has also been well studied.*

Mr Keeley probably did learn something from my efforts, since the Vietnam War was not yet a subject of great public debate. Whereas that other great neocolonial debacle of recent times, the invasion of Iraq, was mounted with fanfare in the teeth of opposition from public and politicians, the Vietnam War gradually escalated from a minor matter of gunboat diplomacy to a massive military effort. The BBC reported the weekly casualties as if they were football results – 'USA 107 dead, Viet Cong 1,135' was a typical score. This helped to normalise the war and gave the impression that a United States victory was imminent. But there was little mainstream scrutiny of US policy at the time; the main sources of critical information were left-wing pamphleteers.

That was to change over the next two years, but meanwhile there were upheavals in my own life. In 1966, pursued by the Inland Revenue, and facing a libel action from Lady Antonia Fraser, my father moved to the United States, where he secured work as a Washington columnist. He never returned; indeed he never again left the US. Soon after, my mother and sisters joined him in a rented house in the well-appointed Georgetown area, while I stayed at boarding school. In the summer of 1966, I flew over for a rather trying holiday in the capital's sweltering humidity.

When I arrived back at Westminster for my sixth term I was summoned to the housemaster's office. Mr Keeley came straight to the point: 'Your father has not paid any bills since you first came here. The school has made allowances in your interest, but I'm afraid this can go on no longer. We have made arrangements for you to stay with a friend of your father, George Gale, who will supervise your education.'

After a few months with the Gales I was packed off to Colchester Royal Grammar School, which, because it served a garrison town, had a small boarding house. Years before, my mother had wisely made me take the eleven-plus exam in the expectation that there might be some disruption to my private school education. She later told me that this was not the first time that my father had failed to pay the school bills. Indeed there was a strong likelihood that he had not paid any of them, but had been bailed out at the last minute by benefactors.

Colchester Grammar was no match for Westminster. It lacked the privileged metropolitan position, the quirky erudite teachers, the long list of famous alumni. However it was an eye-opener for me because I was at last able to become part of a community that was less artificial and more heterogeneous than a private boarding school. I was quick to make new friends. Long hair was not yet fashionable for males, but was affected by a minority as a sign of rebellion, and that made it easy to identify other boys with radical or bohemian tendencies. I gravitated towards a set whose interests were left-wing and pacifist politics, blues and beat poetry.

My friends were also day boys and this meant that I socialised in town, creeping out at night through a window in the downstairs dormitory, visiting pubs at the weekend, going to concerts and parties. I met people from walks of life I had never before come into contact with: lads who had left the 'vocational' secondary modern school at the first opportunity to find work, and blokes who had dropped out of the army (there were several in Colchester since it housed an army prison). Most importantly of all, I encountered a subsection of humanity that I had never had any dealings with, bar my sisters, namely girls. Incarceration in single-sex boarding schools for two-thirds of the year, plus the lack of a stable home the rest of the time, left me pitifully ill-equipped to engage with these alien creatures, let alone try to seduce one of them. Now I had the chance to learn.

So it was that when my father charmed Randolph Churchill into paying the school bills, and arranged for me to go back to Westminster, I was adamant that I wanted to stay at Colchester. This was a disappointment for my father and probably also for the headmaster and housemaster at the grammar school, who by then were keen to get rid of me. I was a disruptive influence: a boy who flagrantly wore flip-flops, questioned the syllabus, and had scant respect for many of the teachers.

The critique of liberal capitalism that was gathering steam amongst my contemporaries did not spare the education system. Ivan Illich had not yet written *Deschooling Society*, but the ideas of anarchists such as A.S. Neill were filtering through, and Summerhill, his experimental school, was not far away at Leiston in Suffolk. Meanwhile we experienced the inadequacies of our schooling and the unsatisfactory nature of the exam system first hand. Life in the sixth form was entirely focused on A levels, which provided a stultifying framework for learning.

Curry, the English master, had carried out an analysis of previous A level papers showing that there were only a certain number of essay questions, which were regurgitated in slightly different form year after year. For instance, if you were studying Keats you always got a variation of the question: 'Keats combines emotional intensity with romantic imagery and intellectual rigour. Discuss.' He was right: it did turn up in my A level exam. We were therefore made to prepare answers to these questions, peppered with suitable quotations, and learn them almost by rote. At the exam itself, you had to churn out these oven-ready essays in a ridiculously short time.

By the time the actual A levels came around, I nursed such contempt for them that I couldn't be bothered. I reasoned that any institution that accepted or rejected people on the basis of them wasn't the sort of place I wanted to go to. In any case I had received rejections from all six universities I had applied to through the Universities Central Council on Admissions scheme, presumably because of the headmaster's report. When my results came through, I had a C and two Ds, which was viewed as disappointing. The verdict, from elders and betters was that, since I was not yet seventeen, I should repeat the year and take the A levels all over again. The prospect filled me with despair.

————

There was one subplot to my school career that I haven't mentioned yet, though if the teachers had become aware of it, it would have been the main plot.

I first heard of cannabis when I was fourteen, listening to a programme on the BBC Home Service in which beatniks, interviewed on the beach at Brighton, talked about getting high on pot. My immediate thought was that I had to try this stuff. I'd seen beatniks on their way to Brighton once or twice when I lived in Lewes. I'd known what they were because they looked just like the ones in *Punch* cartoons. They'd seemed interestingly different from most people. Perhaps 'pot' had something to do with that.

The trouble was that I didn't know how to get hold of it, and in the end I had to go to considerable lengths to find some. Various friends at Westminster claimed to have a source, but none of them came up with the goods. By the time I got to Colchester, pop songs referring to drugs were on the radio and there were several of us trying to locate the stuff. In desperation we tried smoking all sorts of substitutes – nutmeg, ground up aspirins and dried banana skins, the latter inspired by

Donovan's song 'Mellow Yellow'. 'Ooh, I think something's beginning to happen,' we'd say after about ten minutes, but it always turned out to be wishful thinking.

Then early in 1967, I read an article in a Sunday supplement about hitch-hiking to Istanbul on the 'pot trail'. I suspected that the journalist didn't actually hitch-hike there herself because she claimed that it was traditional to start from Trafalgar Square, which was transparently nonsense. But she also wrote about 'the Tent', a marquee on a hotel roof in Istanbul, where hundreds of hippies lay around smoking hash. Was she bullshitting about this as well? There was only one way to find out. I'd read Kerouac's *On The Road* only a few months previously. At the start of the 1967 summer holidays, I bought a money belt and some traveller's cheques, stuffed a rucksack with a sleeping bag and a change of clothes, and set off for Turkey – not of course from Trafalgar Square, but from an appropriate point on the A2 to Dover.

The demise of hitch-hiking is one of the saddest changes to society over the last few decades. In the 1960s, the main difficulty faced by hitch-hikers was other hitch-hikers. Your heart sank if you got dropped off at a roundabout or motorway slip road and there were already half a dozen blokes and couples standing with their thumbs out. Now you can drive for weeks on the motorway system without seeing a single one.

The hitchers of yesteryear have grown old and few modern youngsters do it. They have more money than we did, more cars, better fuel economy, cheaper petrol, cheaper buses and digital lift-share apps. They can fly across Europe at little cost other than a twinge of conscience about their carbon emissions. And they are more risk-averse: they were ferried to school in cars, warned that 'strangers mean danger', the generation for whom the gap year was invented in case they succumbed to the urge to drop out. Young people today move around the world with greater speed, ease and certainty than we could fifty years ago, and that is their loss, since, as has long been known, travelling is often better than arriving.

Hitch-hiking has been compared to fishing by more than one writer. A cod fisherman must 'think like cod', and the hitch-hiker has to anticipate the reactions of motorists, who have a split second in which to decide whether or not to stop. Finding the correct place to stand is crucial: typically at the point where the driver is just about to accelerate out of conurbation onto the open road. A few metres one way or the other can make a big difference.

The bait is also important, and the bait is you. Look young, fresh and just out of college. If you look old people may think you are a loser. Beards are out as they make you look like a tramp. The ideal is to be an attractive young female, or failing that, look like one. A high-vis jacket is essential for hitching at night, the only time most truck drivers will stop, as they can't be seen to be carrying a passenger. An umbrella is a good accoutrement, which makes you look urbane when it isn't raining and competently dry when it is.

And as with fishing, luck plays its part. On an unfamiliar road you might get put down in a lay-by where cars can draw up easily, or on a sixty miles per hour freeway with a five-mile walk to anywhere sensible. You might wait ten seconds for a lift or ten hours. You might hook tiddlers – local motorists going to the next village – or the big one that takes you a thousand miles.

Once inside the vehicle you have to play your fish carefully. You are in a metal box moving at speed, with someone you've never met in your life before. So is the driver. Why have they picked you up? Do they want to talk or not? Are they reasonable? Interesting? Weird? Drunk? The driver has to make similar assessments about you. Once you have established a rapport then conversation can develop freely. You are someone the driver is never likely to meet again and can talk to in confidence. As a hitch-hiker you are habitually engaging with people you would never normally meet, and sometimes you hear things they wouldn't tell their best friend.

All this was something I gradually absorbed as I thumbed my way through France, across the Alps and the necklace of cities strung across the north of Italy. Yugoslavia, after Slovenia, was unpleasant. The four hundred-kilometre road between Belgrade and Zagreb was a death trap, peppered with crashed cars and the odd dead body. I found the atmosphere in Yugoslavia to be uncomfortable, almost as if a war might break out.

I teamed up with an American traveller, and after an abortive lift with a hilarious Czech family of five in a tiny Skoda sports car, we got picked up by a dodgy-looking Asian geezer in a Mercedes. He wanted us to strap a load of watches to our arms as we went into Bulgaria, saying that he would get searched, but we wouldn't. I wasn't up for this, but the American was. When we went through the customs, the Bulgarians pulled the car aside into a shed, gave it a thorough examination and frisked our driver. I was shitting bricks, and so no doubt was my American colleague with the watches on his arm. But the Asian geezer was right, they didn't frisk us westerners, and we all went through unscathed.

Bulgaria was a breath of fresh air after Yugoslavia. There were no cars, just antiquated lorries and buses. You stuck your thumb out and the first lorry that came along would stop, every time. We trundled down the highway bordered by fruit trees and the peasants in the field waved as we went past. At night we stopped in a village where the locals feted us with plum brandy, putting their arms around us exclaiming, 'Bulgaria-England, *Nazdráve*'. In Sofia, the capital, I ended up in the student quarter where I was welcomed into people's homes and had intense conversations about the state of the world and the war in Vietnam.

Over the course of the next few years, I travelled through Bulgaria several times, and its generosity never failed to impress me. It was such a far cry from what we had been told to expect of communist Eastern Europe: there was no evidence of Stasi types looking over your shoulder. I sped through Bulgaria because you had to buy an expensive visa if you didn't leave the country within three days, but one of the regrets of my life is that I focused on the drugs and the eastern promise of Turkey, rather than taking off into the rural hinterlands of Bulgaria.

Once I got to Istanbul, I asked for the Gülhane Hotel. It was barely a stone's throw from the two main edifices in the city, the Hagia Sophia and the Sultan Ahmed Mosque. There was, as promised, a large marquee on the roof and inside there were a couple of hundred hippies whose miniscule territories were marked out by their sleeping bags. It was a cross between Coney Island beach on a hot day and a refugee camp. Joints of hashish were passed around, and it was there that I must have had my first taste of the stuff, though I remember nothing. The place was so weird that mind-altering substances made little impression. After a few days I couldn't take the intimacy of the tent, and opted to pay slightly more for a bed in a hotel room. This was no improvement. It meant I was lodged with the Gülhane elite, who were junkies, skeletal bearded creatures who spent most of their day lying on their bed trying to find a vein. For a sixteen-year-old, it was great example of what not to do with your life.

I spent all the money I had on several slabs of Turkish gold hash, and set out to hitch back to England. From the Turkish border I got a lift all the way to Paris with a genial French librarian. It took three days, and was nearly three thousand kilometres, the longest lift I ever got in my life. From Paris, I hitched to Amsterdam where I hung around for a few days, sleeping on an empty houseboat. On the fourth night the police

raided the boat, arrested me, took all my money, drove me to
The Hague and stuck me on a ferry. My rucksack was in a left
luggage locker in Amsterdam that I was sharing with another
backpacker, but I couldn't tell the police that as there was six
ounces of hash in it. My friend, who had the key, would have
a nice surprise. I landed up in Harwich port in Essex with
nothing but my passport and a shilling stamp, with which I was
able to buy a loaf of bread. That was the end of my career as a
dope smuggler.

Fortunately, I had posted some back to England from
Amsterdam, so I arrived back for the autumn term with some
supplies to turn my friends on. Turkish gold was far from the
best hashish in the world, but it was better than banana skins.

Meanwhile my mother and my two younger sisters, Charlotte and Emma, had come back from the States, leaving my
father behind. The family had split up by mutual agreement
and my mother had to find work and somewhere to live. Fleet
Street came to the rescue. She secured a job with the *Daily
Express* syndication department, and was found temporary
accommodation by Leslie Illingworth, the cartoonist who had
shared an office with Henry during his time at the *Daily Mail*.
Eventually, after fruitless weeks of searching for a permanent
family home, she walked into the office serving four blocks of
flats opposite Olympia exhibition centre in West Kensington,
immediately after someone had handed in their notice.

Flat 10 Glyn Mansions, with four bedrooms, was just £11
per week, which was affordable. Even luckier was the fact that
over the roughly eighteen years that my family lived there,
which included the severe inflation of the early 1970s, the rent
only went up to £14 per week. This was because the blocks kept
being sold from one speculative property company to another,
and the profit was in capital gains, not in rent. Eventually, in the
recession of the late 1980s, the bubble burst and the existing

owners went bankrupt. The flats were put under the management of a residents' association, which decided they all needed
to be done up, and required its members to 'decant' so that their
flat could be gentrified. My mother couldn't be doing with this.
Thanks to the cheap rent she had about £5,000 put aside that
she had used to buy a shiplapped cottage in a part of Sussex
so remote that sukebind might still be found flowering. Some
years later, she sold it at a price that enabled her to buy a house
in nearby Hastings Old Town.

About a year after she left Glyn Mansions, I dropped in
to see what the builders were doing with the flat. They had
changed a spacious four-bedroomed home, which at various
times had housed my mother (plus lover), her three children,
my grandmother, lodgers and other waifs and strays, into two
pokey studio flats, each with its own kitchen, bathroom, hall and
front door, which together probably housed just two people. In
2016, one of them, number 10a, went on sale for £635,000. It
was a sorry tale of greed and social atomisation, but ironically
it was the speculative activities of the owners that had provided
our family, for once, with a reliable and affordable anchor.

I however was down to do another year at Colchester Grammar. My triumphant return with hashish perhaps enhanced
my standing with some of my fellow pupils, but no amount
of dope was sufficient to alleviate the pressure and the tedium
of doing A levels all over again. As I embarked on a rerun of
Keats, E.M. Forster, and the Tudors and Stuarts, depression
set in. One day in November, I jettisoned my school blazer,
put on a trench coat bought at a jumble sale, walked out of
the boarding house down to the A12, and hitch-hiked north. I
spent a night in Morecambe with a friend who had started at
Lancaster University, hitched to Barrow-in-Furness because it
looked interesting, decided it wasn't, and then travelled across
the Pennines to Yorkshire.

There I found work picking potatoes. The weather had turned icy: as we followed the tractor and trailer it was hard to tell frozen clods of earth from potatoes, and I had no gloves. The other pickers were blonde Yorkshire girls who took the mickey out of me. At night the farmer let me sleep in the cab of his lorry, but that was bitterly cold, even with the trench coat. After three days I could stand it no longer and hitched back down to London. My mother had notified the police, but she claimed not to have been unduly worried by my disappearance. 'Like father, like son,' was her comment.

The grammar school had expelled me, which had been the object of my absconding. However, after frantic phone calls between my father in the States and the headmaster, I was allowed back. Since my experience of the potato fields of Yorkshire had been sobering, I acquiesced.

————

Resistance to the Vietnam War was gathering steam. On 22 October 1967, I went on the first of the demonstrations outside the US Embassy in Grosvenor Square. The day before, thousands of anti-war protesters had surrounded the Pentagon in Washington, and attempted to exorcise it by levitating it three hundred feet in the air with the aid of chanting. Nothing like that happened on our demo. It was relatively small, only a few thousand people. Indeed none of the Grosvenor Square protests were anywhere near as big as the anti-poll tax demonstration, the Countryside March, the protest against the Bush/Blair invasion of Iraq, or the anti-Brexit marches. But the October protest attracted attention because it was violent. The police used force to stop us advancing on the embassy, and we responded. London hadn't seen violent demonstrations since the 1930s.

The demonstrations were organised by a number of umbrella groups with names so similar it was hard to tell them apart: the

British Council for Peace in Vietnam, the Vietnam Solidarity Campaign, and the British Vietnam Solidarity Front were the main ones. These in turn were dominated by tiresome left-wing groups with names like International Socialists, International Marxist Group, Communist Party of Great Britain and so on, who wasted much of their energy on internecine disputes. I never bothered to find out what it was that made the Trots such enemies of the Maoists; I had not yet heard of Freud's 'narcissism of small differences'. Pacifists were less doctrinally anal, but often a bit wet and reluctant to take a revolutionary stance. The anarchists were too full of themselves, always pushing to get their red and black flags to the front of the march, causing friction and havoc. Like most of the people on these protests, I was not affiliated to any of these groups, but drew on their ideas to formulate a less ideologically rigid critique of modern capitalism.

I did however find myself drawn to the anarchist end of the spectrum. I read James Joll's and George Woodcock's books on the movement, bought copies of the brilliant little magazine *Anarchy* edited by Colin Ward, read Kropotkin and Voline, Max Stirner and Rudolf Rocker. I never really believed that a completely anarchist society was achievable, through revolution or through any other means, but it was something to strive towards. My understanding of anarchism became clearer when I tumbled on Gustav Landauer's words: 'The State is a condition, a certain relationship between human beings, a mode of behaviour; we destroy it by contracting other relationships, by behaving differently toward one another.... We are the State and we shall continue to be the State until we have created the institutions that form a real community.'

Landauer's statement could just have easily ended with the three words 'an alternative society'. From the fertile ground of the US anti-war movement a new ideological life form was emerging, and we were just beginning to hear about it. Journals such as *Peace News* published photos of protesters offering flowers to rifle-wielding soldiers at the 1967 Pentagon protest. If this was 'flower power' there was nothing soppy about such a highly charged political statement. But in the popular press it was soon eclipsed by a slightly different phenomenon, the 'flower child'. We learnt how many thousands of 'gentle people with flowers in their hair' were converging on San Francisco because, in the words of Scott McKenzie's UK number one hit, 'summertime will be a love-in there'.

It sounds tacky, but in fact the 'Summer of Love' was a practical response to an unstoppable movement. Its catalyst was the Human Be-In, an event held in San Francisco on 14 January 1967 to protest against a California law banning LSD, featuring Allen Ginsberg, Timothy Leary, Gary Snyder, Jerry Rubin and other famous names. According to Chet Helms on the Summer of Love website the Be-In attracted up to thirty thousand people 'with virtually no conventional publicity, mostly word of mouth', but it was subsequently widely reported in the mainstream press. San Francisco community activists 'realised that by the time school let out in April or May we would be inundated by literally tens of thousands of young people from all over the country'. To deal with the invasion they formed the Council for the Summer of Love, which set about providing social services to cope with the expected invasion, including a free clinic, food banks, shelter and support for runaway kids. It was at a debriefing session after the Be-In that Rubin, Snyder and others dreamt up the project of levitating the Pentagon. The shoots of an alternative society were emerging through an unlikely combination of political activism, drug-induced mysticism and community concern.

Back at Colchester Grammar School we heard only tantalising snippets about what was happening in the States, but the next Grosvenor Square demo was on 17 March 1968. I asked the housemaster for permission to go to London for that weekend, which was refused, but I went anyway. The protest this time was bigger, and there was a good throng of us ostensibly trying to take the US Embassy by storm. We were rebuffed by solid ranks of police officers, backed up by mounted police who tried to push us back by driving their horses into the crowd. This tactic only served to make people angrier and the scuffle got nasty. There was however no prospect of storming the embassy. When the occasional protester managed to break through the police cordon, they would run up the steps of the building and then dither, as they took stock of the US military police standing there holding submachine guns. There was nowhere to go; all they could do was wait to be arrested. Perhaps we should have tried levitating the embassy, but we weren't as spiritually advanced as our transatlantic counterparts.

In all 246 people were arrested, including myself and a couple of girls I had travelled up with. We were held overnight, charged and tried in the morning and given a £5 fine, or a day in prison. I chose the latter and was then released within fifteen minutes, to the annoyance of the girls who had paid their £5.

When I got back to school, I thought my escapade in London had gone undetected. But a photo in one of the Sunday newspapers showed my face in the crowd. That was the last straw for the grammar school and they expelled me once again. This time there was no going back.

The March 17 demonstration played a relatively small part in the wave of upheavals that erupted in many other countries throughout 1968. These kicked off in the spring with battles between police and students in Italy and Germany, and spread in various forms to about a dozen countries. The bloodiest repression was in Mexico and Pakistan, while revolts against Franco in Spain, and against Soviet domination in the Czech Republic, gave a foretaste of liberation to come. But it was the events of

May 1968 in Paris that really inspired us, and not only because at one point it looked as though an alliance of students and workers might topple the de Gaulle government. The slogans and graffiti articulated our half-formed insights about the banality of life in an economy fixated on consumption, and the need to transcend it: 'Cours, connard, ton patron t'attend'; 'Métro, Boulot, Dodo'; 'Consommez plus, vous vivrez moins'; 'Soyez réaliste: demandez l'impossible'.* This inchoate soup of ideas and aspirations became the feedstock for more mature critiques of post-industrial capitalism, and inspired solutions that extended the domain of the realistic by striving for the impossible.

I can't remember why I didn't go off to Paris when it was all happening. Instead I went to France in June, shortly after it was all over. I visited the Odéon in Paris where many of the debates happened. It was still technically occupied, but it was like a seaside town in winter – just one or two people packing things up. The best bit was hitching across France down to the south. It was easy to get lifts and as soon as I got in everybody talked enthusiastically about 'the events'. Only one elderly couple opposed the movement: they had picked me up because they thought from my long hair that I was a girl. Everyone said the struggle would start up again in October. It didn't.

———

Despite all the revolutionary excitement, my academic career was not yet over. My parents were determined I should go to university, and arranged individual tuition for me at a crammer near Victoria Station. I got another clear round of rejections, but I also had an interview at Cambridge and was offered a provisional place subject to my performance in their entrance exam.

---

* 'Run, fuckwit, your boss is waiting'; 'Tube, Work, Sleep'; 'The more you consume, the less you live'; 'Be realistic: demand the impossible'.

This was a relief. The format of the Cambridge exam was less deadening than that of the A levels, which there was now no point in me resitting. I opted to do English, while my father advised me to do history, probably wisely. The trouble was that history, as taught in English schools in the 1960s, focused on monarchs – Merovingian and Capetian, Tudor and Stuart, Ottonian and Habsburg – whose political machinations were of zero interest to me. Commoners hardly got a look in, unless the king had to execute some of them after a peasants' revolt. I had an A level in medieval and early modern European history but had barely heard of the enclosure of the commons. Later, I developed an interest in social and agrarian history but only after several years of living and working in the countryside had raised questions that begged for answers.

I took the English exam, and while I think I wrote passable essays on Swift and Blake, I completely flunked the comprehension paper. Nonetheless I was accepted, into Caius College, almost certainly because of the influence of George Gale's friends at Cambridge. That, as my father had famously pointed out, was the way the establishment worked.

I was by no means sure that I wanted to go. I'd had my fill of formal education, and there was a world out there waiting to be discovered. I had fallen in love with a graceful Anglo-Indian girl named Carol who was also seeking to broaden her horizons. We had no long-term plans, and we were held together by, amongst other things, a mutual desire to go to India. However my father invited us to the US for six weeks before the university term started, offering to pay for air flights for both of us and Greyhound bus tickets. I suspected that his motive was to ensure that I didn't disappear into the hinterland of Hindustan, but returned to Britain in time to start at Cambridge. But it was a generous offer. I reasoned it was wiser to see what Cambridge was like, than to reject it out of hand, and so we accepted.

In the interim, however, I was receiving letters from my father that voiced concern about my behaviour and aspirations. Like many teenagers I was often moody, arrogant, lazy, inconsiderate and resistant to doing what my elders thought wise. Like many parents, my father felt it an obligation to steer me back into ways that were productive and wholesome. All this is normal, but if your father happens to be a professional writer who likes nothing so much as the sound of his typewriter or the rasp of his pen on paper, you can expect to be the recipient of a disproportionate quantity of anguished prose.

At one point I received a fifty-six-page letter almost entirely about the length of my hair. The catalyst for his objection was that I had refused to cut my hair for my interview for Cambridge. His argument was: 'You have got this peripheral question out of all proportion – you are making the peripheral central ... You find it difficult to get jobs as a result of your appearance, and so give yourself an unreal excuse for saying the world is against me.'

It was a reasonable observation. There was also a benefit from wearing long hair that my father failed to consider. It enabled us to identify people of a like mind. It signalled who might be worth approaching in an unfamiliar setting, such as a new school or university, who might be able to tell you where to score dope, the best place to hitch from, or where a certain squat or shop was located. It confirmed that one was not alone but part of a movement. When you passed another freak in the street, you would acknowledge the cultural solidarity by exchanging a smile, a gesture or a 'Hi, man!'

It was not just the long hair, which anyway was normal for females, but also your dress, or absence thereof, and your accoutrements, and by that I don't mean the bell-bottoms and beads, which were such a nuisance that anybody with sense soon abandoned them. Dress was practical and comfortable:

ex-army clothing, patched jeans, Indian pyjamas, loose-fitting shirts and skirts, sheepskins, waistcoats, sandals, desert boots, headbands, rucksacks and male handbags. There was an absence of unwanted constraints, notably ties and bras.

In photos from the early twentieth century, radical thinkers such as anarchists, and even Dadaists, dressed more or less identically to the bourgeois they were contesting. There is a photo of Glasgow anarchists in 1915 who could just as easily be a Presbyterian congregation. No doubt they felt that dress was a peripheral matter compared with seizing control of the means of production. But it suggests that their ideology had little impact on their lifestyle, compared to, for example, that of a monk.

———

In summer 1969, the US was in a state of subdued tension. The previous summer had seen riots after the assassination of Martin Luther King Jr, and at the Democratic Convention in Chicago, and there were fears that something might trigger another 'long, hot summer'. The tide of public opinion was beginning to turn against the Vietnam War but there was a long way to go before it would be brought to an end; the farcical trial of the Chicago Seven would take place in the autumn of 1969, and in the following May, the Kent State shootings would precipitate a nationwide student strike. The hippie movement and its culture had spread across the country. Every city had its own underground paper, even towns in the Deep South, and hippie paraphernalia shops were sprouting. But it wasn't clear where all this was heading. The Woodstock festival and the Charles Manson murders occurred within a week of each other, in August 1969.

Carol and I flew out in July, and stayed with my father for a week in Washington and then went off to look for America by Greyhound bus, heading for Berkeley on the west coast, via

New York, Gloucester Massachusetts and Chicago. At the time Greyhounds offered a degree of comfort deemed appropriate for the poorest 10 per cent of the US population. A three-day ride from one coast to the other was more of an ordeal than suggested in Paul Simon's wistful song 'America'. Relief came when the bus made rest stops in seedy bus stations where, over a sandwich, you could study the worn faces of the US underclass – black, brown or white – as they waited by their baggage for their ride to another town.

Berkeley, the university town attached to San Francisco, was largely occupied by hippies. Shops around Telegraph Avenue sold radical books and magazines, health foods and hippie paraphernalia, and the smell of marijuana wafted from groups at street corners. Hitching was a dream come true. You only had to stick your thumb out at an intersection and the first car would take you, even if just for a few blocks. There was little to indicate that less than three months previously there had been a near-massacre round the corner. Ronald Reagan had sent in police with shotguns to clear demonstrators from People's Park, an abandoned plot owned by the university that had been taken over by community activists. One man, James Rector, was killed, another blinded and many more wounded with buckshot. Reagan then declared a state of emergency, and sent in 2,700 state troopers who kept the town in a state of martial law for seventeen days, while the university closed off the park with an eight-foot-high fence.

The people got their park back in 1972 after tearing down the fence, and fifty years later the university is still fighting them for possession. But by the time we arrived, the atmosphere was one of subdued despondency, possibly aggravated by the shadow of the Manson murders. As at Paris, I'd arrived too late for the revolution. 'It's gotten heavy in the city,' people told us. 'It's not like it was in '67. Folks are leaving, going to the country, getting back to the land.' So we went out to the country too, staying with refugees from the city in a house overlooking the Pacific in Mendocino County. Our hosts made homely leather bags sown with thongs, and showed us how easy it was to do.

We went back across the South to New Orleans, and then took the bus back to Washington. When it stopped at Charlotte, North Carolina, I got off to buy food, while Carol stayed in her seat. As soon as I was off the bus a cop came up to me, pulled out his gun and said, 'Spread.' I stood against the bus, hands outstretched, while he frisked me. When he found a tin of McCormick's sweet basil that I had been smoking in an attempt to give up tobacco, he bundled me into his police car, took me down the station and proudly presented me and the offending article to his superior officer. The chief sniffed it, raised his eyes momentarily to the ceiling and drawled, 'Take him back.'

Back at the bus station, the Greyhound had gone, but I found Carol, and we settled down for a wait of many hours until the next bus. There were two cafés next to each other, which respectively had 'coloureds' and 'whites' signs above them, painted over, but still legible. Since Carol was obviously not white, we knew which we were supposed to go in, but it was closed. I tried to buy something at the sweet counter, but the store holder refused to sell me anything. I was rash enough to complain to another policeman who said, 'Tha's right. Ah wouldn't serve you eether; you stink like a polecat!'

I sat back down and dozed in my seat. About 15 minutes before the next bus was due a third cop came up, pulled me to my feet and started frogmarching me out of the building. 'Git!' he shouted. 'We don't want the likes of you round here.'

'Believe me, I'm only too anxious to leave,' I tried to explain.

'You ain't nothin' but a dawg 'n a hypocrite,' he said, bundling me into his car. 'You're comin' down the station.'

The prospect of missing the bus a second time was looming. Fortunately Carol had found somebody with a bit of sanity in this nuthouse who explained to the cop that I had a ticket and if he wanted to get rid of me the best thing was to let me get on the bus. He acquiesced, and as the bus left Charlotte with us on it, I breathed a sigh of relief.

Not long after, there was an item on the news about a 'hippie commune' in North Carolina that had been arrested on suspicion of committing a brutal murder. A few days later it emerged that someone else had been charged with the murder and the hippies were released. The reasoning process of the North Carolina police force had apparently been: Manson committed murder; Manson is a hippie; therefore hippies have committed the murder. I'm glad we got out of town before it happened.

————

A month later I started at Cambridge. On the first day, Enoch Powell was speaking in town and there was a demonstration, which I and some others attended instead of the formal college induction ceremony. In the evening, the master of the college, Joseph Needham, came to the dinner hall to congratulate and welcome those of us who had missed the induction, stating that he would have liked to have joined us. Needham was an extraordinary man, editor and chief author of the monumental *Science and Civilisation in China*, and a communist who lived with both his wife and his mistress for fifty years in Cambridge.

My director of studies was Jeremy Prynne, a scholarly beanpole of a man in his thirties, and a poet of some renown within the fashionable English school influenced by Charles Olson, the Black Mountain Poets and Basil Bunting. I started off on the wrong foot with him when he asked us what we had most enjoyed reading in the holidays. When I mentioned Kesey's *One Flew Over the Cuckoo's Nest*, not yet made into a film, his comment was one of crushing contempt. He was brilliant, if brilliance includes being able to talk nonstop for twenty minutes about five words in Coleridge's 'Frost at Midnight'.

The lectures too were a disappointment. My father had regaled me with tales of eccentric lecturers at Oxford, one of whom, for example, delivered an entire lecture crouched under a table. The only person at Cambridge who matched his description was Prynne, and I didn't need to hear any more from him. Otherwise, the standard of the lectures that I attended ranged from mediocre to dismal. It was quicker and easier to read the same material in a written paper where you could skip irrelevant bits and make notes in the margin, than trek down to a packed lecture hall where there was no chance for dialogue with the lecturer.

The living arrangements were also peculiar. My study was a poky garret in the college, with a kitchen the size of a Greyhound bus toilet. I would rather have been in a shared house with a decent-sized kitchen and living room. But the most bizarre feature was the 'bedder', one of a number of middle-aged women who bussed in every day from housing estates at the edge of the city to clean undergraduates' rooms, make their beds, sweep the floor and whatever. This was already uncomfortable enough, both because of the class structure of the relationship and because I didn't want anybody tidying up my room for me; my own mother would never have dared. But bedders were rumoured to report to the proctor any evidence of illicit activities that might have been taking place, notably drug taking and entertaining girls. Maintaining day-by-day relations with an uninvited servant who might also be a spy was not what I had expected, and more than I could handle.

Moreover, gates to the colleges were shut at about 10.30 pm. To get back into Caius after that time you had to clamber over wrought iron railings topped with spearheads. It's a wonder that no drunken reveller was ever discovered in the morning skewered to these fortifications. At Trinity College, you could get in by edging along the outside of a bridge over the river hanging onto the railings, while avoiding a coil of barbed wire. By the start of the second term we could stand no more of this Victorian regime, so, in addition to my study, Carol and I rented a flat in Mill Road, the bohemian quarter in Cambridge, which we could afford because Carol got decently paid for temp work in London. It was empty save for a bed, a two ringed Belling stove and a one bar electric fire, and it was January. We spent much of the time in bed.

I was starting to socialise with townspeople, and to get a perspective of the university from their point of view. It sat on the town like an octopus with tentacles in every quarter, monopolising the centre with its colleges, its student shops and pubs, its highbrow entertainments, flaunting its privilege and pushing local people out to the extremities. I was having trouble meeting people in the university who shared my outlook, and I was uncomfortable with the prevalence of public school attitudes and accents. I was getting very little out of Cambridge and there was not much to hold me there. At the end of the Lent term I threw the *I Ching* and it came up with hexagram 29 line 6: 'Shut in between thorn-hedged prison walls: For three years one does not find the way. Misfortune.'

That seemed to be unambiguous counsel. I saw my tutor and informed him that I was going to leave. He expressed his regrets and told me I was welcome to come back any time I wanted. If times get hard I might hold them to that.

I wrote to my father saying, 'I hope this doesn't impair my relationship with you,' but he was so disappointed in me, we didn't correspond again for ten years.

CHAPTER THREE

On the Hippie Trail

'If you don't want to go to Cambridge don't go,' my father had written. 'I mean that. Go and drift wherever you please. Go and sit on a beach and become a beachcomber, not just for a holiday, which is delightful, but for the rest of your youth.'

We did go where we pleased, to India. Perhaps I was just pursuing a fashionable trend, but for Carol, who was born in India and left when she was thirteen, this was about retracing her roots. But before we went we had to put some money aside. I found work as a temporary labourer on a large building site in Cambridge. They must have been desperate. The uninitiated tend to think of a building labourer as 'unskilled', but that is far from the truth. However I *was* unskilled. It took me more than three days to chisel out the half bricks in a doorway that was to be blocked up, a job that should have taken a morning. The foreman didn't complain; I think he thought it was a good place to put me when they didn't need me. They thrust a pneumatic drill in my hands which immediately got stuck in the asphalt. One of my favourite jobs was unloading bricks. They hadn't progressed to palettes and forklifts in those days, so we moved the bricks from the lorry to the stack by lobbing them one at a time to one another in a chain. I wasn't too bad at this; I guess cricket practice at school helped.

I managed to amass £125, the equivalent of about ten weeks' work. We applied for visas at the Afghan Embassy; Carol was given hers but I was refused. Friends said it didn't matter, you could get one in the Afghan Embassy in Tehran for a bribe. We packed our bags, took the boat to Calais, and stuck out our thumbs. Five days later we were in Istanbul where we rested for a few days before undertaking the four thousand-mile journey through Turkey, Iran, Afghanistan and Pakistan to India.

If you did the whole trip by local buses, it cost £9, providing you haggled and changed your money on the black market, and you could reduce this further by hitch-hiking some of the way. This route became inaccessible after the revolution in Iran, and the Russian invasion of Afghanistan, and remains inadvisable today. But in the 1970s, when flying was expensive, it was the highway between South Asia and Europe, frequented by American and European backpackers, Aussies taking the cheap route to Europe, various wheelers and dealers usually in Mercedes, and an elite of hipsters with a source of income, such as exporting lapis lazuli, that enabled them to hop more or less indefinitely between the more salubrious hotels in places like Kabul and Kathmandu. Most locals were used to foreigners, friendly, and happy to provide any service that might earn them money.

In Iran, which was then under the rule of the Shah, we saw little sign of the turmoil to come. True, nobody we met dared to smoke dope, because the sentences if you were caught were draconian, and we were keen to get out of Tehran, which was hot, noisy and crowded. We felt sorry for a bunch of travellers who had been marooned there for ten days because their so-called 'Magic Bus' from Istanbul to Delhi had broken down, but in a way it served them right for taking a package trip. The local buses were reliable, flexible, and you met people. The peasants who made short hops on the Iranian buses, sometimes with a few goats or sheep, were often friendly and talkative, trying out the odd word of English on us, making graceful hand gestures as they spoke.

We took a diversion, by bus, to a resort on the Caspian Sea and were amazed to find beach huts, identical to those you might find in Bognor Regis. We rented one, and while we were changing a wispy soprano voice came from the adjacent hut:

Row, row, row, your boat
Gently down the stream
Merrily, merrily, merrily, merrily
Life is but a dream.

We looked outside and there was a six-year-old Iranian girl and her parents, come to enjoy the sand, sun and sea. The father spoke good English, the mother some, and the whole family was delightful. They invited us back to their flat in Tehran where they fed us sumptuously and put us up for the night. The father was a well-heeled businessman, presumably a beneficiary of the Shah's unpleasant regime, educated, as was his wife, and liberal. They were Muslim, but they weren't going to let that get in the way of a western lifestyle. I wonder what became of them after the revolution.

The country I fell for, however, was Afghanistan. It was an extraordinary place before it got done over progressively by the Russians, the Taliban and the US. We entered on a bus from Mashhad in Iran, to Herat, the first city in Afghanistan. As we approached the border the bus driver handed out a duplicated sheet that listed all the goods that you weren't allowed to bring into Afghanistan. The list didn't include things like watches and transistor radios, which you were allowed to bring in, but had to pay duty on. It consisted of banal items like blankets, buckets, saucepans and mattresses – all things that Afghans were capable of manufacturing themselves, thank you very much.

When you got to Herat you could see why this protectionism was enforced. Despite the cars and the backpackers it was still a self-sufficient medieval city, largely because it had never been colonised. Certain streets in the city were allocated to a particular craft such as weaving, leatherwork or blacksmithing. The most striking of these was the copper beaters' street, where in a score of adjacent workshops men were beating out huge cauldrons up to three hundred litres in size. The noise was phenomenal. These workmen 'competing' next to one another must have been run by guilds that regulated prices, set standards and oversaw apprenticeships. It was the opposite of a capitalist economy.

Modern products had been absorbed into this system of indigenous production. You could buy tailor-made tobacco cigarettes in a packet, but the 'tailors' who made them were a line of men squatting in a street rolling them all by hand. There was a locally produced drink called Afghan-Cola that was even more disgusting than the American original. The food was entirely limited to what the country could produce: rice, wheat, lamb, spinach, onions, mung beans, sugar, fruits, tea, eggs, yoghurt and chicken. That was it, and you got the same menu in every restaurant, but it was wholesome and adequate. Everything, even a fried egg or a dish of spinach, came swamped in a puddle of warm grease, carved from the two bags of fat that flap like bosoms on the rumps of the sheep that could be seen hanging in butchers' shops. It was essential sustenance for a shepherd on the slopes of the Hindu Kush, but not so good if you were a foreigner suffering from gastroenteritis.

The problem with Afghanistan was the way women were treated. It was the only country we visited where many women wore a chadri, which is the ultimate form of burqa, a conical tent with a grid in front of the eyes. If you were searching for good things to say about it, it was probably airy and cool, and women could do what they liked inside it without being observed. But it was alien and abhorrent to our western sensibilities and reinforced the idea that a woman was a chattel of her husband.

I wanted to stay in Afghanistan longer, and go round the country by the more remote northern route. But Carol's visa, obtained in London, was valid for only ten days, while mine, acquired for a fiver bribe in Tehran, was indefinite. And worst of all, we were getting on badly. This was because I wasn't doing what was necessary, as a male companion, to protect her from harassment by Muslim men. When they asked me 'Are you married?' I should have said 'Yes.' Instead, being naive and politically correct, I answered, 'No, she's an independent woman', which in their eyes meant loose.

We moved swiftly to Pakistan, where if anything it was worse. Carol, who could have been mistaken for Pakistani, was spat at more than once in the street. The country was teeming with soldiers and the atmosphere tense. The only people we had prolonged conversations with turned out to be from East Pakistan, now Bangladesh, and they told us that a war was brewing. It came a year later.

———

India was a relief after the highly charged gender politics of Muslim countries. We made our way to Moradabad in Uttar Pradesh, where Carol's Anglo-Indian contacts lived. It was a community in decline since more than half had emigrated to Britain, Canada and Australia. Those who remained lived in a neighbourhood of *pukka* houses called the Railway Cantonment, since India's extensive rail network had been staffed largely by Anglo-Indians. The social centre was the once grand Railway Institute, now starting to look underused like a seaside hotel that has seen better days.

But the railways themselves were far from moribund. In 1970 some 3,400 steam locomotives staffed by 1.4 million employees trundled along 100,000 kilometres of track weighed down by their cargo of seething humanity. Over the next five months Carol and I rode much of this network, from the narrow gauge track that runs up to Shimla in the foothills of the Himalayas, to Kanyakumari on the southernmost tip of India. The trains weren't fast, but they were invariably on time, thanks to wide margins in the timetabling that allowed for long stops at stations where *chaiwallahs* would serve you tea through the carriage windows in unglazed earthenware mugs that were thrown onto the track once empty.

To see India, or at least to meet its peoples, we didn't have to look beyond the railway stations, for all life was there. There were clerks in western clothing brushing shoulders with pink-robed sadhus, Brahmims in white homespun next to tribals wearing beads and noserings, businessmen in smart suits ignoring beggars in saris, schoolgirls in salwar kameez, sweepers in loincloths, coolies with four suitcases on their head and police with truncheons. Entire families worked in the stations, hawked goods, hustled or begged, performed music, cooked and ate chapattis, nursed their babies, slept overnight on blankets, prayed there, washed there, sometimes lived their whole lives and died there. As we waited for our train, sleeping overnight on the station floor, all the faces of India would pass by, and small human dramas would unfold before us.

We were also subject to more human contact than we needed as successions of Indians, mostly educated Indian males, would approach and question us, while another ten might form a ring around and observe. 'Where are you from? Are you married?' – these were the two commonest questions, but another common one was, 'Please Sir? Are you a hippie or a Beatle?'

The exploits of John, Paul, George and Ringo at the Maharishi's ashram had been well publicised in India. Prior to the 1960s the Indian people's main experience of the British was the Raj: they wore linen suits and ties, military clothing, or in the case of women, frocks and hats. When hippies arrived and adopted sensible native garb such as pyjamas and lungis (sarongs), perhaps it was natural for some Indians to assume that this was another British caste they hadn't seen before, possibly because it had, like the Indian nation, recently been liberated from the oppressive rule of the Raj (which in a sense was true)? When the Beatles came along it seemed that this was still another caste, though not that different from hippies, and they sought clarification on this matter.

Many Indians were perplexed by the hippie movement. Another common question was, 'Why do you wear Indian clothes?' Because they are cool, comfortable and cheap was the answer, but this didn't explain what made English people adopt the dress of Indians of modest means, when any Indian male wanting to make his way in the modern world wore western style clothes. Answering 'none' to the question, 'What is your religion?' didn't help either. Perhaps from a Hindu point of view, everyone has a religion, and everyone belongs to a caste.

The Hippie phenomenon was disquieting to those amongst the Indian population who felt that India should progress towards an industrial economy and a western lifestyle. One such person was Ayi Ganpat Tendulkar, the father of Gautam, a friend of mine from Westminster school, whom we knew only as Mr Tendulkar. He invited Carol and me to stay on his model farm in a village called Belgundi in the Belgaum district of the state of Karnataka where we remained for a month.

Mr Tendulkar, who was sixty-five and could speak ten languages, was a remarkable man. Born into a poor caste and orphaned at an early age, as a schoolboy he walked penniless to Ahmedabad, applied to attend the Gandhian college there, and topped the list of successful candidates. While there he joined the satyagraha nonviolent resistance movement, became close to Gandhi and was employed as private secretary to Sardar Patel, India's future deputy prime minister. After winning a scholarship that took him to Europe, he stayed in Paris for four years, where he married a beautiful Italian socialite, then divorced her, and in the early thirties, moved to Germany to complete his doctorate. There, after another marriage and divorce, his articles on Indian freedom in a left-wing publication attracted the attention of Thea von Harbou, wife of Fritz Lang, and writer of the screenplays for his best known films. When Lang discovered her in bed with Tendulkar, he divorced her and she and Tendulkar married, in secret because this was 1933 Germany.

In 1938, the targeting of Jews during Kristallnacht convinced Mr Tendulkar to return to India. There he started a nationalist newspaper, but was imprisoned by the colonial authorities until the end of the war. After independence he married again, settled in Belgundi and founded a cement factory as a contribution towards the industrialisation of India.

Mr Tendulkar had built for himself, in the depths of the Mysore countryside, a glass fronted, concrete residence on a farm he owned. It was the only building for miles around lit by electricity, and hence every insect in the vicinity converged upon it at night time. It was an entomologist's paradise. In the evening, no sooner had his cook served us curry and rice at the dinner table, than legions of crickets would hop onto our plates as if to add animal protein to the vegetarian meal. Meanwhile a species of large flying beetle would land upside down on the concrete floor, and then boat noisily around in circles on its back, flapping wings and wriggling legs in a frenzied attempt to find some irregularity in the immaculately screeded surface against which it could right itself. There were so many of them, nobody, not even the dog, could be bothered to deal with them.

I don't suppose Mr Tendulkar ever considered eliminating these problems by going back to oil lamps and earthen floors. He was a modernist and a keen advocate of the IR8 rice that was just triggering the green revolution. But there was a note of disenchantment in his voice. India's bureaucratic inertia pained him. And he was intrigued by what he unhesitatingly called our hippie philosophy. I suspect we awoke in him a tension between his modernist aspirations and the Gandhian Luddism that had influenced his early years.

I had bought a bike in Belgaum, a black sit-up-and-beg boneshaker, with threadbare tyres whose rips had been neatly sewn up. Carol and I agreed to go our separate ways and meet back at Mr Tendulkar's in a couple of months, and I set off on the bicycle down the west coast of India to Kanyakumari in the state of Kerala. In those days, Kerala was probably the world's finest example of ribbon development. A single road, in most places a broad well maintained dirt track, stretched some 700 kilometres from north to south, hugging the seaboard except for a couple of diversions into the hills, and connecting the historic trading ports of the Malabar Coast – Calicut, Alleppey, Cochin, Trivandrum. I trundled down this highway, at a rate of about thirty kilometres a day, often at night because of the heat, with only a dhurrie (a thin cotton rug) and a muslin lungi for bedding under the stars, and my money belt with its precious traveller's cheques.

This was about as far as I was to get away from western civilisation, but it was by no means wilderness. The road made its way from village to village through a patchwork of coconut plantations and paddy fields, peppered with homesteads and shacks. Pedestrians, notably the women carrying baskets of vegetables on their heads to sell at market, were more numerous than vehicles. At intervals along the road there were stone dolmens where they posed their burden at shoulder height while they took a rest.

Kerala was (and still is) one of the most densely populated regions of India. It was also refreshingly sane, and prosperous in a wholesome meaning of the word. Standards of education were high, and the population intermittently voted in a communist government. Malayalam, the official language of Kerala, which boasts fifty-seven letters in its alphabet, was the first in India to provide translations of Marx's texts. In many of the villages there were co-operative weaving workshops, with maybe a dozen handlooms offering employment to men and women producing the gay saris and lungis. Dotted along the coast were fleets of inshore fishing boats, little more than large canoes, powered by sail and hand. At the end of the day when they returned the rest of the community would be waiting to haul the boats up above the tide line, and to buy, process and distribute the catch. By the following lunchtime you could be eating the fish in a roadside canteen where you could buy a thali (set meal) with soup for a starter, three different fish curries, vegetable side dishes, rice and one of the distinctive flaky Keralan parathas. These flat breads were made on the spot by spreading oil over rolled out dough, and casting it across the work surface so that it stretched into a three-foot wide membrane that was cut into strips, gathered into a ball, rerolled and fried. This sumptuous meal was to be found, not in a three-star restaurant, but in shacks that were the equivalent of an English greasy spoon café.

Kerala, as I found it in 1970, was supremely civilised, not in the sense that it was wealthy, or technologically advanced, but because its people were happy, well fed, intelligent, polite and handsome. If there was poverty, or ethnic tension, or vicious class and caste distinction, I didn't penetrate deeply enough to witness it. In Cochin I talked to an Indian Jew who ran a bookshop where, amongst other items, you could buy the works of Marx translated into either Malayalam or English. 'Cochin must be the best place in the world for a Jew to live,' he told me. 'The population of our town is quarter Hindu, quarter Muslim, quarter Christian and quarter Jewish – and we all get on.'

At Trivandrum, the capital of Kerala, I made my way to the temple tank, for a wash. There I was accosted by a distinguished-looking gentleman of sixty or so years of age, dressed in a khadi, homespun lungi. He was the sort of Indian who is at one with the world wearing spectacles and carrying a black umbrella. 'Excuse me, you are English?' he asked. 'Allow me to introduce myself. I am Mr Pannikar. I have been to Oxford.' He produced a faded photo of a younger Indian gentleman in front of what might have been a college. Mr Pannikar explained that in recent years he had become a sadhu, a holy man, and was now practicing what he called water yoga, which in his case involved floating on his back in the temple baths with his legs crossed in lotus position, and he showed me another photograph to prove it. Seeing I was duly impressed he confided: 'I am now learning to do lotus position in water sitting up. Six years I have been trying, but have not achieved it yet.'

When I told him I was bicycling down to Kanyakumari he announced, 'I will come with you. Tomorrow. I have bicycle.' He continued: 'My bicycle is very good, but has punctures and needs mending. Would you be so kind as to?' I agreed to pay for the repairs and the following evening as it was getting dark we set off to ride through the night the fifty-six miles from Trivandrum to the southernmost tip of India.

Mr Pannikar was a charming companion, fitter and faster than I, though three times my age, full of beans and good humour. When I sprang a puncture half way through the journey he knew where to go to get it repaired well past midnight, and engaged in spirited Malayalam banter with the mechanics. The last ten miles of the journey passed alongside a moonlit marsh that reverberated with the sound of thousands of croaking frogs. We arrived at Kanyakumari in time to see the sun rising over the Indian ocean. Dotted around the rocky shore were various sadhus, sitting cross-legged and staring fixedly at the ocean like a colony of seabirds. On an island just offshore somebody was building a memorial temple to Swami Vivekananda who had apparently meditated there for three days in 1892, and made the decision to go to the US. But tourist development hadn't really got under way. Nowadays Kanyakumari boasts a 133-foot-high statue of the Tamil poet Thiruvalluvar on another offshore rock, and onshore a full range of facilities including temples and churches for just about every denomination, a helipad, the Baywatch Theme Park, the Aqua World aquarium and three tattoo shops.

Watching the sunrise was a romantic enough experience, but sunrise doesn't take long in the tropics. To be honest, I had found it more exhilarating to watch gangs of men and boys hauling fishing boats out of the surf. Travelling to the very tip of India was more rewarding than arriving.

My plan was to sell the bike and make my way back to Belgundi through Madras State (now Tamil Nadu). However Mr Pannikar, who was now getting on famously with some of the sadhus and showing them his water yoga photo, made it clear that he hoped, indeed expected, that I would give him the bike or at least sell it very cheap. He deserved it – he had been such a congenial companion – and the price I had paid for it in India, I had earned in England in a few hours. But I was seven thousand miles from home with less than £25 left in my money belt. The look of disappointment on Mr Pannikar's face when I sold it to a local dealer has haunted me ever since.

Hopping from one temple town to another by bus, train and hitch-hiking, I made it back to Belgundi. After a rest, Carol and I set off on the journey home, retracing our steps. We had learnt a thing or two about how to stay sane while travelling, and got on much better than we had on the outward journey.

Back in a grey London winter I mulled over the experience. I loved India, but was aware that I had just glossed over its surface. I was keen to return, but not as a backpacker poncing around the country, acquiring people's goods and labour with cash so cheaply earned in Britain. I had seen how backpackers were the advance guard of a tourist industry that destroyed the very thing it cherished. I decided that I would return when there was work or something else sensible I could do there. That opportunity has never arisen. In any case the revolution in Iran and the Soviet invasion of Afghanistan were soon to make the overland journey next to impossible, and the idea of flying to India in a matter of hours seemed grotesque.

However I gained more from one journey of seven months than I could ever have learnt in three years at university. There were aspects of India it was hard to countenance: the caste system, the gulf between rich and poor. But my exposure to its poverty confirmed for me that the standard of living we pursue in Europe – the machines, the plastics, the consumer goods – contributes little or nothing to human welfare. Provided people's basic needs are met – food, shelter, medical care, a home and community – they require little more to live happily. From a single tree, the coconut palm, the poor of maritime India obtain food, drink, timber, fuel, thatch, mattresses, matting, animal bedding, rope, ship rigging, fishing nets, alcohol, brushes, scouring pads and much more. Why look further afield when nature offers so much potential on our doorsteps?

What that journey taught me was that human nature is mercurial; human societies can be almost anything they choose. The cities of the industrial world may become increasingly indistinguishable as they embrace global capitalist culture, but indigenous and rural societies are all intriguingly different. Belief in this malleability of human nature is indispensable for the revolutionary seeking to create an alternative society. But revolutionaries often underestimate how hard it is to change people who are set in their ways.

CHAPTER FOUR

Work and Lodging

With India 'done' so to speak, and lessons absorbed, I had to knuckle down to the mundane business of earning a living and finding somewhere to live. In fact it turned out to be less mundane than it might have been, for over the next two years I flitted from one job to another, rarely sticking at one more than a few weeks, and moving domicile accordingly. The trip to India had introduced me to ways of living that were utterly different from the culture in which I had been raised; now I was to experience first hand some of the absurdities of late twentieth century capitalism, and that was to be just as educational.

My first priority was to attend to the other missing bit of my education. My job on the building site had revealed how incompetent I was on a practical level. I now considered it ludicrous that I had been admitted to one of the top universities in the country without even knowing what a carburettor was. I therefore began what was to prove a rather long process of addressing this deficiency by enrolling on a course in welding at Hammersmith tech college, two afternoons a week. Since the course began with the assumption that the students knew nothing, I could cope. I didn't take to electric arc welding: it had limited applications and seemed to be designed for mass production on the factory floor. But I enjoyed using the oxy acetylene kit, which is an altogether more convivial tool. With oxy you can do all sorts of things, including copper welding, glass blowing, forging metal, cutting up scrap cars, burglary and sabotage even. And you can do it anywhere as you don't need an electricity supply.

Enrolment at Hammersmith meant staying in London, where rented accommodation was hard to find and expensive. Somebody tipped me off about an attic flat in a street off Tottenham Court Road that was empty, unlocked and ready to be squatted. It was true, I could just walk in. The place was crammed with the previous inhabitant's possessions: his kitchen equipment, his clothes, his books, his mementoes, everything. He had died some months previously, the undertakers had come in and carried his body away and that was that.

The deceased gentleman's name was Filippo Fiorillo. He was a portly Italian who had worked as a pastry chef in the continental cafés that proliferate in the Fitzrovia area of London. He appeared never to have married, nor was there any evidence of kin. For all I know he had been a jolly fellow, but there was a sad undercurrent to his life. He was in awe of his father Giuseppe, and the room and its contents were a shrine to his memory. Giuseppe was no mere pastry chef; he was one of the top artists in cake icing. There were photos of him standing proudly by five-tiered wedding cakes, and certificates showing the medals he had won in international exhibitions. There were wooden slabs housing hand-carved moulds for making shapes such as shells, lilies, and egg and dart moulding out of fondant icing. The centrepiece was a cylindrical glass case, three feet high, which housed a classical tableau made entirely of icing. It depicted a goddess leaning against a fluted pillar, surrounded by acanthus leaves and similar motifs. Time had taken its toll and the floor of the tableau was littered with bits of broken icing-sugar masonry.

After a couple of weeks a note was slipped under the door accusing me of insulting the memory of Mr Fiorillo. I could see what they meant, and felt uneasy. On the other hand I felt I was paying some sort of tribute to his memory. Sooner or later, house clearance people would enter and unceremoniously cart his stuff to the tip. A few days later, an eviction notice came through the door. There was no point in contesting it, so I slipped away,

In May 1971, I put my practical education on hold. I abandoned the welding course and travelled to Somerset to help in the preparations for the second Glastonbury Festival. The first, in the previous year, had been a minor affair, but this one was to prove, by many accounts, a fabulous event, that established Glastonbury as the archetypal festival site and set the standard for the free festivals of the following decades.

I joined a colony of mud-spattered hippies living in tents in the valley beneath the farmhouse. In the middle was an impromptu tipi, covered in transparent plastic sheeting occupied by Sid Rawle and his current girlfriend. Sid, who had made his name as a land campaigner with the Hyde Park Diggers, had a bluff manner and a brazen resourcefulness that cast him as a dominant figure wherever he went, and here was no exception.

Some of the crew were engaged constructing the huge pyramid stage from scaffolding shrouded in silvery plastic that was to become the festival's trademark. My role was to help prepare and run a free canteen called the Communal Knead. We built a ramshackle kitchen and improvised an oven out of a scrap metal tank that could cook twenty loaves of bread at one go. We had virtually no money, but everything to do with the organisation of the café fell into place with magical ease. On one occasion I was in a squat in North London, and mentioned that I was looking for large cooking pans. 'Go through the hole in the wall at the back of next door's garden,' I was told. There was a scrap yard with dozens of stainless steel pans of about one hundred litres. No sooner had I liberated a couple, than someone came through the door of the squat asking, 'I don't suppose anybody needs fourteen five-pound packs of caterers' dried onion soup, do they?'

Not everything was running smoothly, though. For the two weeks prior to the festival it rained almost every day and the site became a mudbath. There were problems securing a water supply for the numbers anticipated, and the organisers up at the farmhouse were becoming edgy. Then on the eve of the festival the clouds dispersed, and next morning some twelve thousand campers woke at sunrise to the sound of Melanie's crystal voice heralding four days of sunshine and music.

The weather was perfect for the next four days, the music could have been a lot worse, the psychoactive drugs were more reliable in those days, and the atmosphere was brilliant. For those of us on the crew, the additional reward was to have participated in the creation of a temporary city, a makeshift Jerusalem, that ran without money and provided its own food, utilities, welfare services, even its own cathedral. I was on the night shift at our kitchen, which ran twenty-four hours a day. Every morning at dawn we drove to Bristol fruit market to pick up waste vegetables for soup and salad; and for fourpence a dozen we bought rubber eggs (rejects that had no shell and bounced when you dropped them) from a local battery farm. Sid ran the other free food gaff during the festival, up in the farmyard. On day two of the festival, a hot dog van drove onto site in front of the stage and started selling to the punters. Sid got his minions to go round with the hat, bought hundreds of sausages and bread rolls with the proceeds, and handed sausage sandwiches out for free right next to the hot dog man, who drove off and never came back.

After the festival was over and the detritus cleared away, a meeting was called by the stage for all those interested in developing whatever achievements might have been made. It was an optimistic affair, everyone feeling that they had witnessed the embryo of something greater. Andrew Kerr, the festival's main organiser, made a speech outlining plans for settling on an Irish island, and building a permanent community with an 'astrological laboratory' and a self-sufficient food production. The island in question, Dorinish, had been bought and lent to the movement by John Lennon, and comprised nineteen acres of tree-less wind-swept sward. Later in 1971, Sid Rawle moved on with his followers, but their commune lasted barely a year. The festival, by contrast, gradually relinquished its alternative aspirations, to become the orgy of consumption that it is today.

Not long after returning from Glastonbury I found myself at Hammersmith Labour Exchange talking to a careers adviser. He seemed friendly enough, and not a great deal older than I. Some days before I had filled in a lengthy and searching questionnaire, and I was here to find out what the future might hold in store for me.

'Mmm, yes,' he muttered as he glanced through the paper-work. 'We get a lot of people like you. It's hard to know what to suggest ... Have you ever thought of being a lighthouse keeper?'

I hadn't. There were, I gathered, a few vacancies for light-house keepers (though none of them in Hammersmith). It made a refreshing change from the labouring and warehouse jobs typically on offer, and I said I'd think about it. Month-long vigils on Flannan Isle might have been ideal had I wanted to write a novel or get deeply into transcendental meditation; but alas! this was not the case, and I turned the offer down.

When I tumbled into the job market in the late 1960s, 'zero-hours contracts', 'the gig economy' and 'precarity' hadn't been invented. Similar opportunities existed then in the casual labour market, but it wasn't quite as precarious an existence as nowadays. The economy was healthy, until it crashed after the oil crisis of 1973, and jobs rather than workers were two a penny. The challenge for a committed drop-out was not so much to find a job as to avoid being made to do one, at least beyond the point where it got boring.

The system worked like this. Casual workers could claim a weekly social security payment if they signed on at the labour exchange every week, reporting any days they had been employed. Every Thursday a cross-section of the less refined elements of the social spectrum would queue up at the labour exchange to receive a cash payment in a little brown envelope: not a princely sum, but worth having and it paid the rent. Meanwhile, suit-and-tie professionals who had fallen on hard times were received privately in a room with carpets.

After six weeks of this, the labour exchange would call you in, offer you three jobs, and if you didn't take one of them, they'd stop your benefit anyway. If one of the jobs looked half decent I would take it. Otherwise I would go off and find something better. Most jobs were temporary, and the permanent ones were ultimately soul-destroying, so after some weeks I'd find myself unemployed once again, but with money in my pocket. This could be eked out for a further length of time until it was acceptable to go back to the labour exchange and start the process all over again.

It was a pattern easy to slip into, but also a conscious choice. 'A career is a headlong rush towards doom,' I wrote at the time. I was not fully aware of how I was benefiting from being a casual worker, but was in no doubt that I was doing the right thing. In retrospect, I see how it compensated for the inadequacies of my monochrome education. It was a foundation course in learning to use my hands; it provided a fresh window from which to observe how society functions; and it put me on the same level and in contact with the sort of people that my upbringing had sheltered me from – namely the working class.

Middle-class youth nowadays do not seem to have this option. University is almost obligatory, and at the end of it, if they don't land a job straight away they enter the limbo of unpaid internship with the prospect of a career sometime in the future, maybe. But then, on reflection, perhaps they do have that option, but don't want to take it. Unemployment, at least in the more prosperous parts of the UK, is lower than it has ever been. The sort of jobs we used to do in the 1960s are now (pace Brexit) performed by Eastern Europeans, because, apparently, Brits don't want to do them. Nobody (except me) is advising the kids of today to 'turn on, tune in and drop out'. When I recently conducted a straw poll of a number of acquaintances, I found that every person over fifty had at some time in their youth earned money picking fruit or vegetables. Not a single person under thirty-five had.

My mother's flat at Glyn Mansions, where I stayed from time to time, overlooked Olympia exhibition hall. The billboard opposite announcing the date of the next show was a permanent outdoor calendar. Olympia also happened to be one of the main centres for casual catering work in London in the 1960s. Maybe it still is. You could turn up at the start of an exhibition and they would hire you, on a daily basis, for 4 shillings 6 pence an hour, which was the equivalent of three litres of petrol, or two pints of ale. Washing up dishes for the Ideal Home Exhibition was hardly an ideal job, but it was an eye-opener for a young school-leaver.

Part of the attraction of working at Olympia was mixing with people from different walks of life, whom I had never previously come into contact with – black people, Irish labourers, criminals … The biggest eye-opener was my introduction to the sexual mores of the working class. It wasn't just the topless pinups on the wall. It was that they adopted a ritual of seduction more animal than anything I had previously encountered. I could hardly believe the crudeness with which one of my workmates at Olympia pursued a particular girl down the corridor every time he saw her, wolf-whistling and shouting that he liked the way she wiggled her bum – and I was almost shocked that he could keep up this unrequited tirade of 'compliments' day after day. It looked to me like harassment, and nowadays it would be regarded as such. But I was still more astonished and a touch envious, when one evening I went into the pub and there she was snuggling in his arms. Was that really how it was done?

Olympia was a good standby, and another was working for temp agencies. This was a better option for our girlfriends who could earn much more than we blokes could. At the tail end of an era when women's liberation, as G.K. Chesterton put it, meant 'taking dictation', lasses had been under less pressure to go to university, and instead encouraged to take shorthand typing courses, which meant they had a skill that was in demand in 1960s London. A male drop-out, or indeed a graduate seeking temporary work, was near the bottom of the employment ladder. The plight of those who had completed a liberal arts degree was epitomised in an advert that appeared in *Private Eye*: 'Need a philosopher? Doctor of Philosophy offers consultations: £1 per hour.'

A few of the temp agencies found work for unskilled males at six shillings an hour before tax, barely half what the girls were earning. It was mostly warehouse work. I did a stint at the British Standards Institution where I amused myself by devising a more efficient system for storing and retrieving their documents, which I was in no position to implement. For Hulton Press I stuffed promotional literature into envelopes pre-addressed to every primary and secondary school in Britain, never failing, when appropriate, to scribble a note saying that it had been packed by an old boy. I did one day at Fenwick of Bond Street before they fired me for having long hair.

Then an opportunity arose to move out of London. A couple whom I knew well from Colchester, Jane Hales and David 'Baz' Barry, had been engaged as housekeeper and butler for the Baroness Edmée Di Pauli, of Stanley Hall, a moated fifteenth-century stately home in the Essex village of Pebmarsh. It was an unlikely arrangement. Jane, a qualified teacher, carried out her duties conscientiously, but Baz, a poet and blues guitarist of bear-like stature and long lank hair looked singularly out of place. The Baroness, who was a supporter of the organic movement, needed help managing her vegetable garden, so I and two mates moved into the lodge at the end of the drive in return for a few hours' work keeping her weeds at bay.

I'm afraid we were a disappointment to the Baroness. She was an intimidating woman and difficult to warm to. In the main reception room of the house was a massive portrait, painted by her husband, the Baron, showing her advancing towards him holding a pair of secateurs at crotch level. It was hard to share her excitement about kohlrabi and celeriac, vegetables we'd never seen before, or to muster great enthusiasm for her endless battle against couch grass. We did the minimum number of hours necessary to pay the rent, and looked elsewhere for cash.

Out of London the jobs were not necessarily better. I did a month on a twelve-hour night shift at Polytops Plastics factory at nearby Halstead supervising injection moulding machines making toothpaste tube tops. Granules of plastic went into a hopper at the top of the machine, and came out the other end in the form of about forty toothpaste tube tops and the plastic grid that had extruded them – just like an Airfix model aeroplane kit, except the machine was supposed to detach the tops from the grid. However it only had a 95 per cent success rate, so my job was to manually remove any recalcitrant tops. The machine disgorged the tops at the rate of one grid every twenty-five seconds, so I had about eighteen seconds free in which I could read a book, interspersed by seven seconds of manipulating plastic.

Then one evening I clocked in for work and they put me on another machine with a ten second cycle. Seven seconds of twiddling tops and just three seconds of relief before the next batch arrived: 240 toothpaste tube tops a minute, 14,400 an hour, 170,000 a night, 850,000 a week, more than 40 million a year. With no opportunity to read, time passed slower than I have known before or since. I tried to ration my glances at the clock, but what seemed like an hour turned out to be fifteen minutes. In prison you can snooze or daydream, or scratch pictures on the wall, but at Polytops I was slave to a machine that demanded my response every ten seconds.

I had to do something. I calculated that a hopper full of plastic lasted about twelve hours. Just before I clocked off, they refilled the hopper, and so before going home I flipped a halfpenny into it. Next evening when I turned up for work: bah! the ten-second machine was still working, and I braced myself for another night of tedium. But barely twenty minutes into my shift the machine emitted a despairing screech and ground to a halt. The line manager came over: 'Ooh, what's happened here? We'd better wait till the engineer comes in the morning.' I was put back on the 25 second machine. Victory! It was my first and only act of silent Luddism.

I left Polytops shortly afterwards, but what perplexed me was that there were people at the factory who worked twelve hours on the night shift, week in week out, on the 10 second or the 25 second machines, and who seemed happy with their lot. A friend who worked for a time in a London biscuit factory told me how she had befriended another woman who had worked there for seventeen years. Happily this woman had saved up enough money to emigrate with her husband to Australia. What was she going to do there? Work for the same company in another biscuit factory.

But the most bizarre job I undertook was steaming and mashing potatoes on a nearby farm. My employer, proud owner of no less than nine tractors, had grown two thousand tons of potatoes, which were piled up in a huge asbestos shed. Britain apparently had an arrangement with the Germans that we would import a quantity of their potatoes in return for selling them some other commodity, so these home-grown spuds were surplus to requirements. The government bought them off the farmer for £18 a ton, and then, without moving them, sold them back to him for £4 a ton. The farmer had thus earned £28,000 and still had a barn full of potatoes. The trouble was that he wasn't allowed to sell them, and to ensure that he didn't, men from the ministry had come round and sprayed them purple.

The farmer had to somehow get rid of the purple potatoes, so he chose to turn them into cattle feed with the help of a vintage potato masher. Our job was to superintend this machine, which had clearly been designed for the war effort by Heath Robinson. We shovelled the purple potatoes onto conveyor belts that riddled them, washed them and delivered them into the boiler, whence, once fully cooked, they were crushed by a vertical revolving augur that disgorged dollops of off-colour mashed potato, like miniature cow pats, onto a further set of conveyor belts. These belts rose into the air over a length of about fifty yards into a field and dropped the substance into a pit the size of a circus ring, dug for the purpose. Nearby was another pit, full of last year's mashed potato, covered by a layer of scabrous skin. 'Don't go near it,' advised the farmer. 'It's still hot. If you fall in you'll scald to death.'

The production line had to be kept going day and night, because it took time to heat up the boiler and there were an awful lot of potatoes to get rid of. Three of us tended the machine: we each did four hours on, four hours off for two days, and then took the third day off. The trouble was that the potatoes had been picked by a brand new £40,0000 state-of-the-art Dutch harvesting machine, which had difficulty distinguishing between potatoes and flints, whereas the steamer was designed for potatoes picked by people who could tell the difference. We therefore had to supervise the incoming conveyor belt to remove any stones. However a flint covered in Essex clay doesn't look much different from a potato covered with the same, and when both are dyed purple it is even harder to tell them apart. Inevitably the occasional flint would get into the augur, and when it did the machine would grind to a halt. The only person who understood it well enough to repair it was the farmer and, unlike us, he was not willing to turn out at unsociable hours, so it was rare that the machine ran throughout the night.

Despite these welcome breaks in the routine, the working schedule was hard to maintain over time, and after a month I jacked the job in, even though it paid well. Before leaving the farm for the last time I peered into the circus ring. There was a pitifully small puddle of mashed potato compared to the mountain of spuds still to be processed. On the other hand a goodly amount of potato had spilled out into the yard. In those days the yards of dairy farms were often ankle deep in cow shit. This one was awash in purple mashed potato.

Eventually I did find a job that I liked. I left Stanley Hall, moved back to Colchester and got a job on the municipal dustcarts. It was the only job I held down for any length of time – five months in all. While it was as fatuous a waste of human effort as a good many other jobs, it had a number of things to recommend it: it was well paid in comparison to casual work, it was to some degree managed by the workers, and it was interesting, indeed fascinating.

I was a stand-in for regular workers while they were on holiday, so I worked with a number of crews, but they all operated in the same way. There were five men to a cart, who had a certain area of town to cover within a week. It was 'job and finish', and each crew could organise its round as it saw fit. All the crews I worked with did roughly eight hours on Monday,

six on Tuesday and Wednesday, four on Thursday and not even
two on Friday – about twenty-six hours in all.

The council's management were aware of these short hours
– you could hardly hide the time when the cart was returned
to the depot – and complicit in maintaining them. The system
secured for them a contented workforce who got a dirty job
done efficiently for a price that society was prepared to pay. The
only time I did a forty-hour week was when a time and motion
man was brought in to calculate the work load of our weekly
round. He sat in the cab making notes, while we worked at a
walking pace appropriate to payment at an hourly rate, rather
than the brisk pace of someone doing piece work.

Domestic refuse collection in those days was different from
what it is today. There were no wheelie bins, no bin bags, and
householders did not have to put their rubbish out the front.
Instead dustmen used to go round to the back of the house,
equipped with a stout rubber skip, as big as a large dustbin,
but more comfortable to carry on your shoulder. This meant
that instead of carrying the householders' bin to the cart and
making a second journey to return it to the house, you could
tip the contents of the dustbin into your skip, and thus make
only one journey.

It was this that made the job bearable. For a start, the back of
a house is a lot more interesting than the front. Each backyard
is different, a tableau reflecting the lifestyle of the incumbents.
You find out who is growing dope in their back garden, who
has an old motorbike or a pile of bricks that might be for sale.

You find out still more about them when you tip the contents of their bin into the skip: what they eat, how wasteful and
messy they are, whether they open their bills and so on. But
at this point your main interest in the shower of detritus is to
see if there is something worth recuperating – anything from
returnable Corona bottles and scrap metal to smart clothes and

collectable bric-a-brac. During the day the cab would become increasingly cluttered with booty, which might be dropped off at a house en route, or taken back to the depot. Amongst my better finds were a decent violin and a Lalique lampshade.

In the first week on a new crew I would be told, 'Don't do that house, it's Fred's,' and, 'Don't do those two, they're Joe's.' These houses, allocated to the most senior members of the crew, were those that customarily threw away their cigarette coupons. Fred would have the Embassy tokens and Joe the Player's No.6. By the end of every week they would have enough saved to buy an electric drill, a coffee set for the missus or a toy for the kids. When I came back to England in the 1980s after ten years' absence, bin bags had come in and cigarette coupons had disappeared.

While I was working on the council's dustcarts, I was also living free of charge in one of their empty properties. Most of the documentation of squatting in the late sixties and early seventies focuses on London, and in particular famous occupations such as Frestonia, Elgin Avenue and Eel Pie Island. But there was no shortage of houses lying empty in provincial towns as well, nor of people prepared to occupy them.

Colchester, where the council's plan was to rip the heart out of the town, was no exception. Every Saturday, the cattle market held at the bottom of North Hill became the social and economic centre of the community (who had just been paid on Friday). At least five auctions were held there: the livestock, the outside deadstock, the interior furniture and effects, the live poultry and veg, and the impounded bicycle auction. The local pubs, including a hippy haunt called the New Market Tavern, had all day extensions in an era when afternoon closing was obligatory. The market was where you headed for on a Saturday and you were bound to meet your mates there.

The council's plan, which they eventually carried out, was to move the market out of town, build a roundabout in its place linked to a new road system to bring more traffic into the town, and sell the rest of the site off for development. The Royal London insurance company built their office block there, which was a fat lot of good to anyone on a Saturday morning. It is a fate that has since been inflicted on virtually every market town in England.

As a result there were a number of houses and other buildings on the line of the projected road, lying temptingly empty, either originally owned, or else compulsorily purchased by the council. Colchester's squatting movement started tentatively when Greg Cox and myself moved into a two-up-two-down in Pope's Lane. We were new to the game then and it was only a few weeks before the authorities had us out. But by that time we had made contact with the remarkable Bernard Brett, whom I had first got to know a few years earlier when a pupil at the grammar school.

Bernard had cerebral palsy. Aged about forty, he was confined to a wheelchair, couldn't sit up properly, couldn't talk, groaned and dribbled constantly and had muscular control over none of his body, save one arm. But there was nothing wrong with his brain; he was as bright as a pin. As a schoolboy I had been one of the people who used to wheel him around town. He communicated by pointing with his finger at letters on a green board with the QWERTY alphabet printed on it. Once you got quick enough at reading it he would make puns by waving his finger ambiguously between two letters and let you know with a giggle. Being unmistakable, he was well known around town, and when people stopped to say, 'How are you', you had to translate Bernard's keyboard response, often a politesse followed by a caustic aside like 'twit' or 'let's go'.

Bernard was secretary of the local Quaker Housing Association, whose main role was to assist people facing eviction, including families. When he got wind that we were squatting he proposed a little conflab. Squatting was just what the Quakers needed to push the council into releasing empty buildings for short-term housing, but a mainstream organisation like theirs could not be seen to be supporting it. We hippies on the other hand needed something, or rather someone, to give us mainstream credibility and get the press on our side. The solution was obvious. Bernard would let us know when there was a family in need, and then we would pounce. The mischievous giggle that spread over his face as we said goodbye that evening was unforgettable.

A couple of weeks later Bernard had a case in need. A couple nearing retirement age had been made homeless; their possessions were literally on the pavement. I owned an Austin FG bread van at the time that I had bought for £33 at Chelmsford vehicle auctions. I had no driving licence, but that didn't matter. We rolled up, picked up the couple's possessions and moved them into a house in Belle Vue Road, while we simultaneously occupied the house next door.

It worked. Local press coverage was sympathetic. The council did not rush to evict us. And other people were being drawn to the idea of squatting. A few weeks later Bernard contacted us with another household facing eviction, and soon after a third. We decided to go for the main prize, a row of about ten houses at the bottom of Butt Road, a stone's throw from the town centre. Soon we had every house in the block occupied either with bona fide homeless or with hippies, artists, disaffected students, greasers and other oddballs. I shared my house with a biker called Greasy Pete and a clean-cut blond couple called Pete and Linda. They might have passed for normal had they not dressed themselves and their small child entirely in white, and painted the entirety of their south-facing room and its furnishings white as well. Visiting them was like walking into a Fellini movie.

Less successful was our occupation of the former police social centre at the bottom end of the block. It was a great place, but we didn't have the skills needed to operate a squatted social centre. We tried to put on events, but the place got taken over by greasers, who embellished one interior wall with a panorama of a town in flames with the word 'Triumph' arched across the sky, but otherwise just smashed the place up. This scared everyone else off and we had to let the place go. Some months later one of the greasers came up to me in the pub and apologised.

After that debacle, we opened up one of the houses as a free shop. We had no problem stocking it since three of us worked on the dustcarts, which, handily, passed by the squat on their twice daily trips to the tip. Every weekday, six municipal lorries would disgorge a cargo of unwanted clean clothes, kitchen equipment, tools, books, sports goods and general bric-a-brac into our shop. This too was not without its problems. Antique dealers would strip the shop of anything of value. A few people would walk out in a complete set of clean clothes, having taken their dirty ones off and left them for us to deal with. But the shop served its purpose of questioning the logic of capitalism and high-lighting the grotesque volumes of waste that could have been recycled. And there were good moments: for example when an ice cream salesman whose equipment had broken down gave us a huge box of ices, that we handed out amongst ourselves and to people in the unsquatted houses across the road.

The Butt Road squat was a focus of radical resistance to the policies of the town council. Graffiti appeared around the town demanding 'Homes not Roads'. The message was not falling on deaf ears: the senior probation officer for Colchester went on record as saying that he and his colleagues could see no alternative but to suggest squatting to their ex-offender clients. On one occasion we occupied the Town Hall, and on a balcony overlooking the High Street spread a massive banner bearing the words 'The Council is Mad'. When a national politician visited the town, a sizable anti-war demonstration turned into a vicious scuffle in which several of the military policemen's caps went flying through the air.

Military police were used to maintain order because Colchester is a garrison town. Normally its annual tattoo, in which regiments, marching bands and tanks parade through the High Street, passed off without incident, but not so in 1972. To offset the pageantry, a fellow called Tony Cornflake and I made some crutches, swathed ourselves in bloodstained bandages and, accompanied by Liz Morris dressed as a nurse, joined the parade in the gap between two marching regiments. Amazingly we were not bundled off, but allowed to hobble along through the entire route.

If Colchester's municipal establishment had ever entertained thoughts of tolerating the squats, this agitprop activity was sufficient to dispel them. While the council undertook the process of obtaining a court order, the police focused on the yellow van that we used to move people's goods into squats. This was now parked on a side street with an expired Ministry of Transport (MOT) test. Ordinary garages couldn't test it because it was too big, and heavy goods vehicle garages couldn't because it was taxed as a caravan. I explained the problem to Swansea Vehicle Licensing Agency and they wrote back saying that as far as they were concerned the vehicle was exempt from the MOT test.

Meanwhile the police had charged me with twenty-one offences connected with the van, including cracked mirror, no unladen weight written and three charges of no MOT. When the first fifteen charges were heard in court I read out the letter from the DVLC, but the magistrate found me guilty and I was fined accordingly. The van was towed away to the police pound.

The remaining charges were heard some weeks later, and this time I was found not guilty, and told that I didn't need an MOT after all. Flushed with victory I went to the police to reclaim my van, to be told that I had to pay a charge of £1 for every day it had spent in the pound, in total £65, which was twice as much as the van had cost. I had to leave it, and shortly afterwards the police towed it to the tip and deposited it on top of a sprawling heap of domestic rubbish. This was the same tip that I was visiting twice a day as a dustman so I had the privilege of watching a tide of filth pile up against my van, engulfing first the tyres, then the engine, then the mandala painted on the side panel, and finally the skylight, till nothing remained.

Meanwhile the council's application for a possession order was progressing through the system. It didn't look as though we had much of a defence, but then a week before the court case we had a stroke of luck. A judge in another squatting case had granted a possession order, but suspended it until the owner of the property could show that he needed the building. This was all we were asking for – to stay in the houses until the council had to demolish them for their wretched road. We put it to the judge and he agreed. The council could only evict us if and when they needed the houses.

But relief was short-lived. The original case had been referred at appeal to the Master of the Rolls, the septuagenarian Lord Denning, who in *McPhail v Persons, Names Unknown* [1973] reversed the earlier decision, stating: 'A possession order ... is an authority under which anyone who is squatting on the premises can be turned out at once. There is no provision for giving any time.'

He famously added: 'What is a squatter? He is one who, without any colour of right, enters on an unoccupied house or land, intending to stay there as long as he can. He may seek to justify or excuse his conduct. He may say that he was homeless and that the house or land was standing empty, doing nothing. But this plea is of no avail in law.'

The inevitable conclusion to be drawn from this ruling by anyone squatting was that the law is morally bankrupt.

The council took us back to court, were granted their possession order with immediate effect and gave us a deadline for vacating the properties. We decided not to resist eviction, but instead paint the town red. There were plenty of half-full tins of paint in the free shop. On our last night we plastered the squats and any nearby municipal buildings with slogans spelling out the councils' idiocy.

The police eventually cottoned on. Towards the end of the evening I was acting as lookout for Greasy Pete while he wrote 'Balls to the Bourgeois' in massive letters on the wall of the Social Security office; I also told him how to spell 'bourgeois'. No sooner had he finished than a police car came round the corner and stopped next to me. Inside was PC Les Bloom, who had been in my class at school. 'Everything alright Simon?' he asked, and after a few polite exchanges he and his colleague drove off, completely failing to notice the dripping wet slogan on the other side of the road, or Pete slipping away with the paint pot. Next day Les came to arrest me and I was charged with conspiracy to cause criminal damage. It was a charge I could not in honesty deny, and I was fined £25.

That was the end of squatting in Colchester, at least for a time, but it was by no means a battle fought in vain. Later in 1973, the council allowed the Quaker Housing Association to take over the management of houses slated for demolition in Denmark Street and elsewhere, no doubt out of concern that they might otherwise be squatted. The episode had been a lesson in how mainstream voluntary organisations and direct activists can work together, a lesson that in years to come Friends of the Earth and some other environmental groups would have difficulty absorbing. Direct activists make moderate progressives appear reasonable by shifting the boundaries of discourse. Much later I discovered there was a term for this phenomenon: 'the radical flank effect', coined by Herbert Haines in 1984, and revived by Andreas Malm in his 2021 book *How to Blow Up a Pipeline*.

CHAPTER FIVE

Alternative Consciousness

A Taxonomy

I n the late sixties and early seventies, when I was in London, I used to sell copies of *International Times*, most often in High Street Kensington Tube station arcade. I'd pick up copies from their office in Endell Street at a shilling a piece and sell them for one and sixpence. With my mock-cockney news-sellers' cry, '*Hinternational Toimes*', that lingered long and high on the first syllable, I normally sold about twelve copies an hour, which earned me more than the four and sixpence I could net at casual labour. Today I feel sorry for sellers of *Big Issue*, who rely on an element of emotional blackmail rather than simply the quality of the magazine to make a sale.

This was one of the tiny parts I played in the flowering of alternative consciousness. *International Times*, which had begun publishing in 1966 as *LongHair Times*, and *OZ*, which first appeared in the following year, were the vanguard of the underground press in the UK. Their innovative graphics, semi-illegible typography and libidinous content (some of which would not be politically correct nowadays) made stalwart radical publications such as *Peace News* and *Anarchy* look tame. They came out of the same stable as Abbie Hoffman's *Revolution for the Hell of It*, and Jerry Rubin's *Do It!*, the book that my father called 'the sustained incantation of the spoiled child ... the cry of a child in tantrum'. He took it a bit too seriously. It was good fun, it made some good points, it made youngsters like me laugh and think, and it baited the bourgeois, who sorely needed baiting.

But repeated attempts to outrage result in diminishing returns. Children grow out of their tantrums. If the counterculture was at its most shocking and flamboyant during the latter half of the 1960s, during the early 1970s the flood of ideas coalesced into something approaching a coherent proposal for an alternative society. In Steve Jobs' words, 'The sixties happened in the early seventies.' There were now dozens of magazines springing up catering to all sorts of subsections of the movement. *Gandalf's Garden* for the spiritual types (1968–1972); *Frendz*, a UK rival to the US's *Rolling Stone* (1969–1972); *Resurgence*, started by the turbulent vicar John Papworth in 1966, subsequently taken over by Satish Kumar; *Spare Rib* the feminist magazine (1972–1993); *Gay News* (1972–1983); *The Ecologist*, founded by Edward 'Teddy' Goldsmith in 1970; *Seed: The Journal of Organic Living* (1971–1977); *Undercurrents*: The Magazine of Radical Science and Peoples' Technology (1972–1984); the *Catonsville Roadrunner*, for anarchist Christians (1969–1975); *Up Against the Law* (1972) for legal activists, and many more. On top of that there were local underground papers such as the *Liverpool Free Press*, *Mole Express* (Manchester), *Grapevine* (Birmingham), *Muther Grumble* (North East) and *Snail* (North Devon). Most of them were short-lived. I contributed to an alternative magazine for Colchester, called *Cymbeline*, which managed just two issues. We were young and in flux.

For those who weren't around at the time, I have attempted to categorise the various directions the movement was taking. I started to list them as a spectrum, with the practical stuff at one end and the spiritual at the other. But the counterculture did mandalas, not lists, so picture them as a 'Wheel of Alternative Consciousness' with the key text of the era at the hub.

The *Whole Earth Catalog*

This was the key text, where you could locate everything else. Compiled in the United States mostly by Stewart Brand, the *Whole Earth Catalog* was subtitled *Access to Tools*, and it was the nearest thing we had to the internet in those days. In its later editions it comprised 450 tabloid sized pages, packed with information about how to acquire anything that one couldn't find on the high street. About half of these 'tools' were books or magazines, encapsulated in a pithy review and a handful of plum quotes; they included anything from *Goat Husbandry* and an Israeli Army keep-fit manual to the works of Buckminster Fuller (who occupied all of page one) and Ayn Rand's *Atlas Shrugged* ('This preposterous novel'). The other half were physical tools such as ram pumps, mud-brick-making machines, batik dyes, baby carriers and five-horsepower steam engines for boats. To emerge from a blinkered academic education and find all this information at one's fingertips was liberating, and we certainly used it. My original copy fell apart years ago. When I recently asked my secondhand book-finder Clare to locate another, she wrote back apologetically: 'The copies I can find are quite expensive and they are all in dreadful condition.'

A comprehensive account of all the ideas and movements that were emerging in the early 1970s would require a work of several volumes. Anybody who does seek such an account should start with a copy of the *Whole Earth Catalog*. Here I present just a flavour of what was on offer at that time, by briefly covering each of the subject headings given in the Wheel of Alternative Consciousness in turn, starting (and ending) with Politics.

Politics

From 1971 to 1975 the United States gradually reduced its presence in Vietnam, and the war faded as a focus for political dissent. What took its place? There was the long-running campaign against the apartheid regime in South Africa, which was still being armed by the UK government. There was a shambolic bombing campaign carried out by the Angry Brigade, that failed to enlist any support from the rest of the movement. There were two successful miners' strikes in 1972 and 1974, the second of which brought down the Heath government, but neither sought anything more radical than a pay rise that would inevitably be neutralised by inflation. I had read Marx and Engels with critical approval, but where was the working-class movement to take over the means of production? It did eventually surface in the inspiring plan formulated by shop stewards at the Lucas Aerospace factories to cease making armaments and convert their machines to the production of socially useful goods, but that was in 1976, and by then I had already left the country.

Academic Marxists informed us that the key issue now was 'alienation' and that rang a bell with alienated youth. But the main text, Marcuse's *One-Dimensional Man*, advertised on its cover as 'the dominant intellectual force behind the present wave of Student Revolutions', turned out to consist mostly of a stream of indigestible abstractions, such as: 'The transformation of ontological into historical dialectic retains the two-dimensionality of philosophic thought as critical, negative thinking.'

I was drawn instead to the French situationists whose revamping of Marxist concepts such as commodity fetishism lay behind many of the slogans of the Paris 'May 68' revolt, though their works weren't translated into English until the 1970s. 'People who talk about revolution and class struggle without referring explicitly to everyday life ... such people have

86

a corpse in their mouth,' Raoul Vaneigem proclaimed in *The Revolution of Everyday Life* (translated 1972). 'Who wants a world in which the guarantee that we shall not die of starvation has been purchased with the risk of dying of boredom?' The other situationist classic was Guy Debord's *The Society of the Spectacle* (translated 1970), whose cover and title were so self-explanatory you didn't really need to read it.

But the more mundane elements of Marxist analysis were still clearly visible in the relationship between the industrialised countries and the Third World. Frantz Fanon's *The Wretched of the Earth* was eloquent testimony, but I learnt a lot about how the British and American empires ripped off the planet from a book published in 1939 by the Pacifist Research Bureau, called *Why Were They Proud?* Susan George's *How the Other Half Dies* brought the analysis up to date in 1976. The consumerist lifestyle that the situationists derided was acquired at the expense of people on the other side of the globe (as it still is), but what was one to do about it? Stand for parliament and lose your deposit? Wear a Che Guevara T-shirt? As Theodore Roszak put it in 1969 in *The Making of a Counter Culture*, 'Political action and organising cannot even provide a full-time career for more than a handful of intellectuals, let alone a pattern of life for an entire generation.'

Social Change

There were better opportunities for revolution at the social level. The most important and effective was women's liberation. Even if you had never read Betty Friedan, Germaine Greer or Kate Millett, if you were part of the counterculture you absorbed their ideas through osmosis. Your girlfriend was likely to have a copy of the Boston Women's Health Book Collective's *Our Bodies, Ourselves* (1970). That's not to say that every male with long hair, beads and a caftan relinquished the patriarchal norms of their upbringing, far from it. But hippie culture was fertile ground for the spread of feminism. The ready availability of contraception, frankness about sexuality, scepticism about the nuclear family, a less demanding approach to domestic tidiness, the fact that most men didn't come home from a nine till five job hungry and that women often earned more than blokes – all of these were likely elements of hippie households that militated against what was then known as 'male chauvinism'.

Some changes in attitude were radical. I have known two women who had babies out of wedlock at the end of the 1960s when they were both very young. One, who had not by then escaped from her straight upbringing, had her child confiscated by the authorities at birth, and never returned. She never had another child and the loss was a trauma whose scar she bore for the rest of her life. The other had left her convent education to mingle with a bohemian set of poets and musicians in London, some of whom sheltered her from the authorities and helped her set up a life as an unmarried mother, a status whose normality we now take for granted.

The counterculture also went some way towards dissolving class distinctions, not least because nearly everybody from whatever background was chronically broke. In squats or in the festival scene, public school and convent drop-outs mingled with Scousers, greasers and Rastas. But on the question of class, mainstream society has moved more slowly than it has with gender. Admission of women to Oxford and Cambridge is now on a par with men's, but Oxbridge remains a bastion of middle-class culture.

There were a number of other aspects of our lifestyle that deviated from bourgeois standards, some of which, such as dress and hitch-hiking, I have already mentioned. The most significant was perhaps diet. 'You are what you eat' we were told, so food occupied a position of high status amongst the range of lifestyle changes. In any case it is relatively easy to control what goes in your mouth. Some folk pursued specialised regimes such as macrobiotics. Meat and two veg were no longer on the menu: a vegetarian diet with wholemeal wheat and brown rice as staples became the norm. I declared myself a vegetarian after I realised that I had not eaten meat for several months, and hadn't missed it.

Psychology

Society was fucked up, so therefore people were. Or was it the other way round? There were all manner of fashionable savants, some of them charlatans, purveying their own brand of therapy for the human condition. I read Wilhelm Reich, but balked at his ridiculous orgone box. I never bothered with Janov's primal screaming. Erich Fromm's *The Fear of Freedom* was more to my taste, and I devoured anything I could find by Ronald Laing, attracted by his view that madness was not an illness but maladaptation to a repressive social structure.

After Laing, I moved on to Foucault's *Madness and Civilization*, which seemed to be making similar points. But I had had my fill of Gallic verbosity with the situationists, and I never reached the end of the book. Little did I know that in fifty years' time Laing, Marcuse and the situationists would be half-forgotten, while Foucault would be venerated as the progenitor of an entire school of academic ideology.

Religion

Some of this psychological pioneering morphed into religion, via the work of people such as Jung, Krishnamurti, and Gurdjieff. Broadly speaking the more religious this became, the less appealing I found it. I had read Alan Watts' *The Way of Zen*, but my feeble attempts at meditating did nothing for me; when I felt like transcending corporeal reality, I found it more effective to go to sleep. These cults were even more disturbing when they were centred on an authoritarian personality. Towards the end of the 1970s there was a wave of 'orange people', so-called because they dressed only in that colour, returning to Europe from Shree Rajneesh's ashram in Pune, Maharashtra. They mostly seemed fairly level-headed so I wondered what they saw in this charlatan who over time accumulated ninety-three Rolls Royces.

On the other hand I had a soft spot for the Hare Krishna people. They were good natured and decorative, seemingly uncomplicated, and cooked good free food. Much later I went to the Bhaktivedanta Manor, the temple near Watford, bought for the Krishna Consciousness movement by George Harrison in 1973. It was thriving, visited by both European and Indian visitors, and producing much of its food with a herd of dairy cows and draught oxen, a happy contrast to the ill-fated hippie community that briefly occupied the island of Dorinish, lent to them by John Lennon.

Communes

There was much talk and media bluster about 'hippie communes', and there was a bimonthly magazine called *Communes* that had run to forty issues by 1972. But there weren't very many actual communes around in the early 1970s, at least not that weren't affiliated to some spiritual or similarly specialised organisation. The only one I visited was a place called Garranes, near Schull, in County Cork.

'Ah Garranes, that's the place with the cauliflowers,' said two of the drivers who picked me up on my way there. Exotic vegetables were a novelty in rural Cork. As I walked up to the farmhouse, I saw the words 'NO FRESH BIRTHS' painted in two-foot-high letters on the wall. Inside the farmhouse, the gloomy living room with its crude inglenook fireplace was carpeted with loose straw, which was swept out and replaced once a week. Upstairs the walls had been knocked out to make one big dormitory where everyone slept, if the bedbugs didn't keep them awake.

There were only three people left in the commune: a languorous English hippie couple in their late twenties, who would have looked at home in a Gustav Klimt painting; and Rory, a muscular Irishman in his thirties who was the personification of self-sufficiency. Every morning he breakfasted on a heap of boiled whole wheat grains, smothered in goats' cream cheese and topped with five fried eggs. All of this, and indeed almost everything we ate, he apparently grew or reared himself on some pretty rough land, with the aid of his horse. The only things the community bought were tea, sugar, matches, horseshoes and one half pint bottle of Guinness a week.

The famed cauliflowers were straggly specimens, with heads no bigger than a tennis ball, which the hippie couple took to Bantry market once a week with the horse and a bow-top wagon – almost the only work they appeared to do. Rory seemed to get all his labours done in a morning and in the afternoon they played chess, and strummed vaguely oriental dirges on the guitar without ever deviating from the key of E minor. Conversation was sparse, but I gathered from Rory that the rest of the community had gone to India with a view to finding a place for them all to move to, because Ireland was now irretrievably corrupted by consumerism (even though it had only just discovered cauliflowers).

After ten days I legged it back to England, getting a lift from Fishguard in Wales to London in which I had to ration my scratching so as not to let on to the driver about my bedbugs. It had not been an auspicious introduction to community life, but after travelling to India I was prepared for anything. And I reasoned, correctly, that all communes are different, just like people.

Architecture and Building

In the early 1970s Christopher Alexander was working on his book *A Pattern Language*, expounding how architectural design could be answerable to the needs of communities. When it was published it claimed to have sprung from the 'observation that most of the wonderful places of the world were not made by architects, but by the people'.

Alexander's material was not available until the late 1970s, and even then not very well known, but there were other sources. The very title of Bernard Rudofsky's book, *Architecture Without Architects* (1964), is inspirational to anyone who seeks to escape from a life paying rent for an abode they can't abide. Its illustrations of vernacular construction around the world were an eloquent indictment of our contemporary built environment.

In 1973 two books were published that showed what was practically feasible for the twentieth-century drop-out. *Handmade Houses: A Guide to the Woodbutcher's Art*, by Art Boericke and Barry Shapiro, contained fifty or so colour photos of mainly timber homes built in the US by hippie backwoodsmen. We'd never seen anything like this before. Some of them looked gorgeous, and all of them could be built by someone with a measure of skill, access to timber and not a huge amount of machinery or money. Lloyd Kahn's *Shelter* was a sort of *Whole Earth Catalog* for builders, presented in the same tabloid format. It lacked the glossy photos of *Handmade Houses*, but it contained a wealth of information about building techniques ranging from the nomadic and vernacular to geodesic domes. It is still available, hasn't aged, and is widely read today by new generations of would-be home-builders.

Back to the Land

Any serious attempt to create an alternative society must go back to basics, and the only human requirement more basic than shelter is nourishment. John and Sally Seymour's *Self-Sufficiency* first appeared in 1973, but the ideas that it consolidated were floating around beforehand. The American magazine *Mother Earth News* (started in 1970 and still thriving) was a main source of inspiration for people considering going 'back to the land'. Organic gardening books proliferated, the most popular in Britain being Lawrence Hills' *Grow Your Own Fruit and Vegetables* (1971). At a time when recycling was at an all-time low (and Americans tipped waste food down the 'trash-masher' unit in their sink) it became standard in hippy households to keep a compost bucket near the kitchen.

For anyone with the ambition to start a smallholding in the UK there was little help. Books that had appeared in the 1940s as an adjunct to the land settlement movement with titles like *Back to the Country*, and *Livings from the Land* were looking dated. More modern material was available from the United States, such as Ken and Barbara Kern's *The Owner-Built Homestead*, which was part serialised in *Mother Earth News*. Best of all was the delightful series of *Foxfire* books from 1972 in which high-school students interviewed old timers in the Appalachian mountains about practices such as hog killing, cabin building, butter making and moonshining. This was testimony, not from people going back to the land, but from people who had never left it.

For anyone interested in the economic rationale behind the back-to-the-land movements, the work of Ralph Borsodi was undergoing a revival. Borsodi's interest in decentralism stemmed from an analysis he conducted in 1920 of the tomatoes grown and canned by his wife. Once labour costs and all other expenses had been factored in, her tomatoes worked out to be 20 to 30 per cent cheaper than the shop-bought equivalent. He went on to examine how the economies of scale, so advantageous to large corporations, were often outweighed by diseconomies of distribution: excessive haulage, processing, packaging, advertising and handling by middlemen. Borsodi's works were difficult to get hold of but he had considerable influence on 1970s radical agrarianism. In the 1960s he had worked in India with Vinoba Bhave whose *Gramdan* movement involved securing land to be held in trust by villages for poor farmers. When he returned he started a similar movement in the United States, which in 1969 established a land trust for expropriated black sharecroppers in Albany, Georgia called New Communities, Inc., widely agreed to be the first community land trust in the country.

Unfortunately going back to the land was just a dream if you hadn't got any land, and most of us were penniless. Even an allotment was out of the question if you were moving from one temporary opportunity to another. It was not until 1976 that Herbert Girardet's brilliant little book, *Land for the People*, appeared with a manifesto calling for land redistribution, and articles about enclosure, land settlement and land taxation. It included an introduction by another disciple of Vinoba Bhave, the editor of *Resurgence* Satish Kumar. Meanwhile, the provisional answer for some who yearned for a rural experience was WWOOF, Working Weekends on Organic Farms, started by Sue Coppard in 1971 from a flat in London, and now an international network.

Alternative Energy

Modern interest in renewable energy can be dated back to the 1961 United Nations Conference on New Sources of Energy, whose published proceedings were advertised in the *Whole Earth Catalog*. As the *Catalog* pointed out: 'They aren't new sources; they're the oldest: sun, wind, earth heat (geothermal). But OK, to us they're new and they're exciting.'

The spread of alternative energy in its early days was substantially due to a handful of technologically minded freaks in the 1970s. Godfrey Boyle started *Undercurrents* magazine in 1972. Its first issue consisted of a handful of leaflets in a polythene bag but thankfully they soon put a stop to that idea. The following year the Centre for Alternative Technology was set up in an old slate quarry near Machynlleth, Wales. Within a few years, wind turbines had become intrinsic to the caricature of the hippie lifestyle, along with lentils and sandals, which may account for some of the more irrational objections to them when they started to become mainstream.

Rarely if ever was there any reference to 'renewable' energy; it was usually 'alternative'. Ecological concerns provided only a secondary rationale for experimentation. More emphasis was placed on independence from the 'technocratic society'. 'Technology,' the *Undercurrents*, manifesto headlined in 1972, 'while still masquerading as mankind's great emancipator, is increasingly becoming the instrument of our enslavement'. The *Whole Earth Catalog* put it differently: 'The prospect of truly self-contained habitable energy systems is romantic country. There you are with your friends on your hill putting sun and wind through useful changes that are ... an integral part of your living.' This view is still reflected in the current enthusiasm for living off-grid.

Green Issues

Over the following decades renewable energy was absorbed into the mainstream as a result of environmental concerns, and ceased to be alternative. Rachel Carson's *Silent Spring* (1962) is often credited as triggering this environmental movement; but it was a single issue book, as was Paul R. Ehrlich's Malthusian *The Population Bomb* (1968). I might be more inclined to award the title to Vance Packard's 1960 book, *The Waste Makers*, since it broached the problem of indefinite economic growth.

However the first book I was aware of that catalogued environmental crises on a number of fronts was *The Doomsday Book*, by BBC *Horizon* editor Gordon Rattray Taylor, published in 1970. Taylor covered matters such as pollution from asbestos, lead, pesticides, deforestation, overpopulation, the unsustainability of the North American standard of living, and global warming – though he also considers the opposing theory that the world was entering another ice age. Acid rain and the depletion of the ozone layer were to come later in the 1980s.

The same year Teddy Goldsmith founded *The Ecologist* magazine, which in 1972 published *A Blueprint for Survival*, covering similar ground to Taylor, though by now the ice age theory had been dropped, while carbon induced warming was highlighted. The *Blueprint* cited another influential 1972 publication, the Club of Rome's *The Limits to Growth*. Next year E. F. Schumacher's *Small is Beautiful* was published.

All of this confirmed what we already sensed. That capitalism was not only killing people, it was killing the planet. In 1971 Friends of the Earth UK carried out its first action, dumping hundreds of non-recyclable bottles on the steps of Cadbury Schweppes offices. Since then millions of people around the world have been involved in a relentless campaign to force the architects of economic growth to cease their planetary debauchery.

Politics (Again)

In the February 1974 general election, the People's Party, with their *Manifesto for a Sustainable Society* based on *The Ecologist's Blueprint*, fielded six candidates, one of whom was Teddy Goldsmith. All the candidates lost their deposit, and Goldsmith got only 395 votes. In the following year it changed its name to the Ecology Party, and in 1985 it became the Green Party.

In the intervening years the party has managed to secure one MP, and a maximum of 3.8 per cent of the vote in a general election (in 2015). The poor performance is a reflection not of potential support for the party's views, but of the fact that the 'first past the post' voting system ensures that the UK has remained a twin party dictatorship masquerading as democracy. Whoever you vote for the government gets in, a state of affairs that explains why many hippies forsook party politics and became anarchists.

The Ideas Pool

In December 1972, a 'freak from Dublin' turned up at the offices of BIT, the London-based information centre that had spun off from *International Times*, and wrote out a cheque for £1,250 (the equivalent of nearly £17,000 in 2021). This was used as prize money for a competition of new radical ideas. I sent in an entry, which is why I have a copy of the 180-page document, which reproduces the text of all 257 submissions.

My proposal was that the money should be allocated for a 'Rural Tribal Squat in a Deserted Village or Army Camp'. I didn't win, and it never happened, though something similar did take place at the Pure Genius ecovillage site in Wandsworth, London, in 1996. The first prize went to a group of radical technologists based in Sheffield called Radtech in Pact.

Some of the entries were sensible, while others were delightfully zany. The following were some of those that were both innovative and have come to fruition or prominence in some capacity later on:

> *A campaign to enable legal adoption of children by homosexuals*
> *Women's refuge centres*
> *Camps/holidays, etc. for misfit or deprived kids*
> *To establish or support communes, including Laurieston Hall*
>   *and Findhorn (both still in existence)*
> *Local community video support*
> *Working Weekends on Organic Farms*
> *Projects to recycle local waste (recycling was almost non-existent*
>   *in 1973)*
> *A rewilding movement called the British Wilderness Movement*
> *An anti-motorway campaign with the objective of returning*
>   *motorways to agricultural land*
> *A Fair Trade project called Earth Exchange*
> *Circuses and Radical theatre groups*
> *A campaign to legalise cannabis*
> *A proposal for Universal Basic Income*

As for things that didn't happen, there were a large number of proposals for alternative schools, few of which materialised and none of which have lasted. On the other hand, offering facilities for kids with deprived backgrounds or behavioural problems was the subject of a dozen submissions, and that is now a significant source of income for many communities and rural projects.

Surprisingly, the only proposal even tenuously related to the growing vegetarian and vegan movement was one to produce human-edible protein from grass. This product was in fact manufactured in the late 1990s under the brand name Leafu, and marketed at festivals, but its taste had to be disguised with something like honey, and it never caught on.

Finally there was one proposal for 'Low Cost Alternative Computer Facilities' from an 'interdisciplinary group of students and engineers who have purchased a secondhand computer'. Little did we know then that in years to come a sector of the counterculture would take off in a new direction, in fact into a new dimension. Had I been ahead of the game I would have read Norbert Wiener's *Cybernetics* (published in 1948 but fashionable in the seventies) and noted that Stewart Brand was rather taken by these ideas. For one entry in the *Catalog* he wrote:

'We are migrating from a world governed primarily by the laws of thermodynamics to a world governed primarily by cybernetics – a weightless world ... whose events are the impinging of information on information.'

Prophetic indeed, but this was lost on me, not least because the price of a Hewlett Packard desktop calculator advertised in the *Catalog* was $4,400, or nearly two years of my take-home pay.

CHAPTER SIX

Maniac Valley

T he quest for an alternative society, pursued to its logical conclusion, requires land. It is the most basic of the means of production, which Karl Marx had advised the working class to reclaim. That was one reason why, after the eviction of the Butt Road squats, I and others started talking about getting hold of some. There was also a less ideological desire to find somewhere to live and work with a degree of independence and security. Lewis Mumford, in *Technics and Civilization* (1934), has a passage explaining what motivated some of the emigrants to the US over the course of the last few centuries:

> *The desire to be free from social compulsion, the desire for economic security, the desire to return to nature ... provided both the excuse and the motive power for escaping from the new mechanical civilization that was closing in upon the Western World. To shoot, to trap, to chop trees, to hold a plough, to prospect, to face a seam – all these primitive occupations out of which technics had originally sprung, all these occupations that had been closed and stabilized by the very advances of technics, were now open to the pioneer: he might be hunter, fisher, woodman, and farmer by turn, and by engaging in these occupations people could restore their*

*plain animal vigor as men and women, temporarily freed
from the duties of a more orderly and servile existence.*

There was something of this pioneering spirit in our search
for land, and I had my share of animal vigour. The question was
where to find land. I and my two mates from the purple potato
farm, Leon and Greg, set off to look for it up north in the bread
van, in the hope that land with derelict buildings on it might be
a bit more available. We didn't find anything promising. Instead
we gained a fuller understanding of the nature of English
landownership when we drove through moorland near Barnard
Castle and every farmhouse for miles and miles was painted in
the same livery, denoting ownership by his Lordship. We went
to Nelson, at the very edge of the Greater Manchester conurbation, where houses were regularly advertised in *Exchange and
Mart* for a mere £200. This frontier between town and country,
where rows of back-to-back terraced houses faced off a bleak
treeless hillside, looked too grimly structured to be comfortable,
though some hippies did make it their home in years to come.

Later in the summer, I received an international phone call
from the South of France. It was Leon. 'Come down,' he said.
'There's land for sale here cheap. I've just bought a hectare
with a barn for £350.' I took a week off work, put most of my
money into traveller's cheques and hitched down to a village
called Arboras, not far from Montpellier, where I met up with
Leon on his newly acquired patch of reverted wilderness. I
forget how we co-ordinated such encounters in the days before
mobile phones and emails, but it wasn't a problem.

Leon was a portly German who worked as a milkman in
Colchester, had artistic pretensions and an eye for a deal, legal or
otherwise. His land turned out to be a hectare of *garrigue* – prickly,
calcareous scrubland capable of keeping a goat alive for about half
a year – with no water, but a sizable stone *bergerie* (sheep shed),

roofless but sound, and good for repair. It wasn't brilliant, but for £350 (about £4,300 in today's money) you couldn't complain.

The next day we went to the local town, Clermont-l'Hérault, and checked in at its only estate agent. 'Do you have any small parcels of agricultural land for sale, preferably with a ruin?' They did. It was 1.4 hectares, also in Arboras, on the banks of a river called the Lagamas. It had two ruined watermills on it, one dating back to the thirteenth century. It was a little over £600, one-third the price of a Hewlett Packard desktop calculator.

There were indeed two ruined mills. The plot was covered in scrubby bushes – broom, juniper, gorse and redoul (*Coriaria myrtifolia*) – but it included half an acre of flat arable land. There was a deep canyon with a ten foot waterfall in the river traversed by a perilous stone arch bridge some twenty-five feet above. We later found out it was called the Pont du Crime because years before a woman had thrown her baby off it. We went back to the estate agents. 'I'll buy it,' I said. I cashed the traveller's cheques and put down a deposit. That was my future sealed for the next ten years.

Back in Colchester, four of us agreed to club together to buy the land: Carol, myself, Baz and Jane. The land cost us £150 each, six weeks' wages on the dustcarts where Baz and I both worked. We resolved to save up some cash, buy tools and provisions, and move down there the following spring.

Meanwhile something else momentous was happening. Carol was pregnant. It was our choice to have a child; but in fact, I was much too young (or immature) to be a father, too young even to realise I was too young. In hindsight, one might regret fathering a child too young, and any problems that may have caused. But of course I don't regret it, because if I hadn't done it, our daughter Jade wouldn't exist.

Jade was born in early December 1973. It was a home delivery, unusual in those days and the first that the young midwife had ever done. She was visibly nervous, but all went well, and I was relieved to see that (unlike some) Jade really was a beautiful baby. Her arrival coincided with the appearance in the sky of Comet Kohoutek, which returns only once every 75,000 or so years, and was predicted by the Children of God cult to unleash a doomsday event. Since doomsday never happened, Carol and I fancied that instead it must have been heralding the arrival of our daughter.

It never occurred to me that starting a family and establishing a community on a plot of abandoned land in a foreign country, with little in the way of practical skills or money, might be a trifle over-ambitious. Just before Easter 1974, Jane, Baz and I set off for Arboras in a Ford Trader 3-tonne van loaded to the brim with kit, leaving Carol and Jade behind to come later. We had two large army bell tents, mattresses, tarpaulins, hand tools of every description, rope, cooking equipment, a couple of the same stainless steel cauldrons we had used at Pilton, a pump, nickel cadmium batteries, a 12 to 240 volt inverter that was basically a dynamo, Tilley lamps, seeds, sacks of lentils and rice, Marmite and Mars bars. We boarded the ferry at Dover, arrived at Calais and were directed into a huge empty hangar by French customs officers. There we were told that we couldn't proceed because we hadn't got the correct paperwork, which could only be obtained from the French Embassy in London.

It was the Wednesday before Easter. I went back overnight on the boat and train to London, and arrived at the French Embassy a few hours before it shut for the holidays. There I was greeted with Gallic shrugs and the supercilious contempt that French bureaucrats (and Parisian bar tenders) show towards anyone who doesn't meet their sartorial standards. 'We can do nothing. Come back on Tuesday.' There were no mobile phones in those days, so on Good Friday I went back on the train and the boat to Calais to inform Jane and Baz about the wait that lay in store.

When I arrived, I found they had spread a tarpaulin out on the concrete and created an entire kitchen and bed/sitting-room from the contents of the Ford Trader. The only thing missing was the TV. On the Calor gas cooker we knocked up lentil curry and rice, cracked open a bottle of duty free wine, and went to sleep under the asbestos roof.

Next day, after breakfast a senior customs officer paced over to our encampment. 'Allez!' he said with barely a hint of a smile. 'Allez! Fou le camp!' making a motion with the back of his hand as if to brush off a fly. We bundled everything back in the van, fired her up and let out a whoop as we steamed out of the customs yard and headed south.

Settling

Except for the birth of a baby, there are few things more exciting than moving onto a new plot of land, and it doesn't happen often in life. We cleared away some of the bushes, erected the army tents, named the land Le Moulin, and surveyed the scene. The river Lagamas was no more than a stream but we had been assured it never ran dry, and the existence of the mills seemed to prove the point. It sprang from the escarpment to the north towering some 500 metres above us that marked the edge of the Massif Central, and gouged a ravine down a narrow valley some five kilometres long. The valley was carpeted from one end to the other in trees, mostly holm oak, and not much else. But if you walked upstream through the woods there were some deserted stone huts and numerous flat terraces defined by dry stone walls, crumbling under the assault of the oak roots. This was a fertile, but largely abandoned valley, in contrast to the next one along the escarpment that had no terraces, few trees and a river bed of parched dry rock that became a torrent when it rained.

Our mills were near the mouth of the valley as it opened out into the great plain of the Languedoc, which was a sea of vineyards. Overlooking this vista, perched on a ridge that separated the Lagamas valley from its rocky neighbour, was the village of Arboras. It consisted of a single street of about twenty-five houses, a small church, a chateau, a *mairie* – a communal bread oven that no one used any longer – and a bus stop. The voting population was fifty-four but some didn't live there permanently. Of those who did, virtually all were *vignerons* (wine growers), about ten families in all. The exception was the owner of the chateau, a Scotsman, who had bought it for a song in the 1960s, from its occupants who were the poorest farming family in the village.

The road running through Arboras carried on up the side of the Lagamas valley and then laced its way up the face of the escarpment in a series of hairpin bends. At the gateway to the plateau was a plantation of pine trees that opened up to reveal another world of wide unfenced expanses of grass and occasional flocks of sheep. There was a historic reason behind this plantation's existence. In the days before motor transport, when horses would bring carts loaded with hay down to the plain for the vignerons' mules, they would stop before they made the descent and attach a few timber logs to the back of the cart. These acted as a brake as they went downhill, and then could be sold below as building material.

One morning before daybreak towards the end of May when I was asleep in my tent, a curious tinkling sound began to colour my dream, almost inaudible at first, but slowly rising in volume and harmonic depth, much as a stream grows into a river. Over half an hour or so this orchestra of a thousand bells swelled to a gentle and distant climax and then began to fade away up the mountain as slowly as it had approached. This was the first of the transhumant flocks of sheep travelling from their winter quarters in the foothills that bordered the Mediterranean to summer pastures up on the plateau. They left Arboras before daybreak so as to reach the mountain pass before the sun became too hot. It was the most beautiful sound I have ever heard, and a fine sight too, since the sheep looked so smart in their hand-carved and painted wooden collars, their bells of different sizes, some as big as a melon, and the red woolly pompoms attached to their coats. About ten of these flocks passed through Arboras that summer and the mayor optimistically commissioned a new larger enclosure to be constructed at the edge of the village to accommodate them overnight. It was a poor investment. Ten years later most herds had stopped coming; either they had been sold, or else they were taken up to the plateau by truck.

The older of our two mills was sited at the bottom of the ravine beneath the Pont du Crime. It had ground flour over several centuries until it was abandoned at about the beginning of the twentieth century. The other, situated just above the older one, was a plaster mill that ceased production in 1924. The last people to operate it were three sisters, who brought plaster down by donkey from a kiln further up the valley, ground it to powder and then took it again by donkey across the bridge up to the village. Our deeds showed that the three women each had rights to use the water on different days of the week.

The mills had been served by a leat that was little more than a ditch taking water from the river about 500 metres upstream, which filled two large reservoirs built of stone and earth. There was not a large flow of water, but there was plenty of head, eighteen metres down to the lower mill. The pipe taking water from the second reservoir down the hill to the mills was half missing; it had been hewn from stone blocks, with a 12-inch diameter hole carved out in the middle, and rebated to fit into one another. Like all old mills it was a marvel of ingenuity.

After clearing the worst of the scrub, one of the first things we did was to dig out the leat and get the water flowing. Part of the leat had fallen away, so I went up to an old bridge upstream that had collapsed and spent the best part of a day sawing through its iron girder with a hacksaw, to use it to span the gap. Aside from that, getting the water to flow again after a lapse of several decades was remarkably easy. The reservoir filled up and didn't leak. To have such a body of water at the highest point in your land is a valuable asset anywhere, and especially in a dry Mediterranean climate.

Our other achievements over the next two years were less successful, indeed embarrassing to recall. At twenty-three years of age, with a head full of dotty ideas, little experience of building or agricultural work, and no money, I was pathetically ill-equipped to undertake the establishment of a smallholding. The days I spent trying to erect secondhand stock fencing along a precipitous hillside that was little more than solid rock in a doomed attempt to keep goats in doesn't bear thinking about, nor does the time we spent double digging heavy clay soil to produce onions the size of strawberries and cabbages the size of onions.

Carol came down with Jade, now six months old, in the summer so I was keen to provide something in the way of shelter and comfort that was superior to the army tents. We decided to sling a roof across the triangular gap between the remaining walls of the second reservoir, which was otherwise beyond repair. We had no money to buy sawn timber so we cobbled together a framework with whatever roundwood I could find, and for the roofing material opted to use a technique I'd found in an alternative building book called *The Owner-Built Home*, which involved rubbing cement mortar into hessian sacks. If anyone as stupid as myself is ever tempted to employ this technique, my advice is don't. There is (predictably) no way that these slabs are ever going to be waterproof, and the impregnated sacks rot over time. But to make matters worse I had underestimated the weight of the mortar, so the whole roof sagged, creating a puddle that instead of shedding water, collected it. No amount of tar and felt was ever going to seal this upside down umbrella. It was a glaring testament to my incompetence.

This did not help endear Carol, Baz and Jane to the place, but it did not put me off. 'If a fool would persist in his folly he would become wise,' was my reasoning. Meanwhile a couple of Germans, Pius and Maria, bought another hectare of land just upstream from our land. Over the summer various freaks from Britain and Germany rocked up and pitched their tents and by the second summer the valley was peopled with young hippies drinking cheap wine, smoking grass (that we *had* managed to grow successfully) and bathing naked in the hot sun and the cool clear river.

The reaction of the local villagers to this invasion was remarkably sanguine, particularly compared to the mean-spirited reaction that settlers on land in Britain so often receive from well-heeled members of the rural community. Perhaps it was partly because that area of France was already accustomed to immigrants; they had received a large quota of Spanish communists and anarchists at the end of the civil war. At first, when they didn't know what to make of us, the villagers called us *les gitanes* (the gypsies), but there was no evidence of any hostility. Once they had established that we could work hard, didn't steal and weren't turning their daughters onto drugs, relations between us and the village were on first name terms.

It also helped that we fulfilled an economic need. Over previous decades, villages such as Arboras had become progressively depopulated. Many poor peasants, like the previous occupants of the Chateau, sold what lands they had and migrated to cities such as Montpellier to take up more lucrative jobs. About half the houses in the village were empty. Deep in the first winter, when only Carol, Jade and myself were living there, the secretary of the mayor of Arboras turned up to interview us. He was completing a census return and wanted to know how many of us were living on site. When we told him that there were just two of us and the baby, he said, 'But surely there are more of you than that? What about Monsieur Barry and his wife? In the summer there were at least ten of you, n'est-ce pas?' He eventually confided that the village population needed to surpass a certain threshold to qualify for additional funding, and so we agreed that yes, there probably were at least six people living here.

Elaine Morgan, in her magnificent 1976 book *Falling Apart*, observed a similar entente between hippies and locals in rural Wales:

> *When they arrive and settle in or near a small village they are often initially unwelcome because of beads and beards and cannabis and carryings-on. But if they stay, and the strangeness wears off, the village benefits. They don't come like second home buyers with a wallet full of cash to push up house prices, they move into places that were empty or falling down, and stave off the decline. The bus service has a few more regular customers. The local school gets an influx of five or six toddlers. The farmer for the first time in years has a reserve of unskilled labour. Oftener than not, the buzz of outrage that greeted their arrival diminishes and becomes perfunctory. The economic effect of these communes over a rural area is like sowing clumps of marram grass on a sand dune – they look sparse, but they serve to halt the erosion.*

And yes, the local vignerons needed our labour. In the depressed economic climate after the oil crisis of 1973, urban jobs were harder to find and the younger generation became more inclined to look to the land for their future. There was much talk of *la sauvegarde de la patrimoine*, 'safeguarding our heritage', and of reviving and improving local wine production. However there was a shortage of agricultural labourers and the Spanish grape-pickers were not arriving for the harvest in the numbers they had done in years gone by. In the September of our first year several of us were working on the *vendange*. By the second year, with the influx of visitors from Britain and Germany, we were supplying harvesting teams to half of the vignerons in the village.

I worked for a bluff, good-natured farmer in his sixties called Lucien Laures who was the only vigneron in the village still making his own wine; the others all took their grapes to be vinified at the Cave Coopérative in the neighbouring village of St Saturnin. Making wine really did involve trampling the grapes in the press, either in bare feet or gumboots, whichever you preferred. It was as much fun as it looks, but surprisingly hard work after a while. There was also work on and off throughout the year in the vineyards: picking up the prunings off the ground, hoeing round the freestanding 'goblet' vines, slashing off excess summer growth, and, if the vigneron trusted you, doing the pruning. The wages were the *salaire minimum de croissance* (Smic), the national minimum wage, plus three litres a day of red wine that could politely be described as robust. On one occasion I worked for ten days on my own hoeing around the base of 20,000 vines with a mattock, 2,000 every day. That job made me realise what a valuable skill it is to be able to enjoy repetitive manual labour.

Amongst the wave of visitors in 1975 were a bunch from England who all knew one another and whom I shall call the OJs, because some were siblings of a large family with a double-barrelled name. Jane had already gone back to England, and Baz's allegiance to Le Moulin was fading. There was friction between us, partly because my name was on the deeds but theirs

110

wasn't. We needed new blood and some of the OJ set moved in on a permanent basis. Meanwhile there were more settlers over on the German side, the land bought by Pius and Maria. Though you could hardly call it an 'intentional community', the place was looking more like a fully fledged hippy commune, now referred to by some as Maniac Valley.

Like many such communes there was a liberal amount of sexual dalliance and partner swapping that ended up in ructions. Maria got together with the senior OJ sibling, and Pius entered into a relationship with Carol. Carol and I split up, reasonably amicably, though it was not what I wanted. She rented a house in a nearby village and eventually moved in with Pius. Jade came to visit me at weekends. She was a cheery toddler, popular with everyone, but our volatile community was not an ideal environment for rearing a child.

Despite these upsets the OJ influx was welcome. The incumbents at the Moulin were now Martin, an incipient alcoholic, and his feisty German girlfriend Brele; Dick Potts, a tidy little fellow with a wry sense of humour; and from time to time, one or other of the OJ sisters. Cheap wine and tobacco were an incentive for them to move to France, and their devil-may-care outlook was a welcome foil to my intense ideological approach, and soon won me over. They also had an infectious taste in music, preferring the 'Great American Songbook' as sung by the likes of Ella Fitzgerald, Fred Astaire and the Mills Brothers, to 1970s rock music. The Sony Walkman had not yet arrived so for entertainment we only had the radio, a 78 rpm wind-up gramophone, my pedestrian guitar playing, and Dick, who after a few jars could do a passable imitation of Dean Martin.

They also had more building experience than I. My intention had been to put a roof on the bottom mill, partly because it was in such a fabulous position right next to the waterfall. I had already stopped up a large and perilous hole in the stonework and put a reinforced concrete ring beam around the top of the wall, which prevented the building from decaying further. It was more or less circular in plan, and since my enquiring mind was stuffed with the concepts of Buckminster Fuller and the images in Steve Baer's *Dome Cookbook*, the obvious solution was to top it with a geodesic dome.

However, fabulous though it might have been, the bottom mill's situation was impractical, requiring a descent of twenty metres down a precipitous rocky footpath to access it. Moreover I had recently read an article by Lloyd Kahn in his book *Shelter* entitled 'Smart but not Wise'. Its preamble read:

> *Our work on domes now appears to us to have been smart: mathematics, computers, new materials, plastics. Yet re-evaluation of our actual building experiments, publications and feedback from others leads us to emphasize that there continue to be many unsolved problems with dome homes. Difficulties in making the curved shapes livable, short lives of modern materials, and as-yet-unsolved detail and weatherproofing problems ... In the past year, we have discovered that there is far more to be learnt from the wisdom of the past: from structures shaped by imagination, not mathematics and built of materials appearing naturally on earth, than from any further extension of whiteman technoplastic prowess.*

In his article, Kahn launched an excoriating attack on computerised architecture and the use of foam and other plastics in building (one that the designers of Grenfell Tower would have done well to read). By championing local natural materials and vernacular design he was taking the ethos of the *Whole Earth Catalog* down one road, whereas Stewart Brand (though I didn't know it at the time) was steaming off in the opposite direction, denouncing self-sufficiency as 'a damned lie' and increasingly focusing on cybernetics and cyber technologies.

The plan to stick a dome on the bottom mill was quietly shelved. There was talk of building a communal roundhouse on the terrace near to the track. In early '76 I went on a short trip, and when I returned Dick had acquired ten railway sleepers and placed them vertically in the ground in what was more or less a circle about seven metres in diameter. It was a start, the question now was how to roof it. That was answered when Florian Geiger, a dropped-out architect who had moved onto some land in the locality, passed by on a visit. He took about eight 15mm dowels out of a kid's playpen that had fallen apart and tied one end of each of them to pegs in the ground arranged evenly in a circle whose radius was a bit shorter than the length of the dowels. He then arranged the dowels so that each one lay on its neighbour to the left. As he tucked the last one over the first, the structure rose of its own accord to create a pyramid with a polygonal hole in the centre. Florian then stood on the pyramid, which, improbably, bore his weight with no sign of strain.

We needed no more convincing. We acquired ten light-weight telegraph poles, attached them with cables to the top of the sleepers and then raised them into position, heaving the pyramid upwards as far as we could to achieve a pitch of about 45 degrees. An eight-inch nail through each pole into the next at the throat made the structure solid.

The reciprocal roof, named as such by Graham Brown in 1983, is in effect a three-dimensional truss and probably the easiest way to span a large circular area without any intermediate support. It can also take the weight of a turf roof, and in that capacity was later popularised in Britain by Tony Wrench in his book *Building a Low Impact Roundhouse*. We, however, planked the roof with whatever we could find, covered it with the cheapest grade of tar paper and over the hole in the roof mounted the lid of a charcoal kiln that had been abandoned on the land by a previous occupant. Much later I found out that this was the first known example of a reciprocally roofed dwelling in Europe.

The construction of each of the ten walls was allocated to different individuals, including some visitors. Everybody chose different techniques, including poplar logs caulked with mattress stuffing, rammed earth with sawn off wine bottles, wattle and daub made from vine prunings woven into stock netting, French windows recycled from the tip and so on. We fitted it out with a fireplace, a kitchen, a bar and a sleeping platform. It wasn't very smart, but it cost next to nothing, was a pleasant enough structure, easy to maintain and we had some great parties there.

Self-sufficiency

Once the roundhouse was finished, other dwellings started springing up. Martin and Brele put a roof on the top mill, Dick built himself a wooden cabin, and I built a lean-to against a stone wall with a tiled roof that was a considerable improvement on my first attempt. A range of similar structures was sprouting on the German side. At one point Lucien, in a new capacity as *mayor*, got in a minor panic about planning permission, but he soon managed to iron things out. He obtained a residency permit for me on the bogus grounds that I was an *'exploitant agricole'*, i.e. a farmer, and then managed to wangle planning consent for four residential structures.

The people who gave us the widest berth were some of the wealthier English expat community who didn't want to be associated with grungy, drug-taking hippies. However these were a minority. Other English and German incomers and second home-owners were keen to employ us on their building projects, not least because we could speak their language and translate for them.

The building work paid a bit more than minimum wage. Together with the vine work and its three litres of wine a day, we were now living more comfortably than in the early years. Maniac Valley had acquired at least some of the hallmarks of an established and successful community, though not a very structured one, and certainly not a spiritual or monastic one. It was more like *Tortilla Flat* and *Cannery Row*, the hand-to-mouth community of bums and misfits that one critic described as Steinbeck's 'utopia'.

We still strove to produce a measure of food from our three acres, though not very successfully. We kept goats, though the amount of work involved in fencing, walking or tethering them was disproportionate to the return in milk. I soon abandoned vegetarianism when it became plain that keeping billy goat kids was impossible, and killing them without eating them was ridiculous. Our chickens laid eggs in the undergrowth, which we would only discover when they exploded in hot weather. Our ducks got taken by the fox within a week, one every night. We bought a young sow only to find, when we got it home, that male pigs have teats as well. Our garden flourished when we planted tomatoes or courgettes, but vegetables of a northerly disposition would never get to be more than stunted parodies of the picture on the seed packet.

Had Stewart Brand come to Arboras in about 1980 he would probably have seen it as vindication of a diatribe that he had written five years earlier. 'Self-sufficiency,' he wrote in 1975 in his magazine *Co-Evolution Quarterly*:

> *is an idea which has done more harm than good. On close conceptual examination it is flawed at the root. More importantly, it works badly in practice. Anyone who*

has actually tried to live in total self-sufficiency – there must be now several thousands in the recent wave that we (culpa!) helped inspire – knows the mind-numbing labor and loneliness and frustration and real marginless hazard that goes with the attempt. It is a kind of hysteria.

There were plenty who agreed with Brand at the time, and his comments are largely accurate about 'total self-sufficiency', but that is the straw man in the argument. Few people strive for anything beyond a measure of self-sufficiency, and we definitely didn't. It is also a common mistake to view self-sufficiency in terms only of the provision of nourishment, which, although of prime importance, comprises only 10 per cent or so of the modern household's budget.

At Maniac Valley we only produced a fraction of what we ate, and we weren't manufacturing our own shoes. But we did supply our own water, our heating and cooking fuel, our accommodation, our laundry, our sewage and waste disposal, our swimming pool and our dope; and though we didn't own vineyards, our labours on our neighbours' produced considerably more wine than the quantity we drank, which represented at least 30 per cent of our entire calorific intake.

More to the point these days than self-sufficiency is environmental impact, and here we scored well. Our resource use was low by Western European standards, as were our carbon emissions (though nobody counted them then). We ran one 2CV Citroën car between the four of us and didn't travel far. We never flew and were most likely to hitch-hike on long journeys. Beyond that the only fossil fuel consumption was a few litres of paraffin, and perhaps a bottle of gas a year between us. We looked into re-energising the bottom mill with a Pelton wheel to produce electricity, but it was a prohibitively expensive investment for the modest amount of electricity we needed.

Instead we fitted out the Citroën with two 12-volt batteries, one of which was charging while the other was used to power our lights and radio. When we parked the car we plugged the spare battery into the electric circuit with crocodile clips. We had no need of power tools, a pop-up toaster or a washing machine: there was time enough to drill holes, make toast and wash clothes by hand.

This low-impact lifestyle was less due to ideology than to the fact that we had a decent bit of land to live on. It was easy for Stewart Brand and others to mock idealistic attempts at self-sufficiency, or to portray the back-to-the-land movement as a way of burying one's head in the sand. Maniac Valley was naive and often shambolic, but it left me in no doubt that having secure access to land is the best way to keep the rapacious treadmill of consumer capitalism at a distance. It is also worth noting that whereas the *Whole Earth Catalog* has been out of print for many years, John Seymour's *Complete Book of Self-Sufficiency* was republished in a new edition in 2019.

Fading Dreams

Towards the end of 1977 I went back to London to visit my mother and was offered a job that took my fancy. It was as a bicycle courier for a firm based in Soho called Same Day Delivery. The job was good, but London was slightly depressing. Not a lot seemed to be happening compared with five years before. The post oil crisis recession had set in, lots of people were on the dole and many of the freaks of ten years ago had settled down and had kids. I soon left London to return to France, but there, too, something of a malaise was beginning to set in. In 1974, when we arrived, we had been in time to attend the last of a series of mass gatherings protesting against parts of the Larzac plateau being taken over by the military. It was a happy festive occasion in a wide open sunny prairie, the culmination of a brilliantly successful campaign that had united green, socialist and pacifist groups nationwide.

The next big green mobilisation was the 1977 demonstration against Superphénix, the fast breeder nuclear reactor at Creys-Malville on the Rhône. It was huge and when we arrived we were near the tail end of a massive file of people marching towards the power station. However as we got nearer we met a file of protesters coming in the opposite direction saying things like, 'It's awful there! It's war! The tear gas is unbearable.'

Our tail end of the march continued nonetheless, only to arrive at the perimeter fencing and find that what the advance guard reported was true. It was war, the tear gas was unbearable, there was absolutely no chance of breaking through the line of police, and after twenty minutes or so of choking there was nothing for it but to retreat, feeling that one had achieved very little. We all returned home demoralised, and it was a long time before there was any environmental protest on a similar scale again in France.

At a local level, radical environmental resistance was at a low ebb as well. Only a few kilometres to the west of Maniac Valley the government decided to open up a uranium mine. They toured the villages with a promotional show, explaining how this was going to provide jobs for local people, and help the country to be self-sufficient in energy. In fact it is doubtful whether there was any intention to produce uranium, or provide long-term jobs, since the mine was mothballed not long after it was opened. It remains a strategic reserve while France prefers to tap the supplies of other countries such as Niger, Mali and Mongolia. Meanwhile the mine site has now become a solar park.

Worse was to come. In Britain, Margaret Thatcher was elected in 1979, and as we moved into the 1980s the economic malaise deepened. Unemployment peaked in the UK in 1983, while in France it tripled over the period 1974–1984. Work became hard to find. In England, every other person we knew was on the dole, but for us expats there was no social security.

Worst of all at about this time there was a spate of deaths amongst friends and acquaintance who, like me, were in their thirties. I am now a 'vulnerable' seventy and as I write have just lived through a year of Covid-19 in which not a single person I know has died. In the 1980s there seemed to be an epidemic of deaths amongst my contemporaries. Three people I knew from Colchester died of drugs. Little Paul fell out of a third-floor window when he was tripping. Ted, a Geordie ex-squaddie went from a heroin overdose. So did my friend Hodge, who was a pianist in the same blues band as Baz, and who shared the Lodge at Stanley Hall with me. He was found stone cold with a needle in his arm in a public toilet in Diss. Then there was Brian, an Englishman living in France, burnt alive in his caravan because he went to bed too drunk to blow out the candle.

There were those who blew their mind out in a car. Christophe, a local lad who frequented the mill died in a daredevil prank along the lines of 'chicken' in *Rebel Without a Cause*. Thérèse, a mother of three who lived in the neighbouring village of St Saturnin, after starting to exhibit delusional problems drove her car over an embankment on the *route nationale*. Closest to us of all was Baz, who died in a crash when he was driving down from England with Jean-Yves, a mutual friend. For no apparent reason he suddenly drove the Renault 4 off the road and over-turned it. Jean-Yves was unscathed, but Baz was pronounced dead at the scene. It seemed he had a sudden seizure, but no one knew for sure.

Possibly there were suicidal tendencies that helped drive some of these people to their deaths. There were also unambig-uous suicides, the most horrific being a young woman I met a few times who doused herself in petrol and set fire to herself. The most surprising suicide was that of G, a young apparently well-adjusted German fellow, one of those people who give off an aura of competence and efficiency at everything they do, the sort of person I would have liked to have been but knew I never could be. In the second half of the 1980s this wave of tragic deaths petered out, to be replaced by a trickle of acquaintances dying prematurely of diseases such as HIV and cancer.

The Reinventing of Arboras

The ill winds of the 1980s were not without their benefits for certain sectors of society. Increasing levels of unemployment in the cities made the younger generation of peasants all the keener to invest their energy in farming. In the early 1970s there had been repeated demonstrations and acts of sabotage by the vignerons of Languedoc, in an attempt to save their industry. Every town in the region had its graffiti condemning imports of Italian wine and the viticultural establishment focused in Bordeaux and Burgundy. The anger culminated in a shoot-out at Montredon-des-Corbières in 1976 in which a police commander and a vigneron were shot dead. Following this tragedy, the approach taken by some vignerons, and certainly those in Arboras, was less combative and more constructive.

This crisis was rooted in the structure of the French viticultural industry as it had existed since medieval times. It is something of a paradox that traditionally the most renowned wines produced in France – those of Bordeaux, Burgundy, the Loire Valley, Alsace and Champagne – are produced at the extremity of the area that is climatically capable of growing grapes. The reason for this is not, as producers from these regions sometimes like to maintain, because of the suitability of the climate, and the uniqueness of the *terroir*. It is because wine is 90 per cent water, and hence was prohibitively expensive to transport over-land before the construction of railways. The best wines were made in the areas closest to the markets of Northern Europe and with access to navigable rivers or ports; the vineyards of Bordeaux were to a large extent created by and for the English after the marriage of Henry II to Eleanor of Aquitaine. Wine for export had to be good, because it had to keep during the journey, and because it wasn't viable to transport cheap wines.

Grape growers in the South couldn't compete because of their distance from the market – the exception being the mus-cat wine grown along the Mediterranean coast at Frontignan and Rivesaltes, since these extra-sweet grapes could not be grown farther north. Wine was made for local production only: it didn't need to keep long, and was at best mediocre. Olivier de Serres, the sixteenth-century agronomist from the South of France, praised the efficient hygienic wine *caves* of Germany, but didn't think it worthwhile to bring his own up to that standard.

Later, with the construction of the railways, wine could be grown in the south and trucked up to Lyon, Paris or Lille to satisfy the thirst of a burgeoning proletariat. As demand increased the great plain of the Languedoc, once a patchwork of grapes, wheat and olives became a monoculture of vines pumping out plonk for the masses, and its agricultural economy became completely dependent upon a single crop.

By the 1960s vignerons in the plain were producing massive crops of up to 20,000 litres of wine per hectare, but often of only about 8 per cent alcohol. And as international transport intensified, Languedoc was outplayed at its own game. In the horse-trading of agricultural commodities that characterised the Common Market, France was designated as a producer of milk, wheat and Golden Delicious apples, while its lamb was to be imported from the UK and its wine from Italy – and Italian wine was even cheaper to produce than the Languedoc wine.

Meanwhile the demand for low-grade rouge in 1.5 litre plastic bottles was declining, as the tastes of the labour force became more middle class, while proletarian work was increasingly carried out by non-drinking Muslim immigrants. The obvious solution was to improve the quality of the Languedoc wine, which would not have been hard. But the French viticultural establishment centred on Bordeaux and Burgundy didn't want to see wines from the south competing with their elite vintages, and structured the industry to discourage this from happening. The northern producers were allowed to bump up the alcoholic content of their wine by adding sugar, whereas this was prohibited in the south. Grants were available in the north for planting superior varieties such as Cabernet Sauvignon, but not in the south, where it was more usual to get grants for uprooting vines. From a national point of view it was a self-destructive policy, since places such as California, Australia and Bulgaria were planting varieties and developing new wine-making techniques that produced quality wines at an affordable price – and France was not keeping up with them.

The weight of all this history was what the rising generation of vignerons were up against. Their demand was for 'quality, not quantity' and the more dynamic of them weren't going to wait for the establishment to change its policies. The vignerons in Arboras were fortunate in that they had access to '*côteaux*', hillside terraces that were less productive but produced better quality wine. But many of the terraces were small or planted with undistinguished varieties of grape.

In about 1980, five of the younger vignerons in Arboras clubbed together and acquired a ten hectare patch of rocky garrigue that was fairly level. Hitherto this land had only been good for goats, but now there were tractors powerful enough to clear the vegetation and plough through the rock to produce a matrix of shattered limestone and earth, ideal habitat for vines. They employed a couple of us from the valley to help, sorting out places the tractor missed with a mattock, extracting boulders with a mining bar. In the first year, as a way of taming the land, they obtained a contract to plant the ten hectares with onion for seed, a crop that we picked by hand.

The land was ready for planting with varieties such as Syrah and Grenache at the end of the second winter. Laying out a new vineyard accurately on this scale is a skilled job and the vignerons employed a crack team of Spanish planters to organise the operation. I and some others from the valley were taken on. When we arrived at eight in the morning there were thirty or more people helping out – farmers, housewives, grannies, children and us hippies, more than half the village was there. We were all assigned various jobs – marking the spots with stakes, making holes, applying fertiliser, planting, filling in and so on. The operation proceeded with military precision and took two days.

It was a unique and a moving experience. Here was an entire village mobilising to reinvent itself, refusing to allow its roots in the land to be torn out by macro-economic forces. I felt privileged to have participated. I can't imagine anything similar taking place in any of the English villages I have known.

Exit through the Arch

By 1982, the malaise afflicting the alternative movement was taking its toll. The 'Cannery Row' atmosphere of Le Moulin was beginning to pall; the death of Baz and others cast a shadow; the revolutionary potential of the early seventies had come to little. I was not achieving very much and drinking rather a lot.

One day I received a letter from my father – the first communication between us for ten years. He invited myself and Jade, now aged eight, to fly over to Washington, D.C., to visit him, and offered to pay her fare. I later found out that my mother had written to him expressing concern about my welfare and worried that I might be suicidal. She was being rather alarmist, perhaps deliberately to provoke my father into action. I was not that downcast, being buoyed up by romance with a lass whom I shall call Ruth. Ruth wanted to visit her brother, who at that time was in Kodiak, Alaska, working as a fisherman, earning good money. We therefore resolved to go to the States to see what fortune would bring.

The only obstacle was that Ruth was penniless, I didn't have much money and in 1982 jobs were scarce. Someone told us there was work picking oysters in La Rochelle, so we hitched there but found nothing. We spent a month or more travelling around looking for casual work, sleeping rough, exhausting the last of our cash. One thing I learnt from Ruth was that if you are down and out it helps to maintain a touch of class. We became adept at stealing food from supermarkets, targeting gourmet cheeses and the less plebeian alcoholic beverages. In our rucksacks we carried a couple of goblet wine glasses, carefully wrapped in socks, which enabled us to sit on a park bench and drink our Pimm's in style.

We did eventually find a couple of weeks' work, and then made it back to Arboras. There I found a few days' work as a labourer on a building site, for an English contractor. We were building one of the clean-cut 'villas' that were popping up all over the place in the Languedoc countryside, thanks to new roads that slashed the commuting time from the hinterland into Montpellier. Aside from their tile roof they were constructed entirely of sand and cement: concrete footings, concrete block walls, a concrete slab floor laid on concrete beams, all covered in cream-coloured rendering in a vain attempt to look vernacular.

While I was working there I overheard a conversation between my boss and the client, who had requested a traditional cut stone arch around the front door. The price quoted by subcontracting masons using sawn quarry stone was a massive £3,000. That, said the client, was outside his budget. I saw an opportunity. I knew of a stretch of common land where rough sandstone boulders were to be had for the taking, the same sandstone as could be seen used in traditional local buildings. I'd never built a cut stone arch, nor had anyone I knew, but it was surely not that difficult? When the boss wasn't around, I approached the client and offered to build the arch for £800 – more than I had ever laid hands on before. He looked at me disbelievingly. I wasn't even the bricklayer; he'd only seen me humping blocks around, and feeding the cement mixer. 'I'll bring you one stone as a sample and you can judge,' I offered, and he said OK.

The local sandstone is an attractive shade of blue-grey, with occasional swirls of russet, peach or salmon pink in the grain. It wasn't difficult to dress one stone and scrape and polish it to get it to look good, and I got the job. I then had to work out how to get all the boulders cut accurately so they fitted together.

The standard method for squaring up a stone and obtaining a plane surface is called boning. It involves chiselling four small flat seatings where you want corners to be and placing small blocks of wood of equal height on them. Place two straight edges across the blocks, eye them up from a distance and carefully chisel away at the seatings until the two straight edges are parallel. Then remove all the stone in between the four seatings to reveal a plane surface from which, with the aid of a square and a rule, you can deduce the orientation of the other surfaces.

I didn't know about boning. I decided that the easiest way to obtain accuracy was to pour an impeccably level concrete slab in the ground. With this I could verify that the initial plane surface sat on the concrete without wobbling and then the opposite face could be determined using a spirit level. It wasn't the orthodox method of doing it – I was inventing a somewhat pear-shaped wheel. But it worked. I carved all twenty-one stones squatting on the ground, using cold chisels and bolsters. When the stones were ready to fix in the building, somebody advised me to use little wooden wedges to hold the arch-stones in place while the mortar was inserted, and then remove them little by little so that the arch squeezed itself together. Ruth and I put it up in this manner, and it looked good. Nobody was more surprised than myself.

This arch served as the graduation piece of my apprenticeship. I had come a long way since the sagging roof of cement-encrusted sacks. It was a self-taught apprenticeship that had taken me some twelve years to absorb what I might have learnt in three if I had been taught as a stripling. As it was, I had achieved a level of competence, but was still basically a cowboy.

No matter, we had £800, enough to get to the States, and some over. We bought the tickets, put nearly all our money into American Express dollar traveller's cheques and hitched off to Paris to get the plane to New York. Jade was going to fly over later.

After negotiating immigration, we paid brief tribute to New York by eating a BLT in an Italian snack bar, and hitch-hiked out on Route 95 to Washington, D.C., 225 miles further south. We made our way to Dupont Circle where my father had his apartment. This hub of Washington's transport system, where no less than ten streets converge on a plaza embellished with a fountain, was a preferred haunt of panhandlers and hustlers. The hum of traffic was punctuated by the clatter of recyclers stamping on aluminium beer cans.

We found my father's front door, where he was listed as residing in the top flat. I rang the bell, and there he was, on the balcony peering down through owl-like spectacles. 'Who are you?' he seemed to be saying. I went over to the opposite side of the street where I could see him better. 'It's me, Simon,' I shouted and waved across the roar of the traffic. 'Your long-lost son.' He shrugged, waved his hand in a gesture of indifference, and went back inside. We rung the bell several more times but there was no response. He apparently thought we were street nutcases. We tried phoning him, but the phone wasn't working – he hadn't paid the bill. We eventually reached him through the *New Republic* magazine where he worked. When we greeted him in his apartment it was all fine. As he shook my hand he observed, 'Good Heavens, that's a working man's hand.' I took that as a compliment.

He hadn't changed much. He was older, of course, and more portly, but at sixty he had kept his mane of black hair. He still worked deep into the night, fuelled by whisky and cigarettes, but now on an electric typewriter rather than his manual Underwood. One morning I found him fast asleep at his desk in nothing but his underpants. Out of his motionless hand protruded a cigarette. It had burnt down to the filter, but the entire three inch cylinder of ash remained on it, intact. For a moment I thought he must be dead.

If anything his views had taken a turn towards the left, the opposite of what is supposed to happen as age sets in. He was profoundly disturbed by the wave of neoconservatives that were emerging, and championed the common man against their elitism. He was a staunch admirer of the women's liberation movement, and American women in particular. His dearest friend was Howard Higman, a hard-drinking liberal professor of sociology, who for fifty years had directed a quirky annual talkshop at Colorado University.

Jade's arrival from France was also a great success. The eight-year-old girl and her grandfather hit it off so well that after ten days Ruth and I struck off westward leaving them to enjoy each other's company for a week, before he put her on the plane back to France.

That was the last time I saw my father.

CHAPTER SEVEN

Thatcher's Britain

R uth and I hitch-hiked across the lower 48 to San Francisco, and then through Canada to Alaska and joined her brother in Kodiak, an island off the south coast, about half the size of Wales. In 1982 it had a population of about 4,000 people, about the same as the population of Kodiak bears on the island, the largest of all grizzlies. This was much less than the 13,000 or more Alutiiq people who lived on the island before the arrival of Russians in the late eighteenth century. Then, so I was told, it had been the most densely pop-ulated locality in Pre-Columbian North America. The Russian colonialists, who were quite as vile as their counterparts in the lower United States, drastically reduced the population through massacre, disease and enslaving all the males to work in the sea otter fur trade.

The reason for the size of the island's population and the magnitude and number of bears was the abundance of salmon and other fish. The Alutiiq were brilliant fishermen. The women made waterproof jackets out of tightly sewn fish guts that but-toned around the opening of their kayaks to create a perfectly dry, hermetically sealed ocean-going capsule. That was why the Russians chose the men for their fur-hunting expeditions.

The abundance of fish was now the reason why this tiny community at the edge of civilisation was reputedly the wealthiest fishing port in the world. Pacific salmon, king crab, tanner crab, halibut, cod, pollock, herring and scallops were all harvested, processed in the town canneries and dispatched to the lower 48 States or exported, notably to Japan. While the rest of North America buckled down to the recession, jobs and money flowed freely in lil' ole Kodiak.

Ruth soon found a job in one of the ten or so bars in the centre of town, some of which never closed. I got a job in a cannery. This was the lowest of the low in Kodiak, and dismal work, but at six dollars an hour was the most I had earned anywhere. After a month at the cannery, someone tipped me off about the skipper of one of the top crab boats who had dug a site for his new house out of the side of a hill, and needed a retaining wall. I left a message for the skipper in his boat and to my surprise got a contract to build a substantial stone wall with a flight of fifteen steps.

I hauled the stone off the beaches; it was greywacke, black and slate-like, polished by the waves and speckled with white barnacles, beautiful material. The only problem was that I was running out of stone. There were not that many beaches that could be accessed by the island's limited road system. Then, one evening there was a wild storm. I went down to my favourite beach where huge waves were pounding the shore hurling slabs of gleaming graywacke onto the shingle. After the breaking of each wave, I scurried down and picked up the handsomest stone before the next wave could reclaim it.

I was the nearest thing to a stonemason for a radius of about 1,500 miles – but the source of material was weather dependent. In any case it would be strange indeed to live in Kodiak and never go fishing. I got taken on as an unpaid novice on the *Topaz*, a 77-foot dragger – what in England we call a trawler – fishing for cod. There was a crew of six men, including one who was cook, and it was a dry boat, no booze allowed. We cruised around for several days, looking in the electronic fishfinder for likely shoals and every so often running a test tow to see what was beneath us. When we hauled in the net there would be a ton or two of fish of all kinds – cod, pollock, flat fish, skate, sharks, crab and all sorts. In one tow we caught a baby whale, whose eyes were blown out by the bends. But the whole lot, except for our supper, would be pitched overboard, including the cod, even though it was our target fish. The reason was that once you started to put fish in the hold, which was full of ice, then you only had a few days before you had to return to port to unload. It was therefore better to hold off from icing any fish down until you had located a decent sized shoal.

I loved the work on that boat, even though I wasn't very good at it. I know of no job that makes so many demands on a man (or woman; there was at least one female-crewed boat in Kodiak). A fisherman, and especially the skipper, needs strength, fitness, stamina, quick reactions, mechanical and electrical expertise, courage, patience, intuition, financial acumen, good people skills, an understanding of the ways of fish and a dose of luck. But the wastage was gross, and the damage to the seabed from bottom trawling distressing, all the more so since the cod we caught was not for human consumption but for bait to catch the lucrative king crab. Compared to the local fisheries I had seen in Kerala, or the techniques that had kept 13,000 Alutiiq alive on Kodiak, dragging looked to me like whiteman technological overkill.

Unsurprisingly, the lifestyle offered by the 'last frontier' attracted more males than females. Men outnumbered women by three or four to one. A saying amongst single women was that 'the odds are good, but the goods are odd'. Considering how much unfulfilled testosterone there was, and how much alcohol was consumed, Kodiak City was surprisingly even-tempered. There were few fights.

But if you turn up with your girlfriend in a town with such a surplus of blokes and she gets a job in an all night bar, you are likely in for a disappointment. It was (in retrospect) predictable that Ruth would ditch me for another, but I didn't handle it well at the time. One day I was in town, got maudlin drunk, went to Ruth's bar, got in a row with her, she (understandably) called the police and I thumped the cop when he arrived. Next thing I knew I was serving a four day sentence in the local jail.

The day before I was due for release, one of the officers called me: 'Simon, there's a telephone call for you.' I picked up the receiver. It was US Immigration. The next day I was escorted onto a Cessna plane to take me to Anchorage. As it took off from Kodiak I could see the theatre of my life over the previous nine months, even down to my caravan at the end of the road system, becoming smaller and smaller until lost from view. At Anchorage I was held in a remand centre that was smarter and more modern than a good many hotels. Each prisoner had his own private cell, which opened out onto a polygonal blue-carpeted common room where about thirty inmates enjoyed free access to telephones, television and a limitless supply of coffee and tobacco. There were several of these modules surrounding a hexagonal exercise yard. About half the detainees were black, even though less than 4 per cent of Alaskans are black.

On the second day I was interviewed. Like every other detained illegal immigrant, I was offered a choice. Either I could waive my rights to a trial and 'volunteer' to return home, with nothing about being deported entered on my passport, or I could fight deportation in court, in which case I would be kept on remand for perhaps six months and then find myself officially deported. Like most people, I took the first option. Two days later I was put on a flight to London and became one of the 57 million illegal immigrants who since 1880 have been ejected after waiving their rights.

I arrived at Heathrow, in the rain, in my fishing wellies and my Carhartt's brown ducks, with $20 in my pocket. This was the low point of my life: I had made a right cock-up, not least because I had already bought an airplane ticket for Jade to fly over to Alaska, and now I had to tell her it was all off. I went into a depression that took me well over a year to emerge from; but the less said about that the better.

But depression did not prevent me doing things. I found a temporary building job in London, and then accepted an invitation to visit a friend, Gill Barron, in Rossendale, Lancashire. I had known Gill since Colchester days, when she reigned over two regency town dwellings on East Hill that were in a state of benign neglect, not squats but town houses rented pending gentrification. On the door she had screwed a brass plaque bearing the legend *Institute of Metamorphysics*. Inside, once stately reception rooms were furnished with paraphernalia from the auction across the road: oil paintings in Rococo frames, a stuffed moose's head, an epidiascope. One room was entirely full of theatrical clothing gleaned from jumble sales. Bohemian types made art or tea, or adopted feline poses on the sills of the sash windows. Gill had rechristened all these characters with exotic names, akin to T.S. Eliot's 'names that never belong to more than one cat'.

But now Gill was living, with her two sons, in a millstone grit farmhouse, dripping with mould and damp, on a blighted stretch of moorland that marked the edge of Greater Manchester. She was married to Walter Lloyd, twenty-five years her senior, whom she described in a letter as, 'The acme of eccentricity, England's leading Tory anarchist, a doer of great deeds, a charmingly dotty old one-man earthquake.' Walter's many achievements are described in an obituary by Gill in *The Land* magazine (issue 23); but the one for which he is now best remembered, kick-starting a revival of the British charcoal industry, did not occur until a few years later, when he was in his sixties.

The eye-opener for Gill, and later myself, was Walter's familiarity with the Gypsy, Roma and Traveller community. After moving onto the farm he inherited in the late 1940s, he built up breeding herds of Welsh black cattle and hardy Fell ponies that roamed the surrounding moorland, not to mention local parks and school playgrounds. Through the sale of the ponies he became friendly with north country horse-drawn Travellers, and in 1967 he helped one of the most influential of these, Silvester Gordon Boswell, to prevent the closure by the authorities of the centuries-old Appleby Horse Fair.

I arrived at Duckworth Farm in May, and was invited to travel with Walter, Gill and her two sons the hundred-odd miles to Appleby Fair, which takes place at the beginning of June. We set out with a bow-top wagon and a flat cart, but didn't get far. We were trotting along the Clitheroe bypass, a fast single carriageway road. I was sitting on the flat cart with my legs hanging over the off-side of the cart (something I won't do again) when something inspired me to look behind. A car was heading straight for my legs at about five miles an hour. 'Oi! What's going on? Piss off!' I lifted my legs out of the way. Crash!

The car, screeching its brakes, nose-dived into the cart right underneath me at more like thirty miles an hour – I'd perceived its approach in slow motion. It severed the wooden bed of the cart from the chassis and pitched myself, Gill and her son Mike up in the air and onto the tarmac. The horse bolted and dragged Gill, who valiantly hung onto the reins, 100 yards down the road. The driver had started overtaking another car when we were a mere spot on the horizon, not realising that we were travelling at ten miles an hour until an oncoming car forced her to complete her manoeuvre in haste. She had a choice of hitting us or a head-on collision. It was a sobering introduction to the perils of horse-drawn transport on a road network where people drive at speeds that should never have been invented.

We carried on with just the bow-top wagon, this time without incident. As we approached Appleby, we met other Travellers converging on the fair in wagons. There were traditional stopping places where we would gather round a fire in the evening playing music that ranged between Celtic and Country and Western, and singing, notably Ewan MacColl's 'Freeborn Man of the Travelling People'. The fair itself took place on a broad hill where hundreds of these wagons were lined up in rows with ponies tethered nearby, typically black and white gypsy cobs, stocky yet sprightly, with plenty of mane and feather. Young lads and lasses showed them off, riding bareback up and down the alleys, while deals were sealed with slaps of the hand.

This was a new subculture to me. Most of these folk didn't live year-round in horse-drawn wagons. They had chrome-lined caravans, and used a pick-up truck for their work. But they had pride enough in their heritage to make it their summer holiday; you wouldn't find them in Benidorm or Torremolinos. Their gender relations were intriguing. The gypsy women were a tough lot and probably gave as good as they received. In the Appleby pubs during the fair, there was strict sexual segregation. All the men were in one bar, and all the women in the other. The toilets, inevitably, were in the women's half, and if you were a greenhorn male like me you had to run a gauntlet of merciless ribbing to get to them.

After Appleby I stayed on at Duckworth, thanks to Walter and Gill's hospitality. There was plenty of stone around, in fact there wasn't much else. The grass was nibbled down to an inch-high sward by free-ranging livestock, and trees were almost non-existent; the combination of sheep and coal spells the death of woodland. Towering canyons had been hewn out of the hills by generations of quarrymen to provide sandstone paving slabs for the metropolis. For two centuries they had rung with sound of hammer and chisel, now they were silent, made redundant by concrete, serving as rubbish tips and places where wayward youth could set fire to stolen cars. The main industry was scrap, undoing all the infrastructure that had once brought wealth to Lancashire: demolishing the Victorian town halls, mills and factory chimneys; weighing in the metal, cleaning the bricks, pulling up the floorboards and cobblestones and selling them down south. This was my first taste of Thatcher's Britain, and it was, as they say, grim.

Seacoal

In the spring of 1984 I made friends with a Scots lass, Moira, who worked as a horsewoman for a travelling theatre company based in Rossendale called Horse and Bamboo. Towards the end of the year we hatched a plan to move to Lynemouth, just north of Newcastle, where a living could be made collecting seacoal that washed up on the beach. At Appleby I had met Brian and Rosie Laidler who lived on the beach at Lynemouth and who were generous in helping us get set up there.

The beach is a featureless strip of shingle that faces the full force of north-easterlies blowing in from Russia. It is overlooked by a low ridge where at that time some twenty families, mostly Travellers, lived in static caravans, each with its makeshift stable and hay barn. All of these people derived at least some of their living from seacoaling, for which the required equipment was a small 'gallowa' pony, a breed derived from the old pit ponies, and a two-wheeled tipping cart. With Brian's help we bought an old static caravan, a cart, and a fine three-year-old pony with a bit of Highland blood, who was only thirteen hands but looked like a miniature Shire. We called him Brick because he was dependable and built like that kind of shithouse.

The seacoal was mine waste from the nearby colliery at Ashington, tipped into the sea because it was too full of slag.

The ocean swished it around like a washing machine until the buoyant coal became detached from the heavier slag, and then regurgitated it onto the beach whenever there was an east wind. A good drop could deliver perhaps forty tons of coal in a black band along the high water mark, up to a foot deep. The sea graded the coal, with the larger lumps at one end of the deposit and fine grit at the other end.

On a good windy day you might see up to a dozen horses standing belly deep in the surf while men scooped coal out of the breaking waves with nets and ladled it into the cart. When the cart was full the horse would haul out the load through the soupy wet shingle, to drop it above the high water mark. Moira and I, being newcomers and not wanting to compete for the resource, worked the night tides using Tilley lamps. You could claim all the coal that landed on a section of the beach during a single tide by inscribing a line in the sand beforehand with your boot. Not too long a line, mind, for evidence of greed would imperil your standing in the group. By studying the wind direction, the lift of the waves, and other arcane matters, you could try to anticipate where the coal would land, but mostly your share would be due to luck. Five tons of coal might wash onto your patch of the beach or none at all. But once it had landed there it was yours until the tide came in again, unpoachable by others – as was the heap you needed to make safely above the high water mark, prior to carting it up to the road.

This was, as I later came to appreciate, an example of an open access commons operating within the shell of a capitalist transaction. There was an enterprising fellow, let's call him Johnson, with considerable influence, who claimed to have bought the rights to harvest the coal off the Coal Board – or was it the Crown? No one really believed him, and he was maligned by some of the Travellers for having collared what they viewed as a common resource.

In fact, he was its protector but got little credit for it. Every so often, under certain wind and tide conditions, there would be a huge drop of inferior gritty coal, of too poor quality for domestic use. Johnson would arrive with a JCB, scoop it all up and sell it to the Coal Board for use in their power station. The rest of the time he left the beach alone but made sure that nobody else came onto it with machinery. The sole access to the beach was a steep and muddy cutting in the bank that could only be negotiated by well-trained ponies, or on foot by locals, who came to pick a couple of sacks by hand and push them into town on their bicycles to sell for beer money. Johnson had imposed a technological restriction that allowed open access to the beach to anyone with a horse or bicycle, but prevented a potential turf war between coal merchants with JCBs and tractors.

The seacoalers' site was disliked by the authorities and subject to mean-spirited discrimination. The Coal Board, for no apparent reason other than spite, erected a fence across the footpath from the site to the nearest shops in Lynemouth village, necessitating a long detour. Requests for piped water and a telephone box on site were repeatedly turned down. The telegram service had been shut down in 1977 so there was no way of getting an urgent message to someone on site.

The winter of 1984–1985 saw the culmination of the year-long miners' strike. The price for coal was high and striking miners and their neighbours could buy our seacoal with a clear conscience. By March, when the strike was coming to an end and demand for coal subsiding, Moira and I had saved a decent amount of cash. We bought a bow-top wagon, sold our cart and static, and in April set off to Rossendale with Brick and a mare that Moira had acquired – through Newcastle and Gateshead, past Durham and Darlington, crossing the Pennines via Hawes, and down through the forest of Bowland. It was a happy journey.

Three years later Ashington colliery was closed down, the seacoal stopped coming and the people who made a living from it dispersed. The camp was levelled, landscaped and replaced by an eleven pitch council-approved Travellers' site run by a warden. Brian and Rosie moved to a council house forty miles away. The site's demise was one small step in a process that has been gradually shoehorning the travelling community into bricks and mortar, through the obsolescence of work opportunities, the enclosure of traditional stopping places and the cultural homogenisation that springs from schooling and the reach of mass media.

But the process is slow. Like that other persecuted diaspora, the Jews, Gypsies have a strong sense of their own distinctiveness. Both groups have a word for people who are not one of them: gentile (or more insultingly *goy*) and *gorgio*, which apparently means house-dweller. The morals, standards and cultural preferences of travelling communities are rooted in centuries of history, and resistant to change. The hippie's alternative society, which in the 1980s was partly manifest in a so-called 'New Age Traveller' movement, looked by contrast rather flimsy.

Formal Education

When we got back to Lancashire, Moira rejoined her theatre group, taking Brick with her. She rented some grazing for him, but the fencing was not up to scratch, he escaped, walked down a railway line and was mown down by a train. A sad end to a horse that would have gone on to other great things.

I holed up in a brick building in a yard in Accrington belonging to a couple of mechanics. They specialised in taking two cars that were write-offs from accidents and splicing them into one functioning machine. I called them Ford Siestas. I made a bit of cash picking up scrap metal off derelict sites and weighing it in; the price for light iron had attained dizzy heights during the coal strike because it was needed as ballast for the ships that had been bringing in coal.

I spent the rest of my time carving a headstone for Baz's grave. It was an overdesigned piece of work, encrusted with flowery hippy symbolism; I would choose to do something more minimalist nowadays. But it was heartfelt and quite good in its way, and encouraged me to pursue that line of activity. I discovered that there was a two-year course in stone masonry and carving at Weymouth College on the Dorset coast, applied, and was accepted, beginning in September 1985. Since I had only done two terms at Cambridge I found I was eligible for a tiny grant, just enough to keep me alive.

The other people on the course were nearly all mature students, most of them like me in their thirties. The paths that had brought us to converge on Weymouth College were broadly similar. Some were university drop-outs like myself; others had completed an academic course but found that it wasn't what they wanted to do, or wasn't providing them with a decent income. One of the requirements of the City & Guilds exam that we were entered for was to take a paper in Use of English. When we attended the first lesson in this subject the tutor announced, 'You are all better qualified in this subject than I am, so we are not going to cover it and you are all deemed to have passed.' It was a good course and wide ranging, including masonry, carving, conservation, lettering, using a saw bench and 'setting out'. The tutors preferred teaching us to the other class for kids of school-leaving age, since we wanted to learn, unlike many of the youngsters.

In the second term I was carrying a stone I was working on out of a shed, tripped over a bicycle wheel and broke my wrist. It put me out of action for a whole term, but as is often the case was something of a blessing in disguise. For a start it gave me a doctor's certificate stating that I should not be using pneumatic air tools because of the vibrations, and I was more than happy just to stick to hammer and chisel. It also enabled me to spend plenty of time on the drawing board. I had gone to both a public school and a grammar school, but the missing link in my education was the secondary modern, where I could have learnt technical drawing. I worked through a number of the drawings in what was then the stonemason's 'bible', Warland's *Modern Practical Masonry* (1929, second edition 1953) culminating with an A2-sized replica of page 239, 'Gothic Vaulting'. All I did was copy it, but in order to copy it you had to understand it. I still have that drawing, and when I look at it now my mind fogs over. I never actually built any gothic vaulting, I don't think anyone does these days. Perhaps what I most derived from the exercise was heightened admiration for the masons who designed medieval cathedrals without access to drawing boards, or even to paper.

During the second year of the course I rented a tiny cottage with three other people on the edge of Puddletown Forest, about six miles from Weymouth. It was situated on a particularly dangerous blind corner where there were two fatal crashes in the year that we were there. On one occasion there were bloodcurdling screams of pain coming from the road over our breakfast. We wrote to the Council suggesting a 30 mile per hour limit. They wrote back saying they couldn't do that because it was a trunk road.

Nikki Houghton, who lived in the house, had a horse, a Welsh cob, and we would take him into the woods with a trolley to scavenge for firewood. Towards the end of the year we noticed that somebody had come along and knocked in a load of wooden survey stakes. It turned out that the Dorchester Bypass was to be routed through the woods only a stone's throw from our house. It was part of a development scheme for the town focused on Prince Charles' architectural idyll, Poundbury. We gathered up the stakes: they burnt well in our fire. But soon after we moved out the bulldozers moved in. It was a taste of things to come.

The Cathedral

The stonemasonry course was handy because at the end of two years you came out of it with a job. In the white heat of the technological revolution (to borrow Harold Wilson's words), stone masonry was regarded as passé, and the number of apprenticeships in the craft had declined drastically. What the white hot technologists had failed to observe was that although not many carved stone edifices were being constructed, there were a lot of existing stone structures that needed maintenance and repair, some urgently. Several cathedrals were embarking on major repair programmes and, while the rest of the building industry was in recession, they were desperate for masons.

I went for an interview at Salisbury Cathedral. I happened to be reading Thomas Hardy's *Jude the Obscure* at the time and bizarrely, as I was waiting in the Cathedral Close for the interview, I came to the point in the story where Jude gets a job at Melchester (i.e. Salisbury) Cathedral. Jude, readers of the novel will remember, wanted to go to Oxford University, but had to settle for stonemasonry, whereas my own preference was the direct opposite. I got the job and started there not long afterwards. Being penniless, I slept in a bus shelter by the park for the first week, until I plucked up courage to ask for an advance.

The cathedral was carrying out works to its tower and four hundred-foot spire, the tallest in Britain. When I started work there, stone and materials were hauled up by a medieval windlass installed near the top of the spire. This is a huge two-person treadmill; operating it was like carrying a rucksack weighing a hundredweight up a steep hill. The rope, which was as thick as an arm and more than three hundred-foot long, weighed more than the load you were pulling up. Meanwhile personnel had to reach working height at the top of the tower by walking up a 332 step spiral staircase. It paid to make sure that you had forgotten nothing when you went up in the morning. After a year or so, a lift was installed on the exterior scaffolding.

Work proceeded in defiance of any normal health and safety or building regulations. The cathedral was so short of experienced masons that novices fresh out of college like myself were put in positions of responsibility with undue haste. I found myself lifting three hundred-kilo stones with block and tackle, two hundred feet above the public milling around in the Cathedral Close, with no previous experience other than verbal instruction from the college on the art of shifting heavy weights. As if to remind us of the dangers, there were repairs to flagstones in the centre of the nave where not long before a large stone had crashed to the ground when being hauled up by the windlass.

Within a year I was put in charge of replacing the south west pinnacle, one of four that sprang from the corners of the tower at the base of the spire. Simply getting to it was a challenge for anyone susceptible to vertigo. We had to climb up a vertical ladder on the outside of the scaffolding, with a hundred-foot drop down to the nave roof, holding all our tools, and it was even worse if you were carrying a hangover as well. On one occasion, when I was working on the scaffold at the top of the tower, a gust of wind lifted up a saw and sent it sailing through the air like a kite. Fortunately it landed in a gutter on the nave roof, rather than decapitating one of the tourists in the close.

Standing on top of the scaffolding that enclosed the twenty-three-foot tall pinnacle you could grab hold of its finial and rock the entire structure backwards and forwards for about six inches in any direction. When we took it down we found that one of the iron clamps that previous masons had inserted had got wet and expanded in layers until it was the size and form of a mille-feuille cake. The pinnacle, weighing several tons was pivoting on this small pile of rust. After taking it down, my job was to make a full-size drawing of the pinnacle, develop from that all the moulds and templates for the individual stones, get them carved by the team of masons and then fix them all in place. It took me fourteen months. Before hoisting the stones up the tower, we erected the pinnacle dry in the Cathedral Yard, and it all fitted together as planned. My time on the drawing board had stood me in good stead.

After about three years, I left the cathedral and worked for a local masonry firm as a banker mason. Unlike the other guys at the firm, I wouldn't use air-powered chisels, but that didn't worry the boss, since they are only about 30 per cent quicker than a hammer and chisel, so a fast hand tool worker can keep up with a slow air tool worker. In fact he decided that I must be some kind of artist and put all the interesting jobs my way, describing me in his publicity leaflet as his 'Italian trained carver' because I had once been to Carrara for a week.

I was now, finally, competent enough to pass myself off as a professional stonemason. Yet I have never entirely dispelled the feeling that I am an impostor in the world of manual work – that the basic skills and understanding of materials are not as ingrained in me as they would be if I had picked them up when younger, in the same way that anyone who learns a new language later in life inevitably speaks with an accent.

Eventually I went self-employed, doing carving for the National Trust and others. I also dipped my toe into the art world, because I was producing for myself a few works that classed as sculptures, rather than architectural features. I subscribed to the *Artists Newsletter*, took loads of photos, drew up a CV (something I'd never needed before) and entered a couple of competitions. It didn't take me long to realise that the art world is full of bullshit, and that success depends upon whom you know.

Thatcher's Legacy

After a few months at Salisbury, I and two other Cathedral masons clubbed together and obtained a three-year lease on a ten-roomed house on a large estate seven miles out of Salisbury, called Druid's Lodge. We found another three people to share the rent, and with partners there were sometimes as many as ten people living there. It was a great house. The central part, which included the kitchen, was built in 1911 as an experimental cob house, and was cosy. Two wings had been added in the 1930s with spacious rooms and Crittall Hope windows, giving the place the atmosphere of a Noël Coward garden party. We all got on well, and we had a couple of great parties. We looked after the place well, paid the rent and were on good terms with the estate office. It was also a good place where my daughter could pay a visit, something that had been proving more difficult than I anticipated.

The estate was called Druid's Lodge because it was only a couple of miles from Stonehenge, and this turned out to have a certain tactical advantage. It was the era of New Age Travellers, whom Douglas Hurd had compared (with some justification) to 'medieval brigands'. We had seen the footage of the 1985 Battle of the Beanfield, when police launched a vicious and unprovoked attack on a convoy of harmless vans and buses headed for a free festival at Stonehenge. For the next few years there was a ritual re-enactment by hippies and police of this confrontation, which happily never attained the same levels of brutality.

For about two weeks before the solstice, the police would impose a four mile exclusion zone around Stonehenge. However Druid's Lodge was within the exclusion zone, so they could not stop us entering, nor could they stop anyone from coming to visit us. None of us who lived at Druid's Lodge were particularly keen to attend a Stonehenge festival, but we knew a fair few who were, and we had no objection to them taking advantage of our privileged situation. A little garden party on the eve of the Solstice was our contribution to the festivities.

The house was also a useful meeting point for another activity. About once a month the military would carry out an exercise that involved transporting Cruise missiles on huge articulated trucks at great speed in an easterly direction along the A303 at midnight. Why, we didn't know, nor was it clear why they never seemed to come back in the other direction. There was a network called Cruisewatch whose mission was to let these transporters of mass destruction know that they were being watched. The Salisbury branch, consisting of about six people, would convene at Druid's Lodge before driving out to the Amesbury roundabout, where we would hang around for up to an hour waiting for the convoy. It was boring. When the convoy finally came it would tear round the roundabout at a breakneck speed, while we waggled our banners, and then it was gone, into the night. Then we went home. Ostensibly it was a pointless exercise, but it had a sort of religious significance: something to do with bearing witness. Ungodly activities should not be allowed to proceed unobserved.

I might have become more involved in resistance to the military industrial complex if the dominant campaign at the time had not been closed to half of the population. Arriving back in the UK after ten years abroad, I found the women-only policy at the Greenham Common protest camp perplexing, along with the climate of puritanism that was emanating from much of the women's movement. Gone were the egalitarian libertinism and sex-positive feminism of the late 1960s, championed in the extreme by *Suck* magazine, with Germaine Greer at its bowsprit, and echoed in the graphics of *Oz* and *International Times* or the capers that went on in Robert Crumb's buttock-heavy cartoons. Now the dominant voices in the women's movement were those who railed against being a 'sexual object', without making any semantic distinction between being the object of someone's desire (which is potentially a good experience) and being treated as a mere thing (which is not). My sympathies lay more with the plain women and gawky men I have known who were rarely if ever the object of someone's sexual attention, and who yearned to be loved.

Sexual politics aside, the Greenham Common camp was an inspirational campaign which single-handedly established permanent occupations as an effective protest tactic. However, towards the end of the 1980s, and especially after the fall of the Berlin Wall in 1989, the prospect of mutually assured destruction through nuclear warfare was becoming overshadowed by another existential threat: the assault on the planetary environment by unbridled consumer capitalism, compounded by increasing population. Initially there were panics over problems such as acid rain, and the depletion of the ozone layer, but these issues could be painlessly addressed by regulating the behaviour of corporations, and indeed they were. They were a foretaste of the much more intractable problem of global warming that came to the fore in about 1990.

The rise of environmental concerns came as a vindication of the inchoate rejection of consumerism that had surfaced twenty years previously. Low-impact living, renewable energy, growing organic food, vegetarianism, communal living, hitch-hiking, dropping out of the system – once these had been tokens of independence from the excesses of capitalism, now they became reinvested with the more noble purpose of protecting the planet.

In Salisbury, we campaigned against tropical hardwoods and plastic waste, published an alternative local magazine that ran to a dozen issues called the *Sarum Gleaner*, and in 1989 oversaw the count at the European election when the Green Party to everyone's surprise won 15 per cent of all votes across the country – more than it has received in any election before or since. At that time the UK European Elections were decided according to the 'first past the post' system, which meant that with 15 per cent of the votes, the Green Party got precisely no Members of the European Parliament (MEPs). So much for democracy. In 1999 the UK was forced by the EU to adopt a system of proportional representation, so after that we did get green MEPs – including Molly Scott Cato, the only person I have ever voted for who actually got elected. That very welcome representation has since been taken away from me through withdrawal from the EU, courtesy of a government that received only 43.6 per cent of the vote in the 2019 general election, yet as I write has 56 per cent of the seats and an unassailable majority of 80 in parliament.

Towards the end of my stay in Salisbury, survey stakes began to appear on the downs not far from Druid's Lodge, the same sort of survey stakes as I had seen in the woods at Puddletown. It turned out that they were there for the same purpose. There were plans to construct an 11-mile bypass around Salisbury, part of a long-term plan to turn the A36 into a de facto motorway linking Southampton and Bristol. At an exhibition in the public library the people of Salisbury were invited to choose between the red route and the blue route. Those of us who wanted no route formed a Stop the Bypass group, and stop it we did. But that is part of another story.

Along with rising environmental concerns, there was growing resistance to Thatcherism. The year-long miners' strike of 1984 failed to enlist much support from middle class left-wingers and *Guardian* readers, partly because the miners' union leader Arthur Scargill made little attempt to bring them on side. Ironically, shutting down the mines turned out to have been a green policy, but that was not Thatcher's reason for doing it, and the way she went about it was brutal and imperious.

Her victory over the miners was probably what made her arrogant enough to think that she could get away with imposing a poll tax. That drew opposition from a much larger swathe of liberal opinion. Thousands refused to pay. In Salisbury alone the courts had to deal with scores of us, one after another, pleading not guilty and arguing our case with or without the help of a lawyer.

A nationwide demonstration was called on 31 March 1990. It was to start at Kennington, in London, south of the Thames. When we tried to board the Northern line Tube at King's Cross the platform was packed with demonstrators who filled the train, when it arrived, to bursting. At every station down the line, the platforms were thick with people who couldn't even attempt to board our train. Everyone was smiling and joking, because it was clear that this was going to be a massive turn-out. The police afterwards estimated it at two hundred thousand but I suspect it was bigger than that.

When we got to Trafalgar Square it was already nearly full and crowds were surging up Whitehall and into Northumberland Avenue. It was then that the police started to kettle large sections of demonstrators into enclosed spaces. I climbed a lamppost and could see clearly what was taking place in Northumberland Avenue. For reasons best known to themselves, a line of police was pushing the crowd backwards even though there was nowhere for them to go. If the police wanted to provoke a riot it was the best way to go about it.

It was not long before the scuffles and the arrests erupted into a full-scale battle. There was scaffolding covering a large office block on the corner of the square called Grand Buildings (funnily enough I had been carving some stone work for it only a few weeks before). Demonstrators clambered all over the building and set fire to the builders' cabins and other material. Soon after smoke and flames were coming from the

South African Embassy. Eventually the police muscled in with horses and vans, divided the crowd and pushed our section northwards into the shopping centres of the West End where some went on a window smashing and looting spree.

It was great! Just what was needed. Photos of London in flames were in the newspapers across Europe and the rest of the world – a warning to any heads of state who might be considering following in Thatcher's footsteps. The Iron Lady had lost her grip. The Labour Party and various Marxist groups officially condemned the violence and blamed it upon 'anarchists', but they were smirking once their backs were turned to the camera. It was the beginning of the end for Thatcher. Speculation grew within the Conservative Party about replacing her, and in November 1990, after a leadership challenge from Michael Heseltine, she resigned.

But though it was the end of Thatcher, it was not the end of Thatcherism, which had a lasting legacy, not least in the housing sector. She had launched her premiership with her attack on council housing in the right-to-buy legislation of 1980. She followed it up with the 1988 Housing Act, a landlords' charter that abolished fair rent controls and removed security of tenure for tenants.

We were soon to find what that meant for us at Druid's Lodge. Towards the end of our three-year lease the estate changed hands. It was bought by a farmer who, so we were told, had sold farmland for development around Gatwick Airport for upwards of £50 million. Suddenly, instead of dealing with a friendly farm office, we were facing verbal harassment from an uncouth henchman of the owner who told us in no uncertain terms that we would soon be out on our arses.

Then we learnt that the posh estate agent Savills had been engaged to manage the estate's tenancies. A Savills representative came to inform us that although we had paid the rent and maintained the property in good condition, they had a policy of never allowing shared tenancies, and so we would have to leave. It was sickening, since it was a lovely house, and we made good use of it. After we left, Savills rented all ten rooms to a couple who could afford the rent that we had shared between six of us. I concluded that renting was for mugs, and bought myself a clean white Renault Trafic van which I kitted out for living in.

But the event in my life that summed up the ethos of Thatcherism occurred a few years later when I had moved to Somerset. I was returning on the train from Oxford, but dozed off, missed a connection and ended up at midnight at Salisbury Station, with the next train to Yeovil at six in the morning. The railway staff wouldn't allow me to wait at the station, even though I had a ticket. It was bitterly cold, at least -8°C, and I had no sleeping bag, inadequate clothing and not enough money for a hotel. I phoned up people I knew in Salisbury, but there was no reply. I got a number from directory enquiries for a night shelter, but that too didn't answer. Suddenly I was faced with the challenge of how not to die of hypothermia. I decided to try the police; perhaps if I made a sufficient nuisance of myself they would put me in a cell for the night. I rang the door bell of the police station, and a voice came over the intercom: 'How can we help you?' I told them my predicament and they said sorry, they couldn't do anything, they were speaking from forty miles away in Bath.

I wandered down the road, peering into people's gardens to see if there was an unlocked shed that I could borrow for the night. Then I came to the site of the Old Manor mental hospital. I walked in and every building I peered into was empty. I tried one of the sash windows: it was unlocked. I opened it and a blast of warm air hit me in the face. I clambered into a large completely bare room that was so hot – I kid you not – that I had to sleep with the window wide open to the frosty air. It was, I mused as I went to sleep, the very epitome of Thatcherism: closing down a hospital, but leaving the heating on. But it saved my bacon that night.

CHAPTER EIGHT

Road Alert!

Death came to my father, as it did his father, by way of a taxi. In about 1987 he had been evicted from his flat in Dupont Circle, and might have found himself on the street had not the *New Republic* come to the rescue. In return for providing an idiosyncratic regular column in the magazine, they provided him with a modest stipend, and a 'live–work' office just big enough for a typewriter, a bookcase and a sofabed. From here he wrote his last dispatches, worked on a novel that would never be published and supplemented his income by flogging review copies of books in secondhand bookshops in order to subsidise his patronage of various local bars, high- and low-life.

In 1990 he stepped out of a taxi cab, after a well-lubricated evening, slipped and broke his hip. He was taken to hospital, where shortly afterwards he had a stroke that paralysed half of his body. According to a young female employee at the *New Republic*, who had befriended Henry, and looked after him during his last few days, the stroke was brought on by being allowed neither cigarettes nor whisky to alleviate the stress. I can believe this. The only time I have experienced shock was when I tripped up and lay trapped underneath that heavy stone I was carrying with my wrist broken. My flatmate removed the stone, laid me down on a sofa and stuck a cigarette in my mouth. Those first few puffs sorted me out.

Lying in a hospital bed with half his body paralysed and nobody to stick fags in his mouth, Henry must have thought 'sod this for a game of soldiers'. Within two days he had a full-scale heart attack that put him on life support. The doctors at the hospital phoned me up in Salisbury, saying there was no hope, and asking for permission to switch it off. I said yes. A few days later I flew over to Washington to help my sister Charlotte sort out his affairs.

His body was cremated at a bottom of the range crematorium somewhere in the suburbs of Washington, D.C. I was to pick up his ashes, from an employee who would be waiting for me in a white Pontiac in the 'kiss and ride' car park at the end of a subway line. When I eventually identified the vehicle amongst the ranks of commuter cars, the driver, a sinister young man in a sharp suit, didn't bother to get out of the car, but opened the door for me to sit in the front passenger seat. 'Mr Fairlie?' he said. 'That'll be $900.' I counted out the cash and he handed over a box containing a white powder that could have been anything, or anyone. Had a cop witnessed the transaction he would have suspected that something quite different was being traded.

A few days later I flew back to England with the ashes. Thankfully the customs officials did not search my luggage. After twenty-five years in the United States, never once leaving its soil, Henry Fairlie made it back to Britain without being apprehended by the authorities. His ashes were interred at the family graveyard in Monikie, Angus.

The Ecologist

Within a few months of my father's death, I became a professional writer. It was sudden and unexpected, as if my father's legacy had been dumped on my shoulders.

A friend told me that *The Ecologist* magazine needed book reviewers, and drove me to their office in Sturminster Newton, Dorset, where I browsed through the shelf of hopeful review copies and selected an unglamorous textbook that few people would want to read called *Agroforestry in Dryland Africa*. Apparently I did a good job of bringing the book to life, because *The Ecologist* printed it, and then hired me to do some part-time work updating an environmental reference book they produced called *The Earth Report*.

This proved to be an essential introduction to a skill that had hitherto passed me by, namely research. I was given a number of subjects to update such as 'Acid Rain', 'Bhopal', 'the Montreal Protocol' and shown all the relevant reports, the back issues of magazines ranging from *New Scientist to Earth First!*, the files full of newspaper cuttings and press releases. Identifying and filing this stuff as it arrived, mostly in the post, was part of the job.

Since this was before the days of the internet, all of this information took up space – several rooms full of book shelves and filing cabinets. Together with all the other libraries and offices throughout the country it must have made a useful contribution to carbon sequestration. Today it can all be stored in a laptop and accessed using Google rather than a card index. But whether the internet saves time as efficiently as it saves space is questionable. Now there is a surplus of information and time is wasted winnowing out the dross and pursuing distractions.

On the strength of this research I was offered a full-time job as assistant editor. I handed in my notice at the stonemasons and the following Monday showed up at *The Ecologist*, worried that my inexperience – notably my two-finger typing – would let me down. To my relief Nick Hildyard, the editor in chief, was a two-finger typist as well. He stuck me in front of an Apple Mac, showed me how to use the PageMaker layout programme and gave me a couple of manuscripts to hammer into readable articles.

Nick had been trained as an anthropologist, but at an early age became a protégé of Teddy Goldsmith, *The Ecologist*'s founder, who had made him an editor of the magazine in 1976 when he was in his twenties. He was, and still is, an astute campaigner and a fine polemicist. The other member of the editorial team was Sarah Sexton, who joined the same time as myself and who had a background in ecofeminism. And in a backroom stuffed with cardboard boxes overflowing with photocopies of learned articles, was an American, Larry Lohmann, who acted as a sort of intellectual *éminence grise* to the magazine.

Between us we turned out six copies of the magazine a year. We each took total responsibility for certain pages, liaising with authors, hacking the text, running it past the other editors, providing the photos, title and captions and laying it out as camera-ready copy. This is preferable to having art editors, sub-editors, designers and so on messing around with your copy.

Nick was a good person to work with and I learnt much about writing, and almost everything I know about editing from him. Over-verbose copy would be returned with diagonal pencil lines slashed across entire pages, and comments such as 'purple prose' in the margins. Nick's recipe for a good article was 'structure, structure, structure' – a motto I have often repeated to myself, not least when trying to hammer this memoir into shape. My other guiding principle is 'write drunk, edit sober'.

When I first joined the magazine I privately thought that it was too dry and could do with lightening up with shorter items, cartoons, better graphics and so on. I changed my mind when one day I went to do some research in the British Library, and as I walked with my requested books back to my place, I passed no less than three readers with back issues of *The Ecologist* on their desk. At that time, the magazine occupied a unique and strategic position in the market midway between academic journals on the one hand and the middlebrow press and weeklies on the other. Typically we would take academic papers or reports from NGOs and recycle the content as articles that were well-referenced, but readable and with a judicious level of polemic. Some academics whose work we repackaged couldn't write for toffees, and editing their copy was a major endeavour; or their submission might have to be stripped of an overlong postmodern preamble about 'discourse'. Occasionally we'd get a submission that looked good but needed restructuring, and when you had done that you could see that actually the argument didn't stand up to scrutiny.

Sometimes we would issue a press release publicising an article or a themed issue. I'm not sure that the immediate uptake on these was very great, but I noticed that often within a year or two the matter that we had been highlighting would be gathering steam in the popular press. *The Ecologist* was particularly effective at exposing the problems caused by the International Monetary Fund (IMF), the World Bank, and their structural adjustment policies that in a few years' time were under attack by the antiglobalisation movement.

The highpoint of my stint at *The Ecologist* was the July/August 1992 issue entitled *Whose Common Future?* Stretching to ninety-six pages it was ostensibly a response to the Rio Earth Summit that had taken place in June, but its focus was the management of common resources by local communities and their enclosure by corporate and state power. Nick and Larry had absorbed the work of a school of anthropologists whose fieldwork demonstrated that the 'tragedy of the commons' thesis, beloved of economists as an argument for privatisation, did not hold water. There was ample evidence that commons regimes are capable of managing resources sustainably, and that, more often than not, it is the exterior forces of 'enclosure' that precipitate their demise.

The moment was right for propagating these ideas, and *Whose Common Future?* struck a chord with many in the green movement. In a 2018 interview in *The Land* George Monbiot recalled, 'I was influenced at the time by a special edition of *The Ecologist* magazine about enclosure. They took the concept of enclosure and said originally it's been applied to land, but actually it's been applied across the board, in all sorts of ways – think of genes, plant varieties, academic papers, the privatised utilities. And so in a way this describes the history of the world.'

Other writers such as David Bollier have taken commons analysis further, and the concept is now regularly applied to the internet and open-source software. In 2009, Elinor Ostrom was awarded the Nobel Prize for Economic Sciences for 'challenging conventional wisdom by demonstrating how local property can be successfully managed by local commons without any regulation by central authorities or privatisation'. Without diminishing Ostrom's achievements, the prize could perhaps have been awarded collectively to the dozens of anthropologists and political economists who were working on these issues – not to mention Hildyard and Lohmann who had the wit to realise, before anyone else, the relevance of these matters to late twentieth-century Britain.

Not long after I left *The Ecologist*, Nick, Larry and Sarah resigned, in protest at the increasingly right-wing stance taken by the magazine's founder Teddy Goldsmith, who took back editorial control and passed it onto his nephew Zac. Under his regime the magazine did adopt a more popular format, but I'm not sure that that made it any more influential. In 2009, it ceased paper publication and went online, and three years later it was sold to *Resurgence* for £1.

———

The Ecologist's offices were in a former shop and town house in the centre of the Dorset town of Sturminster Newton. For six days, 'Stur' was little more than a large village, with a couple of pubs, a hardware shop and a creamery making award-winning Double Gloucester and Cheddar cheese. It had once boasted a railway station but that had closed down in 1966, along with the entire Somerset and Dorset railway and upwards of forty stations.

But once a week, Stur was transmogrified into a bustling market town. Its Monday cattle market was one of the biggest in Britain and, as had been the case in Colchester, attracted a host of fringe activities: an outside deadstock auction that sold everything from vintage furniture to trays of eggs, market stalls, a Women's Institute market, and church coffee mornings. Jumble sales were invariably held on Monday mornings. And a large hall near the former station was converted for the day into a greasy spoon café where farmers with thick West Country accents would josh raucously with one another over very full English breakfasts.

All this activity got every week off to a good start. But I hadn't been very long in Stur before it emerged that the market's owners wanted to close it down and sell off the land for development, ideally to a supermarket. I was beginning to wonder if I was some kind of Jonah since everywhere I moved to either had its market scheduled for closure, or was in the firing line for a dual carriageway road scheme. The weirdest thing about the proposed development was that nobody (with the exception of the vegans who picketed it) wanted the 700-year-old market to close, but nobody lifted a finger to save it. The local authority planning department stated that they were against closure, but refused to oppose the planning application to shut it down on the grounds that the developers would inevitably win at appeal.

The market closed in 1997, but the town did manage to fend off a large supermarket, and instead now boasts a locally funded community centre whose webpage highlights appearances by Des O'Connor and Michael Portillo. Three years later the creamery was closed down by its owners, Dairy Crest, partly because 'the market had brought in a lot of business from farmers and traders far and wide'. Dairy Crest's manager told the local MP Robert Walter that his firm was determined to pull out of Sturminster Newton, and to prevent anybody else producing cheese there; no way would they consider any offers for the cheese factory from local farmers.

'I deplore this attitude to undermine the skills of local cheese makers,' the MP told the *Dorset Echo*. 'I will not let this issue die.' But it did. In response the town began to host an annual cheese festival, so now, instead of producing cheese, it celebrates it. Meanwhile Dairy Crest, and its brand Cathedral City, have been taken over by the Canadian firm Saputo.

Twyford Down

While there was little resistance to the closure of markets and the corporatisation of the food chain, there was a growing movement against road building. In 1989, Margaret Thatcher's government had introduced a trunk road enlargement programme that promised to deliver 2,700 miles of new or improved roads, including 150 new bypasses, one of which was the Salisbury bypass. Many of the schemes were opposed by local groups of objectors and in 1991 a national umbrella group called Alarm UK! was founded by John Stewart to co-ordinate resistance.

Its first major campaign was at Twyford Down near Winchester where the last three-mile stretch necessary to complete the M3 from London to Southampton required a 100-foot deep cutting to be gouged through an Area of Outstanding Natural Beauty, peppered with archaeological remains and Sites of Special Scientific Interest. In October 1991 the European Commission declared that the government would be acting illegally if it developed the site without a proper environmental assessment, but the government defied the ruling and brought bulldozers onto the site to begin preliminary works. Opposition to the cutting was spearheaded by the Twyford Down Association, headed by a former Conservative Party councillor, David Croker, and other respected local citizens of Winchester. They were supported by Friends of the Earth (FoE) who helped organise and publicise a demonstration that brought in objectors to the roads programme from around the country. *The Times* commented, 'The protest has brought together an unlikely alliance of Tories, New Agers, neo-hippies and eco-radicals.'

However in the summer of 1992, during the negotiations over the new Maastricht Treaty, the EU transport commissioner dropped the ruling on Twyford Down in return for other concessions from Britain; and a court injunction was issued against protest camps on site. Friends of the Earth pulled out of the campaign, their acting director, Andrew Lees, explaining: 'We must separate matters of principle from those of pragmatic reality. One of the hardest things is to know when to say "that's it, we've lost".'

Not everybody pulled out. A bunch of hard-core hippies set up a bender camp on Twyford Down, calling themselves the 'Dongas' after the local name for a network of ancient sheep tracks etched into the hillside. But with the disappearance of FoE and the almost total lack of support from other mainstream environmental groups, there was little to bridge the wide social gulf between the concerned citizens of Winchester on the one hand and the Dongas on the other.

Winchester College, the public school, owned the land the Dongas occupied, and applied for an eviction order against the camp. On 9 December 1992, the day the eviction order was to be heard, yellow-jacketed Group 4 Securicor security guards, accompanied by representatives of the Department of Transport and the police, stormed the Dongas' camp, beating up the occupants and groping the women, while bulldozers followed behind to rip up the Donga trackways. The eviction, dubbed 'Yellow Wednesday', attracted considerable press attention, and occupies a similar position to the Battle of the Beanfield in the annals of the alternative movement.

The January 1993 issue of *The Ecologist* carried an editorial condemning the eviction, and criticising Friends of the Earth and other environmental organisations for their failure to support the Dongas because they were 'afraid of being tarred with a radical brush'. The editorial also acknowledged *The Ecologist's* own failings noting that, 'not a word was published in this journal about Twyford Down until a reader wrote a letter stating that it was one of the "commons" she felt inspired to defend'.

Soon after publication, two of the Twyford campaigners, Becca Lush and Emma Must, invited me to come over to Winchester because they wanted to pool ideas on what to do next. We were agreed that the best approach was to try to muster nationwide support for direct action by emphasising the strategic significance of Twyford Down at a national and European level. This was not just a fight to save one valley, but a symbolic attempt to stop the Conservative's massive road expansion programme. We might lose the battle of Twyford Down, but there was a war to be won. I told them that *The Ecologist* would do what it could to promote the campaign on a national level.

It so happened that the senior editor of *The Ecologist*, Nick Hildyard, was about to take a six-week visit to India to meet grass root groups there. He spontaneously offered the use of his office to the Twyford Down campaigners for the extent of his absence. It was a generous offer, and for the next two months or so Becca, Emma and I, together with Tim Allman and Phil Pritchard, became the nerve centre of the Twyford Down campaign in respect of national outreach, travelling regularly back and forth between the office in Sturminster and the camp at Twyford. We kicked off with a 'National Demonstration

Against Reckless Roadbuilding' on the weekend of 6 and 7 March, which drew several hundred people. It also attracted new recruits for the protest camp, whose occupants were carrying out minor acts of direct action on a daily basis.

It was interesting to see how a bunch of undisciplined and penniless misfits living under canvas on a diet of veggie slop, fraisers (flat bread made with self-raising flour) and dope could nonetheless demonstrate military acumen, sending out scouts to reconnoitre the enemy's manoeuvres and mounting operations at the crack of dawn to take them by surprise. The classic tactic involved two or three people crawling under an earth-moving machine and locking themselves on to it often by the neck, while the remainder of the posse clambered all over it.

One factor in the protesters' favour was that they could and would do anything that came into their heads, whereas the response of the police and the security guards was subject to orders, and predictable. On one occasion I was present at a face-off between a cordon of police and several dozen protesters in the middle of the cutting. After a while a senior officer gathered his men into a huddle to consult on what to do, whereupon one of the protesters, Donga Alex, left our ranks and started circling them performing a frenzied war dance, shaking her dreadlocks, whooping, and making gestures of exorcism. She was doing such a good job single-handed, none of the rest of us joined her. The chief officer tried to keep his men focused, but they were so distracted and disturbed that after a few circumambulations by this whirling dervish, the group disbanded and the cordon of police simply melted away.

Stuff like this was happening on a daily basis on the site, requiring the deployment, at considerable expense to the Department of Transportation (DoT), of large cohorts of police and Group 4 security guards. But back at the office our main job was to promote the big national weekends of action, by sending out photocopied posters to a list of several hundred activists throughout the UK. Much of our time was spent stuffing envelopes, deep into the night – recycled ones where you had to scrub out the old address and stick them up with tape. In 1993, email and the internet were in their infancy, and Facebook and Twitter were unheard of. Instead we had snail mail, a list of addresses and a phone tree.

It was hard work compared to sending out an email to a list, but it was fun, and it was effective. Other groups, such as Earth First!, posted out the flier we sent them to their list of contacts. People came from all over the country in their hundreds to participate in acts of civil disobedience. On one of the marches I overheard a resident of the protest camp saying, 'Isn't it magic how all these people have come down here spontaneously?' Little did they know the long office hours spent getting them to come; magic, like genius, is 90 per cent perspiration. The success of this postal campaign has made me rather sceptical of claims that social media help to foment protest. What matters is word of mouth, and it doesn't make much difference what is the dominant medium by which that word is conveyed.

The other main activity was sending out press releases – again a more time-consuming business than is now the case, as they were either sent by post or by fax. We published about two a week and for more than two months the mainstream media wouldn't bite. It was like trying to tickle a dead elephant. I remember the excitement when we got a little mention in *Private Eye* about Winchester schoolboys on the protest, and *The Guardian* gave us a few column inches. But mostly it seemed we were sending these press releases off into a black hole. I think we had sent off thirteen press releases when finally, and suddenly, the media took the bait.

That was at the Bailey Bridge protest, where we set ourselves the aim of capturing a temporary steel bridge that the construction company was erecting over a part of the cutting. When we massed our troops in the early afternoon, some distance away from the bridge, our scouts reported back that the bridge was stoutly defended and we would probably not succeed in taking it. An air of resignation was prevalent, so to raise morale a few of us got everybody to practice the Roman formation known as the Tortoise. We didn't have the shields to cover us, but nonetheless we did manage to get all these hippies to link arms and bunch together in a solid and irresistible formation.

We set off towards the bridge, escorted by the police, but one of our scouts had discovered a short cut down a little used footpath and a substantial section of the march set off along it without the police clocking what was happening. We arrived at the bridge benefiting from an element of surprise. There was a tall metal fence crowned by razor wire and within it a circle of security guards and police. But this was no match for even a shambolically formed tortoise. And razor wire, although it is sharper than barbed wire, is a lot easier to barge your way through because all the spikes point in the same direction. A hundred or so of us, arms linked in ranks of ten, stomped down the fence with ridiculous ease, brushed the police aside, then scattered and clambered all over the iron girder bridge.

Once we were installed, the police and security guards spent several hours deciding what to do. When dusk came they obligingly set up a stand of floodlights, so everybody could see what was happening. By banging on the girders with D locks or a lump of wood we could make the whole structure reverberate like a huge tuning fork. With a hundred people silhouetted on bare girders against the floodlit sky, and the tension of knowing that the police sooner or later had to get us off, it was an awesome spectacle in the days when the word awesome still carried some weight.

Somehow (and I like to think that the build-up of thirteen press releases had some influence here) word got around Fleet

Street that there was good copy to be had and by nightfall there was a mass of photographers and reporters in attendance to watch us being prised off the girders inch by inch, in my case by a policeman grabbing my thumbs and twisting them until it became too painful to resist. Given that there was a fifteen foot drop down to solid concrete, I thought the police did this with expertise, and a measure of good humour. It was the small hours of the morning before they had removed the last of us from the bridge.

The next day every newspaper, and notably the tabloid press, was packed with pictures of the Bailey Bridge. We had arrived: a red carpet had been laid down giving road protesters unparalleled access to the media, culminating within two years in the much publicised Battle of Newbury, the celebritisation of Swampy and eventually the collapse of the road programme.

When Nick Hildyard returned from India, he reclaimed his office, but *The Ecologist* continued briefly as a centre of operations until Lush, Must, Allman and Pritchard rented premises in Southampton, where they set up as an organisation called Road Alert!

Pentonville

The next step taken by the DoT and their contractors, Tarmac, was to chase up the people who they regarded as ring leaders with a view to getting an injunction preventing them from coming anywhere near the cutting. With this end in view they employed a detective agency called Brays to take incriminating photographs and to serve us with the injunction. Brays weren't very competent, so even someone like myself, not accustomed to being followed, noticed their presence one day in the car park outside *The Ecologist*'s office, waiting for me to emerge from the only door. I therefore spent the day coming and going through a sash window at the back and over a garden wall. By the end of the day I felt so sorry for the poor chap stewing in his Montego that I surrendered myself to him and was duly served with the injunction papers.

These, of course, were a godsend, because it meant that on the next big protest on 4 July we could hang our number round our neck – I was Action File Number 39 – and invite prosecution, with all the media attention that that entailed (thankfully this was the UK, not Syria). Brays compiled a photographic compendium of all those who defied the injunction, and eventually six of us were brought to court on that count: Becca Lush, Emma Must, Phil Pritchard, Bob Baehr, Jason Torrance and myself.

We were tried in London, by Lord Justice Hoffmann, who had no choice but to find us guilty, and sentenced us to a lenient month in prison, commutable to two weeks. He did memorably state, 'Civil disobedience on grounds of conscience is an honourable tradition in this country, and those who take part in it may well be vindicated by history.'

I and the other three men were taken down and escorted to HM Prison Pentonville where we were given the prison uniform – a set of pyjamas – and lodged in two adjacent cells. My cellmate was Bob Baehr, a wiry swarthy fellow, a couple of years older than I, who when young had got strung out on heroin in India, and nearly died, but survived to father four children. The fortnight provided a well-earned rest in an environment that was like boarding school, except you didn't have to do anything. Since there were four of us, we spent much of the time playing bridge and canasta, and I got *Don Quixote* out of the prison library and read it from beginning to end. The food in particular was reminiscent of school: three unappetising meals were crammed into a period of eight hours, between nine and five, so that they could all be prepared by the same staff in one shift – which meant that you went sixteen hours without any grub.

My pangs of night-time hunger were exacerbated by the fact that my cellmate, Bob, was a vegan, and as such was entitled to a daily hamper, stocked with goodies such as marmite and baked beans, which he could eat whenever he felt like it. A further disadvantage of being in a cell with a vegan is that they have loose bowels, or at least Bob did. Pentonville had a slopping out regime. That is, throughout the long night your only lavatory is a bucket in the cell that you empty out in the morning.

Our mornings were enlivened by the arrival of the postbag. The press had christened us the Twyford Six – an unwarranted honorific given the minimal degree of martyrdom we had to undergo – and we received hundreds of letters of support. The pleasure these gave made me realise how valuable letters must be for people who are locked away for years. We were also visited in our cell by politicians wishing to distance themselves from Tory road-building policy: Chris Smith, the Labour shadow minister of the environment; Simon Hughes, who occupied an equivalent position in the Lib Dem Party; and Carlo Ripa di Meana, the European Commissioner for the Environment. At no other time – or place – in my life have I been visited by people of such eminence.

I can speak blithely of my prison experience because we were only in there for two weeks. If it had been two years that would have been a different matter. Moreover the women, Becca and Emma, had a more gruelling experience in Holloway, since a high proportion of women held there were distraught or disturbed. In Pentonville, by contrast, none of the inmates we met appeared to be mentally unstable; prison seemed to be just a normal part of their existence, like bad weather. Solace could be acquired by smoking cigarettes, or taking drugs, and some sort of purpose to life could be found in the lengths it took to acquire these things.

But the most striking feature of Pentonville was that everyone interned there, except ourselves, was working class;

if there were other exceptions, we didn't meet them. As a well-grounded lefty, I was aware that the purpose of the judicial system is to protect the interests of the upper classes. But it is not until you go to prison that you experience the blatant and numerically irrefutable truth of the matter at first hand. Even though we were hippies, in jail we enjoyed the patronage of a middle-class liberal establishment, which nobody else in Pentonville benefited from.

Moreover getting on for 50 per cent of the inmates of Pentonville were black, mostly Afro-Caribbean, whereas the proportion of black people in Greater London at the time was 8 per cent. I declined to go to the voluntary exercise sessions while I was there, because it would have reminded me of school drill. But I did go to the Sunday Christian service. The chapel was packed, but every single face, including the preacher's, was black – not a white man there, bar myself. I was hopeful that I would be treated to some gospel shouting or a hellfire sermon. But no, the service was as tame and as dull as any other. The only touching moment was when the preacher bade a sad farewell to those members of the congregation who were about to leave.

The M11 Campaign

I met more interesting people at Twyford Down than at any other point in my life, and many of them I still know. For nearly all of us it was a catalytic moment. Some years later, for Helen Beynon's book about the campaign, *Twyford Rising*, I wrote the following:

> *The alternative movement collapsed for me in 1977, when 500,000 'soixante-huitards' marched in single file on Malville Superphoenix nuclear power station, got tear-gassed one after the other, went home, got a job, had*

kids and gave up. Twyford Down for me was the rebirth of the spirit of 1968.

By the end of 1993, the Twyford protests were attracting more supporters, but the cutting itself was on the way to completion. Stopping construction had been the ostensible aim of the protests, but we knew all along that that was unachievable; the real objective was to disrupt, discredit and sink the entire road-building programme. Twyford Down was a Pyrrhic victory for the road builders, a battle that we would lose, along with some others, in a war that we ultimately won.

In January 1994 a huge column of people filed down the now asphalted cutting at Twyford in what was effectively a funeral procession. After that the protest movement spread across the country. Almost every road-building scheme that ventured off the drawing board was greeted with a protest camp where hardened eco-warriors spent months living on platforms precariously tied to the canopies of trees or holed up in tunnels underground, while concerned local citizens supported them with letters to the local paper and deliveries of cake.

I was not deeply involved in the organisation of any of these, but went to a number of actions in their support: Solsbury Hill near Bath, where protesters dodged bailiffs by swinging through the trees like gibbons eighty feet above the ground; Fairmile on the A30 in Devon where Daniel Hooper, aka Swampy, briefly became the darling of the tabloid press after going on hunger strike in a tunnel he had built; and the Newbury bypass where 800 of the estimated 7,000 protesters were arrested and the security operation cost £35 million, five times as much as had been budgeted.

Most memorable for me were the evictions of Wanstonia, and Claremont Road, squatted properties in the path of the M11 link road in East London. The resistance movement to urban road construction had a different flavour from the rural counterpart. It was communities that were threatened more than nature, rooftops occupied rather than treetops. The counterculture was as much punk as hippie: at Twyford protesters sat around wood fires with guitars and tin whistles, singing songs about raggle taggle gypsies and wells down in the valley-o; at the M11 you were more likely to hear a sound system blaring out the Clash or hard-core techno. Twyford protesters had support from Tory dignitaries who cared about their landscape; M11 squatters had support from working-class folk who were being thrown out of their homes.

The climax of the campaign was the eviction, in November 1994, of Claremont Road, a Georgian terrace of a dozen or so houses. All of these had been occupied by squatters bar one, the home of 92-year-old Dolly Watson who had lived there all her life, and now refused to budge. Once the possession notice had been secured, the police let it be known in advance when the eviction was to take place, enabling hundreds of supporters like myself to come to East London to reinforce the defences. No one tried to stop us entering the houses as we arrived, but once the riot police and the bailiffs arrived in force on the afternoon of the 28 November, they cordoned the area off. Why the forces of order allowed Operation Garden Party, as they called it, to swell to such a scale I never worked out. Incompetence? Overtime pay? I rather think they were looking forward to the spectacle.

And a spectacle it was. The houses were decorated, inside and out, with graffiti, garish paintings and sculptural collages made from shop mannequins and plastic detritus, while from the middle of the terrace roof sprung a scaffolding tower 80 feet high, with people clambering all over it and a loudspeaker blasting out music to match the sculpture. The surrounding trees were strewn with bunting, motorway tape, rope and any bric-a-brac that came to hand; cargo netting, stretched between the trees and the rooftops allowed the protesters to move from one to the other or to dangle their bottoms tauntingly over the heads of the police and security guards beneath them.

The hard-core protesters had specified roles. Some sat in eyries on the tower or in the trees; some had their arms locked into shafts sunk into the street; others were entombed in bunkers in the basements covered by heaps of rubble. As for the extras, some were barricaded in the houses, while I was one of a hundred or more prancing around on the rooftop and shouting comments on the proceedings. Beneath us milled untold numbers of police – Keystone Cops in riot gear – plus security guards in yellow jackets, and bailiffs in municipal blue, all mute.

Nothing much happened on day one, and we passed the night on the roof, kept awake by the cold, the floodlights and the clanking of heavy machinery. Early next day the eviction began in earnest. Security guards and bailiffs began battering down doors and smashing their way through the fortified windows with sledge hammers; a fleet of JCBs swept away the sculptures; pneumatic drills were brought in to extricate the people locked onto the roadway; and hydraulic cherry pickers homed in on protesters in the trees or on the cargo netting, to the accompaniment of boos and cat-calls from the chorus on the rooftop.

It required two or three bailiffs to haul each struggling protester clinging to a tree into the cherry-picker cage; sometimes they held on for fifteen or twenty minutes in a mid-air tug of war as breath-catching as a high-wire circus act, more so because it was unrehearsed and there was no safety net. Other protesters clung onto cables attached to chimney pots; one fell twelve feet into a digger bucket, apparently without injury. After one treetop protester had performed an intricate ballet within a whisker of the whirring teeth of a chainsaw, the crowd roared, 'Tree-geezer, you're a star,' and the security man who brought him down did a sarcastic little bow.

In the most tense moments, the mood of the crowd turned from one of taunt and banter to fury: 'Murderers!' came the cry. 'You're not just killing the planet, you're killing us.' Thankfully nobody did get killed, and once safely in the cherry picker the protagonists were lowered sedately to the ground to cheers, as if they had done a turn on the stage. More than once, protester and bailiff put their arms around each other and raised their hands to acknowledge the applause – and the bailiffs deserved it for getting everyone down without any serious accident. The spectacle was street theatre of an order and a scale that had probably never been witnessed before in London. It would have made great TV. The pity was that because the police had cordoned off the area from the public and the press, few people got to see how it really happened.

Once they had secured all the downstairs rooms, the bailiffs started picking off those of us on the roof – again a precarious business on a 35-degree slope over a 20-foot drop. For some reason they didn't seem very interested in me, and as the evening began to fall, apart from the people up the scaffolding tower, which was unscalable, there were just two people left on the roof, myself and the filmmaker Julia Guest. We assumed we were next in line to be chased and pulled off, but the bailiffs changed their tactic. 'We're going home now,' they said. 'You can either come down in the cherry picker, or you can stay up here all night and we'll get you in the morning.'

Since we were hungry and knackered, another cold night on the roof for no tactical advantage was unappealing. On the other hand, volunteering to go down after so many other people had resisted was humiliating. After a moment's consideration, and knowing that the media had only limited access, we said: 'OK, we'll come down, but only provided you secure an interview for us with a national television station.'

They agreed in principle, went away and came back some time later saying that it had been arranged. We were lowered in the cherry picker, and there, true to their word, was a national TV camera team to interview us. Whether or not the clip was broadcast, I don't know, but at least honour was upheld.

End of the Road

After much delay, construction work on the M11 link went ahead and the new road was opened without public ceremony in 1999. The campaign at Newbury in 1995–1996 also failed to prevent construction of the bypass, which opened in 1998. Apart from one brief visit early on, I kept away from Newbury because by that time I had found out that a 48-day prison sentence had been imposed on me in my absence for non-payment of poll tax. Two weeks in Pentonville as a roads martyr was fine; seven weeks without remission for non-payment of a fine was less attractive.

Newbury was the last gasp of a dying industry that had been on the defensive since 1993. In 1994 the Tory transport minister John MacGregor withdrew forty-nine schemes from the road programme, including the M12 motorway, which was what the M11 link road was intended to link to. Then in July of that year MacGregor was sacked and replaced by Brian Mawhinney who immediately initiated a 'great transport debate' that cast doubt on the future of the road-building programme. By the time Labour came to power in 1997, the 500 schemes that were in the pipeline in 1990 had been reduced to 150, and the new government scrapped most of these. The last brand new motorway built in Britain, aside from a few spurs and missing links was the Northern Ireland M3, opened in 1994, and since then the number of trunk A roads (those which are immune from local authority speed limits, bus lanes, etc.) has declined. Within a period of less than five years the road-building programme was dismantled and the philosophy of endless traffic growth that lay behind it comprehensively debunked.

This was a phenomenal achievement, perhaps the most successful environmental campaign the UK had ever seen, and much of the credit for its success was due to direct action. The protesters brought the issue into the public eye, added to road builders' costs, and devised a form of good-humoured riot that was threatening to the establishment, yet appealing to the media and acceptable to large swathes of middle England.

But direct action was only part of the story. Riot, however good-humoured, is ineffective unless mediated through negotiation: the poll tax riot got rid of Thatcher, but only once the Tory party had worked out other reasons why she had to go. While the road protests were centre stage, behind the scenes academics such as Phil Goodwin, John Whitelegg and John Adams were developing the economic rationale to disinvest in road building. Journalists such as Christian Wolmar of the *Independent* and John Vidal of *The Guardian* used the protests as a peg to introduce these concepts to a wider public; and for every road proposed there was now a group of objectors who would challenge it, not by direct action but through the approved procedures of letters to the local paper, consultation exercises and public inquiries.

New roads were then (and to an extent still are) justified by a cost-benefit analysis methodology known as COBA, which allocates a financial value to every minute of time supposedly saved by every motor vehicle expected to use the new road, and tots these up to show that they outweigh the cost of construction and maintenance. COBA, unsurprisingly, is economic fairyland. The methodology takes no account of time lost by pedestrians, cyclists or people escorting children to school because of increased danger. It fails to recognise that easing congestion in one place tends to increase congestion at other pinch points elsewhere. It doesn't allow for the extra time motorists spend travelling to facilities that are sited further apart than previously because of the time saved by faster driving conditions. In John Whitelegg's words, 'When people save time, they use it to buy more distance.'

The collapse of the road-building programme was an admission that growth cannot be maintained indefinitely, and I have been waiting ever since for this view to spread to other sectors of the economy. Much of my life has been spent pissing against the winds of capitalism, so it was good to find that the winds of change were behind us for once.

Debriefing

In December 1994, at a packed meeting in a large hall in Oxford someone organised a sort of debriefing after Twyford Down for the environmental movement. Three anti-roads activists – Emma Must, George Monbiot and myself – shared the podium with senior representatives of the National Trust, Greenpeace and Friends of the Earth, and the question we were asking them was: 'Where were you?'

Speaker after speaker from the floor commented on the NGOs' conspicuous absence from any of the public demonstrations, and in particular Friends of the Earth's abandonment of the campaign in the face of an injunction. I compared their approach to the glee with which Bernard Brett of Colchester Quaker Housing Association had co-operated with squatters. The NGOs hadn't grasped the dynamics of the radical flank effect – that it was the threat of riot and chaos that made their demands seem reasonable. FoE's representative at this meeting, Charles Secrett, had only recently taken over as its director. He listened to the criticism, took it in good grace and acted on it. According to one account: 'The Newbury Bypass campaign became the case where this new FoE policy was put into practice. FoE act[ed] as a bridge between the direct action movement and the environment "Establishment".'

The meeting was also notable for a fiery speech from Monbiot who argued that an entirely new movement was required, one that created positive alternatives, and that focused on the control of land, for that was where power lay. Two months later Monbiot published 'A Land Reform Manifesto' in *The Guardian*. 'Political change does not take place,' he said, 'until the opponents of government fight for what they're for, rather than simply fighting what they're against. Nothing of substance will alter until we tackle the continued enclosure of our land.'

For many young people in the late twentieth century, the road protests, along with the women's camps at Greenham Common, were the first opportunity to experience anarchy in action. Living on a protest site was a formative experience in itself, so much so that the medium – land occupation – became as important as the environmental and political message. The camp was the campaign: it was the germ of an alternative society, and those who built and defended it were, to borrow George Monbiot's words, fighting for what they were for, rather than simply fighting what they were against. This outlook was to colour many of the campaigns that were spawned by the road protests, such as The Land Is Ours, Reclaim the Streets and, later on, the Climate Camps.

CHAPTER NINE

Tinker's Bubble

I however was no longer a young person, even if I still behaved like one. I had already spent ten years in France in a botched attempt to create an alternative society. Now after a further ten years aspiring to be vaguely normal, even holding down PAYE employment, it was time to try again. Revolution was in the air once more, and a new generation of hippies was eager for change. Besides, I was fed up with the precarity of rented housing, and the inconvenience of living in a small van with my possessions stored in a leaky farm building. The option of once again building my living quarters on a secure plot of land was clearly preferable.

While I was in Pentonville, my cellmate Bob talked enthusiastically about a plot of land near Yeovil in Somerset whose current owner wanted to sell and had given Bob first option to buy, at the very reasonable price of £1,300 per acre. (Land was still relatively cheap in the early 1990s, especially woodland. By 2018 the land at Tinker's Bubble would be worth closer to £8,000 per acre.) After our release he took me to view it, and it was stunning. Some twenty-six acres of conifer and deciduous woodland overlooked thirteen acres of apple orchard on the south-facing slope of Ham Hill, one of the largest Iron Age forts in Britain, and since Roman times the site of a stone quarry. Bang in the middle of the forty acres was a spring from which flowed a stream known as Tinker's Bubble, so called because it was where the Gypsies had stopped when they came to do the apple picking. It was conveniently close to the village of Norton-sub-Hamdon, with shop, pub, school and bus service, and on the edge of a satellite hamlet called Little Norton.

This looked promising, though I did wonder how Bob, who could easily pass for a tinker himself, had managed to charm the owner into reserving the property for him, rather than putting it on the open market. Shortly afterwards we held a meeting that brought together a number of people interested in founding a land-based community, most of whom were active at Twyford. Besides Bob and myself they included the journalist Oliver Tickell, and a fellow from Glastonbury who I hadn't met before called Chris Black. Bob's parents had offered to stump up £12,000 and the rest of us could put up some cash – I could spare £2,000 – but we were still a long way from the target. We resolved to find others who would buy a stake in the property.

I was entrusted with drawing up and distributing a publicity leaflet, proposing a non-hierarchical community, living on the land in something akin to Iron Age-style roundhouses, aspiring to a measure of self-sufficiency, and using no fossil fuels on the land. This attracted a couple more interested people willing to pitch in £2,000 for a share in the project, but we were still some way from the £52,000 needed. At this point Chris Black offered to front the balance of the money, on the basis that he would be paid back as other people bought into the project.

Chris, I learnt, was the great-grandson of a certain Donald Smith who had made his fortune by rising from apprentice in the Hudson's Bay Company to its governor, and then financing a good chunk of the Canadian Pacific Railway. Part of this fortune had passed down to Chris, who had apparently made it an aim in life to spend it all on hippie land projects, a mission he has successfully accomplished. Before bank-rolling Tinker's Bubble he had won a groundbreaking planning appeal allowing a tribe of misfits to camp for a year in benders in the curtilage of his house in Butleigh, near Glastonbury. And he went on to acquire four acres overlooking Worthy Farm, the site of Glastonbury Festival, where he founded a bender camp known as Infinity Fields, though the name was subsequently toned down to King's Hill. If there can be such a thing as an anarchist property developer, Chris Black is it.

It looked as though the purchase of Tinker's Bubble could go ahead, but a hitch occurred. Bob's parents announced that the £12,000 they had offered was for a piece of land in Bob's name and not available for a collective project. Chris was unwilling to stump up any more cash. On the road-protest grapevine we had heard that someone, whom I shall call Geoff, currently on the M11 site, was interested in putting up some money. I hitched up to London and found him in a squatted house in Wanstead. It didn't look promising: the house was a tip, and Geoff himself was a wild-looking bloke with dreadlocks, a laugh that was a leer, and only one functioning eye. He had lost the other in a fight.

I mentioned that I'd heard he was interested in putting money into Tinker's Bubble 'Oh, right,' he said nonchalantly, as if I'd been delivering a takeaway meal that he'd forgotten about, and without much more ado took out his chequebook and wrote out a cheque for £8,000. I hurried back to Somerset, the cheque didn't bounce, and with an extra £4,000 from Chris we had enough to purchase the property.

We moved onto the land on 1 January 1994, planting a ceremonial mulberry tree, and sleeping in a yurt pitched in a sheltered corner on the edge of the woodland, overlooking the orchard. I say we, but the number of people committed to stay-ing there was tiny. I was the only person who had put money in who planned to live there. Otherwise there was the now penniless Bob; a local couple, Louise and Andy Chant with their four children; and Mike Zair, a friend of Bob's who was in his fifties, but already had a patrician air about him. All of them were fresh from a successful protest in Yeovil against the construction of a relief road, during which they had squatted in benders on the roof of an abandoned supermarket.

It was an inadequate crew for a monumental task. Reinforcements were to come shortly. Word got around that Chris Black had bought the Dongas a homeland, and within a week they started arriving. Soon there were up to forty of them, pitching their benders on a flat area some distance up in the woodland. Individually many of them were good people, but collectively they were the last thing we needed. A Batman flag flew from a tree at the lowest corner of the woodland in full view of the hamlet of Little Norton. At night the villagers could hear drumming emanating from the forest, as if 'the natives were preparing a war party'. On Thursdays, the top deck of the bus into Yeovil was monopolised by dreadlocked grungies with nose rings travelling into town to collect their income support. This was not the kind of public relations that was helpful.

The Dongas also had an approach to land management that was at odds with our own. When Oliver Tickell dug some steps up a bank to link one terrace with another the Dongas were appalled and named the cutting Twyford Down. One of their number took it into his head to rip out the barbed wire fence that surrounded the orchards and leave it in a tangled coil in the nettles and bracken. But the clearest manifestation of the difference between us was the felling of what came to be known as the Karmic Ash.

We needed to remove a mature ash tree that was terminally rotten at its base and leaning ominously over our yurt. Since we had to fell it in the opposite direction from the one it was leaning in, we called in a friend with forestry experience to manage the operation. We guyed the tree with ropes and a Tirfor winch and had just sawn a large gob out of the trunk when a posse of chanting Dongas came charging down the hill and surrounded the tree while some started climbing it to prevent its demise. The forester who had come to help was freaked out by this, and fled, leaving us with a rotten tree, almost half severed at its base, leaning over our yurt and prevented from falling only by the guy ropes – whereupon the wind almost immediately decided to increase to gale force. I didn't sleep in the yurt that night; in fact I didn't sleep much at all. The next day we contacted an ex-fireman we knew in Yeovil who completed the job of helping us fell the Karmic Ash.

Somehow a collective vision had to be forged out of this mess. The first requirement was to get the numbers of people down to those who were interested in working the land and forging a stable community. The Dongas outnumbered us by about five to one. We called a meeting on site that about twenty people attended where it was decided that anybody who wanted to live on the land had to pay at least five pounds a week towards the acquisition of a £2,000 share in the property. Since Chris had paid more than half the cost of the land and his name was on the deeds (together with mine), no one could argue with this. The share offer was extended to individual Dongas, but none of them took it up. We also impressed upon them how their presence was prejudicing our chances of getting planning permission. Eventually, to our relief, they did move on, initially to another plot of land owned by one of their number, Brian, who was sharp enough to appreciate the problems they were causing. Besides, summer was coming and they were getting itchy feet.

But the damage was done. The locals were terrified, leaflets calling for our eviction were posted into every house in Norton-sub-Hamdon, virtually every inhabitant of Little Norton signed a petition against us, the pub wouldn't serve us, the local press carried stories about a Traveller site, and the planning department was notified.

Norton-sub-Hamdon

Norton-sub-Hamdon when we moved there was a village in the last throes of gentrification. Like Arboras, it had a history of fruit growing – not grapes, obviously, but mostly apples. For several decades prior to our arrival most of the productive land around Norton had been orchard; in the centre of the village was a factory known as the Fruit Farm where the apples and other fruit were sorted, processed and packed – the equivalent of the Cave Coopérative that served Arboras. In recent years imports from France and other countries had undermined the viability of the English apple industry, just as imports of from Italy, Spain and Algeria were undercutting French wine producers.

That was where the resemblance between the two villages ended. The crucial difference was that in Arboras, and throughout the whole of the Languedoc, the vineyards were owned by independent farmers, with typically five or ten hectares of vines, whereas the orchards in Norton had all been owned by a Mr Shuldham, Lord of the Manor and owner of the Shuldham Estate. In Arboras most farmers delivered their grapes to a co-operatively owned winery. In Norton, the Fruit Farm was again the sole property of Shuldham.

This resulted in a different response to the challenge of globalisation. Whereas the young vignerons of Arboras joined forces to defend their livelihoods by planting improved varieties of grapes, and in all probability supporting the angry protests against wine imports, the Shuldham estate sold up, and pocketed the profits. The people who worked in the orchards had no stake in them, so no interest in fighting to save them. When we arrived our orchard – which like the whole of Tinker's Bubble had once been Shuldham's – was one of three that remained in the village. Today it is the only one. The Fruit Farm, which had been sold to a developer, lay abandoned, an empty complex of sheds near the church that you

181

could just stroll into. We retrieved apple boxes, ladders and picking bags from there, as well as a horse-drawn plough – nobody cared.

Soon after we arrived the Fruit Farm became the centre of a different local controversy. The owners had been refused permission for residential development on what was the only employment land in the village, so they put in an application for a factory that would be processing potatoes and other vegetables for Oscar Mayer, a chilled food firm based in Chard some fifteen miles away. Since Oscar Mayer's business model was based on just-in-time deliveries this involved umpteen trips by heavy goods vehicles, in the middle of the village, including on Sundays.

I was, of course, opposed to such a transport-intensive operation and went along to a meeting about it in the village hall, expecting to find the village in uproar. In fact there was a balance of views, and it didn't take long to see that most of the objectors to the factory were incomers, while those who supported it were mainly locals. Most people brought up in the village wanted to keep industry alive in the village, perhaps so their sons and daughters could have a summer job (though in fact Oscar Mayer became well known for employing Portuguese and Polish labourers). The objectors' case was tarnished by the woman who stated: 'I have driven all the way down from London this afternoon to oppose this development.'

The district council's response was to allow the development but with so many restrictive conditions that Oscar Mayer pulled out, which was perhaps what the developers wanted. The parish council argued for a hub of workshops along with the housing, but the developers claimed this was not viable, and eventually got planning consent for a 100 per cent residential development, with a few token affordable houses, sealing Norton-sub-Hamdon's fate as a dormitory village.

After that meeting my allegiance veered towards the locals' viewpoint. I also noticed that many of the shrillest voices against us came from incomers, and that many of the indigenous villagers were not that bothered. The neighbouring farmers were helpful, especially a couple of old boys called Lyle and Horace who were the last of the grey Fergie generation. We made friends with a family who lived in one of the few council houses and who from June onwards every year erected a massive Guy Fawkes Day bonfire on the village green, made from hedge cuttings, pallets, old furniture, mattresses and God knows what, until health-and-safety killjoys put an end to it.

We also had some supporters amongst the well-to-do of the village. Val and Richard Constable organised a public tea party in their house for villagers to meet us, but not many who objected to our presence came. Paddy Ashdown, leader of the Lib Dems, who lived in Norton, was personally, though not politically, supportive. On our second Christmas Day at the Bubble, at about nine o'clock in the evening we had surprise visitors: Paddy and his son Simon, in a merry state, had made their way through the woods to our yurt in the dark.

Enter the Planners

However our opponents were loud, especially our ward member on the South Somerset District Council, whose planning officers were quick to respond to the complaints. At first they tried to dispatch us from the land with a stop notice, but the legal basis for imposing this measure on tents was questionable so they backed down. Instead they invited us to apply for planning permission, which of course they refused, and followed this up in August with an enforcement notice, against which we lodged an appeal.

The appeal was not due to be heard until April 1995, so we had nine months to prepare our case. Chris employed David Stephens of Battens Solicitors in Yeovil to represent us, but we had to produce evidence explaining what we were planning to do on the land, and why that meant we should be granted planning permission. Since I was still working part-time at *The Ecologist*, and the only one of us with access to a computer, it seemed logical that I should be the one to take on that role – and no one else volunteered.

Like so many other people who have moved onto land, and been confronted by local authority planning officers, I had to do a crash course in rural planning. There were, I learnt, three main things that we had to prove: that our project was financially viable (the financial test), that it could not be carried out without us living on site (the functional test) and that it did not harm the landscape or environment. This required a business plan, a management plan, and evidence on various other matters such as the amount of traffic generated and the impact upon badgers. It was all new to me, but I knuckled down to the task of pulling this all together.

The financial test was the trickiest. At that time planning authorities expected applicants for agricultural dwellings to be aiming to earn an income of about £14,000 from farming – a sum we had no need for and no hope of attaining. Our approach was that the government considered Income Support of approximately £2,500, as it was then, to be sufficient for people to live on (excluding their rent) and that was what we were aiming to generate. We also maintained that the subsistence produce that we enjoyed, including food, water, fuel wood and off-grid electricity should be valued at retail prices, and constituted about a third of the target income.

These arguments, and the documents I submitted, were approved by all the resident shareholders at Tinker's Bubble, but I don't know whether any of them realised how difficult it would be to get an income of £2,500 from the land without machinery and with few skills. I did have an inkling of what a challenge it was, but I had to put something down on the planning application and there was a logic to the income support

184

figure. Some people, I was to discover, thought all this was just a smokescreen to fool the planners, and had no intention of striving for this comparatively modest target.

My private feeling at the time, however, was that the planners' demands were something of a blessing in disguise. We had to forge something workable out of the primal soup of the first few months, and the management and business plans provided a structure for achieving this. It would have been hard to get agreement on them without the threat of enforcement over our heads.

Samson

With the Dongas gone, it was easier to get to work creating a new settlement. A handful of new people joined us, including Steve Friend, a competent market gardener, while others were dropping in for a few days or weeks to lend a hand. The journalist George Monbiot bought a share and became a frequent visitor. The Dongas had got one thing right: the weather had been very wet, and our site outside the woods, next to the stump of the Karmic Ash, had become a muddy quagmire, so we moved our yurt up to the glade in the woods they had been occupying. It was drier, and more importantly at that point, it was out of sight of the villagers and the public – a matter of overriding concern to the planners.

The Douglas fir woods in which we were now ensconced were a revelation. Like so many green-minded people I had learnt to think of conifer plantations as taboo: dark, sterile, monocultures planted as a financial scam or by a brutalist forestry bureaucracy. Our proclaimed objective when we moved onto the land was to remove all the Douglas and larch and replace them with native broadleaves. Little did we appreciate what a Herculean task that would have been with handsaws and axes.

It was not very long before we realised that we were living in the middle of a congenial ecosystem and an exceptionally generous resource. In winter the bare boughs of our five acres of mixed deciduous woods offered scant resistance to wind and rain, and the fallen leaves in the paths turned to a soggy sponge, but the thick evergreen canopy of the Douglas provided shelter in winter, shade in summer, and a constantly renewed carpet of dead pine needles that kept things dry underfoot. As firewood, Douglas burns readily with plenty of flame, being quick to dry but slow to rot. And you couldn't hope for any better source of kindling than the brash from a felled Douglas fir.

As for timber, the 35-year-old plantation had undergone only one thinning, and there were plenty of long, thin, straight poles perfect for the sort of low impact roundwood structures that we could most easily build in the absence of sawn timber. In fact, we sold quite a few for tipi poles and boat masts. And these were just by-products. The real wealth of timber was visible in the dominant trees that were already up to 18 inches in diameter at the base and bearing 40 foot or more of straight sawlog. Douglas is a high-quality durable softwood, much more amenable for building and many other uses than the sycamore, ash and hazel that dominated our broadleaf woodland.

A report that we commissioned from Devon-based forester Dave Wood for our planning appeal described in almost lyrical terms the volume of timber and piles of cash we could expect from progressive thinning of the Douglas. As long as we kept removing trees, those that remained would keep growing until, in some forty or fifty years' time we would reap the 'bonanza' of mature trees, majestic 120-foot tall giants that the eponymous botanist David Douglas had described as 'one of the most striking and truly graceful objects in nature'. The sums of money Dave Wood spoke of were beyond our comprehension, and it all seemed too good to be true, like Norman Lindsay's 'magic pudding', which never got smaller no matter how much you ate of it. But twenty-five years later, hundreds of tons of timber and firewood have been removed from that plantation, yet there is probably more biomass there now than when we first found it.

The experience with the Karmic Ash had taught us a lot about felling trees with axes and two-man saws, but there remained the problem of extracting logs weighing up to half a ton without any petrol-powered machinery. It was possible to pull them out with eight or so people on a rope: the plantation benefits from almost entirely down-hill extraction routes, and the soil is free draining, so it wasn't that difficult. The tricky bit was getting eight hippies all in the same place at the same time. Obviously it would be easier to enlist the services of a single horse, which could also be available for other jobs required on the holding, such as carting materials up the hill, ploughing, chain harrowing the grass and so on.

We learnt of a landowner nearby who had a number of draught horses for sale so I paid a visit. Alan, the vendor, had apparently started an abortive Heavy Horse Centre, and was now trying to get rid of eleven shires that did no work, and were costing him a small fortune to feed. We told him what we needed and he said he had just the horse for us. Samson was a grey seven-year-old shire-cross gelding, 16.3 hands, who was halter trained and had been used for chain harrowing in previous years. The horse had a charming placid temperament, so Alan said, and was his stable girl's favourite.

We expressed interest, so he got the horse, tacked him up and put him in the shafts of a two-wheeled flat cart. No sooner had Alan mounted the cart than Samson spooked and bolted at breakneck speed clean through the hedge into the next field, taking with him the cart and its hapless driver. Undeterred, Alan put Samson back in the shafts and tried again. This time he behaved impeccably, walking, trotting and halting on command, and reversing. Buying a horse that had just bolted through a hedge was risky, to say the least, but there was something appealing about

Samson. Alan said we could have him on four weeks' approval, and lent us some harness, so we took him and tried him out.

For the next month we worked Samson pulling logs and a makeshift sled for carting stones. He performed well with only minor mishaps, so we bought him. Inevitably, as soon as I'd sealed the purchase he started playing up. On one occasion he bolted down our drive onto the lane, took a right turn into an open gate and deposited two logs like giant turds on the immaculate front lawn of the neighbouring bungalow.

He was also testing my authority and balking at commands that he understood. After one trying episode in which he obstinately refused to move a few metres forward, I resolved to take the matter in hand. The next day I tacked him up and attached him to a couple of light logs to exercise him. Again, he refused to move, completely ignoring my commands and entreaties. Flicking the reins was of no avail. I took hold of his bridle and tried to lead him forward, but he just dug his heels in. Finally, when he shied his head in a gesture of rebellion, I lost my temper and spontaneously struck him across the cheek with the back of my hand. There was something perfect about the timing of this thwack, which surprised him even more than it surprised me. He lurched forward and for the next half hour he shifted the logs back and forth, never putting a foot wrong.

I could never recommend striking a horse as a means of training it, but from that moment on Samson never questioned who was boss, and we became firm friends. I was lucky enough to be given assistance in training him from Lee Hughes, an 18 year old from a local Traveller family who knew more about horses than I did. Once he was confident about his place in the community, Samson proved to be a docile and friendly character, and remarkably gentle with children. He enjoyed his work and was a quick learner.

Although with his high centre of gravity Samson was not really the right build for a logging horse, he became adept at manoeuvring 16-foot logs around densely spaced trees on a steep slope without getting his huge hoofs caught up in the chains. You would never have thought that such a massive creature could move so delicately. I was particularly proud of the way he could back blindly into cart shafts lying on the ground without treading on them, guided only by a flick of the long reins on his right or left rump.

With a horse in operation, we could fell and extract sawlogs and sell them. We were helped in this by a wonderful old boy of well over seventy with a cheeky grin, called Charlie. Although he was local, and had a thick Somerset accent, he had spent years in his youth working as a lumberjack in Canada in the days before chainsaws. The sight of us felling Douglas fir with two-man saws, however ineptly, brought it all back. He loved our bender camp in the woods, for which he had one piece of advice: 'Floysheets ... Whatcher need is floysheets.' Charlie put us in touch with someone who bought the logs we were extracting.

However a draught horse has needs and one of these is adequate amounts of work. Meeting these needs didn't just provide a focus for my activity, it injected an irresistible impetus. Samson required a stable, fencing, hay-making and muck management for his well-being, and a cart, navigable tracks, an arable vegetable plot, ploughs, harrows and other tools to make good use of his abundant energy. As the sole horseman, all of this became my responsibility. And since the activity encompassed more or less all of our land, it gave me an overall view of the holding and its potential that many of the other residents didn't have. That, combined with my role as planning spokesman, gave me rather more managerial responsibility than was wise for one person to hold.

But by no means everything revolved around the horse. Besides the horse-ploughed communal veg plot, people had their own hand-dug gardens. At a farm auction we picked up an old apple press for £100 that we needed for making cider and apple juice.

We built a shelter using a pile of logs that we had felled and hadn't been able to sell. Since they were too short to make a decent sized rectangular log cabin, I embarked on the ludicrous project of creating an octagonal one, which involved cutting notches at an angle of 135 degrees. The end result didn't look too clever but we put a reciprocal roof on it and covered it in copious volumes of earth. The structure still survives, though it no longer houses the cider press and the roof now has ash trees growing out of it.

In the glade uphill where we lived, the structures we built were better conceived. Around the yurt we planted a dozen larch posts in the ground, the uprights for what was to become the communal roundhouse. From these we mounted a reciprocal roof at an angle of 50 degrees; it required a central pole through the centre hole with several pulley blocks to force it up to this angle. The conical roof was battened with roundwood and thatched with secondhand Turkish reed that had been used for demonstration thatching on a TV programme – the reason being that we wanted to be able to argue that the building was movable.

Gradually the project was shaping up. We had gained a useful new member in Pete Wright, whose aim was to run a market garden, but who had trained as an electrician. He set up a 12-volt electrical system with solar panels. But the device that really brought civilisation to Tinker's Bubble was the ram pump. For a year or more we had carried all our water from the stream up to the settlement, a rise of some 20 metres, in 25-litre jerrycans. At the point where we took the water there were the remains of what had once been a ram pump system sending water up to the quarry at the top of the hill. We were told that someone had blown the system up during an industrial dispute and nobody had bothered to repair it.

I had read about ram pumps years before in the *Whole Earth Catalog*, and been intrigued. They use no electricity or petrol: just the power of a stream to pump a proportion of its flow uphill. We got in touch with a firm supplying them, and it was a relatively simple matter to re-install one that, to this day, pipes water uphill continuously day and night. The pump is situated almost exactly in the middle of the holding, and it ticks remorselessly like a clock. When that heartbeat ceases, it will signal the end of Tinker's Bubble as a community.

Low Impact Development

In early 1995, I was still working part-time at *The Ecologist*, driving every few days the twenty-nine miles between Sturminster Newton and Norton-sub-Hamdon. But my time at *The Ecologist* was coming to an end. I didn't see eye to eye with one of my colleagues there, and I was keen to get stuck in at the Bubble. However I needed a source of income since it was clearly going to be some time before any of us could make a living from the land.

The solution appeared effortlessly, and arose out of my personal circumstances and my work on the planning appeal. Since arriving back in England, I had been looking for some land on which to build a modest home. It had been easy enough in France, and it was what billions of peasants, nomads and landless shanty town dwellers did throughout the Global South. Why was it so hard in Britain, even when you owned the land? As I grew familiar with the workings of the planning system, I became more and more intrigued with its impact, not just on social aberrations like myself, but on wider society.

A century ago access to land had been restricted by private ownership and by enclosure; now in 1995, when land was still quite cheap, the main impediment was not ownership, but the 1947 Town and Country Planning Act. Yet comparatively few people, and almost none of the people I knew, understood how it worked. There were plenty of campaigners fighting harmful corporate developments, such as roads, quarries, or urban gentrification programmes through the planning system, but almost nobody was examining how and why the same system was stifling individual and collective developments that were low impact and affordable.

I applied for funding to write a report tackling this matter, and without much ado was granted enough money to research, write, print and distribute it, and keep me in food and drink for a year. This was a good break.

I started by trying to ascertain the depth of the problem. A few adverts in relevant magazines brought in a postbag full of evidence from smallholders explaining how planning policy was stacked against them and decision makers biased. 'We must put a stop to these quasi-agricultural activities which are springing up all over the country,' one planning committee member stated after refusing permission for a free-range chicken shed.

As well as the smallholders, I also heard from people with craft or light industrial skills seeking to build live–work accommodation and people who wanted to downsize to live a simple life. As one correspondent who had been removed by the planners from land in Galloway put it, 'There doesn't seem to be any place for people to fulfil themselves outside the system. To grow a bit of food and live cheaply. I don't want to get a house and a mortgage where you have to earn £100 a week before you can even breathe.'

And then there were the Travellers, in trucks and buses or horse-drawn, who were subject to appalling attacks from vigilantes whipped up by Tory party rhetoric, and many of whom would have welcomed the opportunity to settle on a secure site.

All this needed repeating because it was rarely reported in the press. It was also apparent that this was the tip of the iceberg of a much larger number of citizens who had similar aspirations, but lacked the bottle to do anything about it in the face of bureaucratic censure. To tackle the problem at its source I needed to work out why and how the British authorities had made it so difficult for people to build their own home.

The root of the problem, it dawned on me, was the motor car. Prior to the invention of motorised transport most people had to live close to their place of work. The arrival of the railway in the nineteenth century brought with it a new kind of citizen, the commuter, whose productive life was divorced from their role as a consumer. However, development remained confined to areas around railway stations until the 1920s and 1930s when, with their newly acquired motor car, the well-to-do could move beyond the railheads into rural hinterlands where land was cheaper. Ribbon development spread like a rash along roads within commuting distance of urban centres. Worse still, in the eyes of the newly formed Council for the Protection of Rural England, the working class started buying parcels of subdivided farmland and building shanty villages of plotland shacks on sacrosanct English countryside. With the growing use of the car, planner Thomas Sharp complained in 1932, 'All the land in the country can be regarded as building land and consequently all the land in the country is being laid out as a gigantic building estate.'

The free-for-all was brought to a halt by the 1947 Town and Country Planning Act, which was widely regarded as necessary to protect the countryside from untrammelled suburban development. It was necessary because the private car allowed commuters to live anywhere, on land that could be bought for agricultural prices. The Act replaced this sudden proliferation of accessible building land with an artificial, government regulated scarcity that restricted house-building to certain allocated areas, usually on the edge of existing settlements. The British public had unwittingly exchanged the right to build anywhere for the right to drive anywhere – a poor exchange in my view.

As a result the price of house-building land started its exponential ascent towards today's dizzy heights, and huge profits were (and still are) to be made from converting agricultural land to building land. The Labour Party, who introduced the 1947

Act, planned to capture this increase in value for the taxpayer, through what was known as a betterment tax, but successive Conservative governments made sure this never happened. As a result in 1995, some 45 per cent of the cost of a home was attributable to this increase in value, and represented a massive levy paid by mortgagees and renters to landowners, developers and investors such as insurance companies and hedge funds.

The solution I favoured at the time, and the one I still favour, is to do away with private cars and thereby increase the friction of transport so that people choose to live in sensible places, either close to their work, or close to public transport. This would eliminate the need to reserve certain allocated areas for housing, and hence the artificial scarcity and price increase that that entails. Professor John Whitelegg and others at the time were cataloguing the hidden costs of the motor car, such as pollution, global warming, accidents and time spent chaperoning children; but none mentioned the rural planning system, and the near doubling of housing costs.

Unfortunately, the powers that be had no intention of imposing a ban on private cars, and advocating that would have consigned my report to irrelevance. I therefore proposed instead that developments which could demonstrate a very low environmental impact and high levels of sustainability should be permitted on land where development would not normally be allowed – i.e. agricultural land – and suggested that this could be termed 'low impact development'.

When the report was nearing completion I bumped into Jon Carpenter, a publisher of environmental material. He proposed that, rather than distributing the work as a report, I should publish it as a book, with a potentially wider readership. The book, published in 1996, only sold about 2,500 copies, but I was able to live off the proceeds for three years and fund further publications.

The Appeal

With the Dongas gone and some progress made in terms of land management, we had gained some friends in the village. But 144 people, nearly all of them local, had written letters of objection to our application and were waiting for the show-down in anticipation. Channel 4 television had picked up on the story and were filming a full-length documentary whose working title was on the lines of 'Fear and Loathing in an English Village'. They sought out the more extreme voices on either side of the fence, focusing on Bob, the most outspoken and least diplomatic of our number, and collaring objectors in the local pub, where tongues were loosened by drink.

The inquiry, scheduled for two days, took place in the village hall, which made it convenient for local objectors and support-ers to attend. I was the main witness for our side, along with a traffic consultant we had hired. My evidence explained, in exhaustive detail, what our objectives were, and how we hoped to achieve them, our environmental policy, our business plan and every other matter of potential interest. After delivering it, with the aid of questions from our advocate David Stephens, I was subject to curiously aggressive cross-examination from the council's barrister, which was easy to stand up to because I had nothing to hide. All I had to do was tell the truth.

Irrespective of what the decision might be, we felt that the appeal had been a success, because it gave the people of Norton the opportunity to hear, in dispassionate detail, what we were aiming to do, and how we addressed the criticisms laid against us. Even if they didn't agree with us, I hope some of their fears were dispelled.

After a few weeks we received the appeal decision letter. The inspector viewed that our project should be given planning permission for a trial period of three years. Our impact upon landscape and amenity was negligible, he said; we had a need to live on the land because 'the agriculture and the alternative life-style are manifestly part of the one experiment'; and the benders 'could be easily and swiftly removed if the project failed'.

However, the appeal had been 'called in' by the Secretary of State for the Environment, John Gummer. This means that the decision is not, as in most appeals, made by the inspector; instead, as a letter to our solicitor put it, 'the Secretary of State considers that he should determine this appeal himself'. Gummer did not accept the inspector's recommendations. He dismissed our appeal and confirmed the enforcement notice, giving the following reasons in his decision letter:

> *Your clients submit that they are carrying out an experiment in living simply on the land and deriving a subsistence existence from it, a pattern of living which is sometimes called 'permaculture'. It is accepted that your clients would have to reside on site to have any chance of achieving their aims. But those intentions are personal preferences which do not justify setting aside the planning objection. Any benefit of these aims to the rural economy would be negligible, since minimal agricultural and other produce would be available for wider consumption ... The view is taken that the provision of groups of tents or similar residential accommodation in the open countryside, merely to provide a subsistence living for the occupants, is not a practical pattern of long-term land use.*

Progress

We hadn't been given permission but there was hope. Our case was deemed good enough to challenge Gummer's decision in the High Court, which we did in 1996. We lost. The judge, Nigel Macleod QC, had two months before found in favour of a development of forty-two holiday chalets on green belt land in the New Forest, but he didn't see fit to allow our seven tents. We were allowed to take the matter to the Court of Appeal in 1997, where we lost again. Some of the legal expenses were paid for through legal aid – something that would be out of the question now – but Chris Black also put in £15,000 to enable the proceedings to continue.

The legal wrangling revolved around Gummer's reasoning that 'any benefit of these aims to the rural economy would be negligible. Providing a subsistence living for the occupants is not a practical pattern of long-term land use.' Our argument was that only one-third of our projected income was subsistence. Two-thirds was from sale of produce, at a level comparable to what could be earned per acre from a lot of agricultural holdings.

No matter. All this litigation was buying us time, since the council could not evict us from the land while it was continuing – time in which we could build up the community's infrastructure. We finished the roundhouse and added a kitchen extension to it, a bathroom was built, and then a guest house. Individuals were improving their private accommodation. Outside of the woods we built a stable-cum-barn for the horse and the hay, erected polytunnels and extended the cultivated areas.

Improved facilities and productivity were attracting new blood. The Chant family and Steve Friend moved away, but others moved in, notably Mary Durling with her son Joe. Mary and I got on well and after a while became lovers. Other people came for a few weeks or months or would drop in from time to time to help. Emma Must had a spell there. Chris Black and Lee Hughes were frequent visitors. Oliver Tickell and Theo Hopkins came from time to time, as did George Monbiot, who bought a share in the community. There were many other volunteers who helped out, such as the nameless plumber who installed a brilliantly efficient wood-fuelled hot-water system in the bathroom, which still functions. When I complimented him for his expertise he said: 'Easy. All you need to know about plumbing is that water runs downhill and you get paid on Thursday.'

Others were not so welcome. We were a magnet for nutcases. One visitor decided to bury his dog beneath the roots of our symbolic mulberry tree, curtailing its growth by several years. Another laid into the Douglas fir next to our outdoor kitchen with an axe, on the grounds that he was creating a totem pole. We had to remove him bodily while he was still wielding the axe. Most problematic of all was Geoff who after an absence of two years arrived on site claiming his £8,000 worth.

It was a visitation waiting to happen and as disruptive as I had feared. Geoff dug himself a tunnel to live in, outside the area we had negotiated with the planners; he set fire to a heap of brashings in the woodland that sent flames thirty feet into the air; when no one was around he tacked up Samson without permission, lost control of him and drove the cart into a ditch. And that was only half of it. It took a long time to get rid of him, and we had to borrow £8,000 to buy him out.

Despite the incident with Geoff, Samson was working well, and we were cracking on with thinning the woodland. But we were only getting the standard price of £40 a ton for sawlogs. If we could saw them into planks or construction timber, we could earn three or four times as much. Most people in our situation would have bought a mobile sawmill, but that would have contravened our no fossil fuel policy. One member of the community at least spoke in favour of ditching the policy, but Chris Black was having none of that. Aside from initiating land settlement projects, Chris's main talent was, and still is, locating and amassing secondhand material – anything from exquisite but threadbare Persian carpets to heavy industrial plant. Within a matter of days Chris had found a 1921 Stenner and Gunn rack bench saw with a four-foot blade for sale, and hired a man to transport a Burrell traction engine to the Bubble to demonstrate the saw in action.

The sawmill demonstration was a great success. The steam engine, the sawbench and the horse, with their respective drivers, all worked in harmony, converting 12- and 16-foot logs into planks, which were removed and stacked by other members of the community, while intrigued locals looked on. We completed fourteen logs in all, with a value of several hundred pounds, and on that basis decided to buy the sawbench. However in all the time we had it I don't think we ever managed to equal that performance. We failed to take into account that the sawbench operator, now approaching retirement, had been doing it all his life and had learnt it from his dad, who bought the machine in 1921. He knew the saw and its quirks like Django Reinhardt knew his guitar, and none of us quite managed to master this ticklish machine.

A few weeks later, Chris purchased a 1937 Marshall portable steam engine. It was not just a good buy, it was ideal. It had been built in 1937 for export to the colonies, and so had an extra large firebox designed for wood fuel rather than coal. Before it could be sent abroad, the Second World War had started, and the machine was mothballed. By the end of the war, steam engines were redundant, and it had been kept in storage ever since. In other words it was sixty years old but brand new. What's more, because it was a so-called 'portable' engine – i.e. it could not motor under its own steam, but all seven tons of it had to be towed – it only cost £8,000, compared to £30,000 or more for a well-used traction engine.

We set the steam engine and sawbench up near the car park and gave it a few test runs. It all worked fine. I'm no great lover of machinery, but this machine was captivating. The industrial marriage of iron, fire, water and steam brought all four elements together in one body that had something animal about it. Like a horse, its power derived from repressed energy that if mismanaged might explode.

I also liked its simplicity. The steam engine was the missing link between the pedal cycle and the internal combustion engine. Most of the workings were on the outside so you could see clearly what was going on. And it was held together with brass nuts the size of cupcakes that you could easily shift with a huge adjustable spanner.

Best of all, it ran on wood, something we had plenty of. It wasn't fussy; it would consume any old fence post or other rubbish that we wanted to get rid of. But in fact the offcuts from the logs we processed were sufficient to keep it running indefinitely. With this machinery and a horse, we now had everything we needed to profitably manage the woodland that comprised two-thirds of our holding without using any fossil fuels. Everything, that is, except permission.

Consent

There was one annoying issue with the steam engine. When it rained, or even drizzled, the drive belt running between the steam engine and the sawbench got wet and slipped, making sawing impossible. For that, and other reasons, we needed to house the sawmill, and so we put in an application under agricultural and forestry permitted development rights to build a barn around it – 70 feet long, and built, of course, from the timber we milled.

The planning department turned down our application on the grounds that we had no permitted development rights because we were not a trade or business, so we carried on using the sawmill outside when the weather was fine. However another problem soon arose. A neighbour living at Tinkabee Cottage complained about the noise from the steam engine, even though we carried out all our forestry work without using chainsaws. The council's environmental health officer slapped a noise abatement notice on us, making us liable to a £20,000 fine if we operated the sawmill.

We had to shut down the sawmill. But the noise abatement order proved to be a blessing in disguise, since we found out that it could only be imposed upon a trade or business. The environmental health department was at cross purposes with the planning department – and since environmental health had imposed a legal order, that view prevailed, to the annoyance of the planners.

We therefore resubmitted an application for a barn, this time insulated with straw bales to minimise the noise. The planners responded that they required evidence from a noise expert that straw bales would reduce the noise sufficiently. We searched around and the cheapest consultant we found wanted more than £2,000 for writing a report. Besides, even if we did get permission for the barn, how could we saw up the timber we needed to build it?

Instead we wrote to the council offering to build a temporary structure around the sawmill, insulated with straw bales, that would cost less to build than the consultant's report. They could test whether it was effective and we would pull it down and replace it within two years once a sufficient degree of noise insulation had been confirmed.

To our surprise the planners allowed us to go ahead and build it. Nearly all the work was done by Chris and myself. Using logs that had been waiting to be sawn up, we sunk sixteen uprights in the ground, on a 70-foot by 20-foot rectangular plan, which we spanned with eight trusses, ten feet apart. None of the timber was jointed or nailed: it was all lashed together, boy-scout style, with sisal baler twine, so that when we came to dismantle the barn, we would be able to run the timber through the sawmill. The roof and walls were covered with old white marquee canvas. Hay bales lined the southern and western walls, facing towards Tinkabee Cottage, and stock fencing was strung across the tie beams of the trusses to support an 11-foot-high ceiling consisting of 70 mattresses, recuperated from Crewkerne town rubbish tip. The chimney of the steam engine poked through this layer and emptied its smoke out through the gable end.

It was a monstrosity, but it stayed up and it worked. The council came with their decibel meter and declared that the noise had been duly abated. The straw bales and mattresses had done the trick. The only thing that didn't happen as planned was the dismantling of the barn after two years. Nine years later, the structure was still standing, thanks to a few judiciously located eight inch nails; the roof canvas was leaking and the mattresses were soggy sponges.

In 1998, we lodged another planning application for low impact dwellings since it was more than two years since we had been turned down at appeal. Having triumphed in the courts, the planners could have used their enforcement powers to evict us, but they didn't. There was now a sizable number of Lib Dem councillors who quite liked us; and even councillors who didn't like us were forced to agree that having us living on the land was better than having us camped elsewhere in trucks and driving onto the land every day, which was what we intimated might happen. Public hostility had died down as well. There were only twenty-seven letters of objection to the second application, as opposed to 144 to the first.

Our application differed only in scale from the first in 1994. We increased the maximum number of people living on site to twelve adults, who would be earning between them an average of £2,650 per person, of which a third was from subsistence produce, and the bulk of the rest from timber and apples. At the committee meeting when they voted to give us temporary planning permission I was chuffed; it was the culmination of five years' work. But I also had a sinking feeling. Permission was tied to the implementation of the five-year management plan. I wondered whether I was signing myself away for another five years of hassling people to attain targets that nobody was very interested in attaining.

CHAPTER TEN

The Land Is Ours

T inker's Bubble had become something of a showpiece
for a burgeoning rural land rights movement, though
it was by no means the only one. In 2000, not long
after the Bubble's success, King's Hill finally won permission
for what was effectively a bender housing estate on four acres
near Glastonbury, and there were other similar projects around
the countryside.

The modern land rights movement's beginnings can be
dated to George Monbiot's speech at that meeting in Oxford
in December 1994, and his 'Land Reform Manifesto' published
two months later in *The Guardian*, which lambasted the environmental irresponsibility of large landowners and announced that
an action would take place on 23 April, St George's day, 1995.

This was the occupation of the abandoned Wisley Airfield,
close to St George's Hill, the original site of the 1649 Diggers'
land occupation, which had become (and still is) a millionaires'
gated housing estate with golf course. You couldn't hope for
a more graphic symbol of enclosure. Although the action was
small and nothing happened, it was covered by a live broadcast
on *Newsnight*, and out of it emerged the Land Reform Group,
soon to be renamed The Land Is Ours (TLIO). It was, as
Monbiot confirmed, 'A movement rather than an organisation.
Anyone endorsing our statement of principle – "The Land Is

Ours campaigns peacefully for access to the land, its resources and the decision-making processes affecting them, for everyone" – can join or set up a Land Is Ours group of their own.'

TLIO's most inspired action occurred the following year: the 'Pure Genius' occupation of a large riverside site in Wandsworth, owned by the brewers Guinness and awaiting permission for a supermarket and penthouse development. The capture of the site was planned with military precision, and a makeshift wood and canvas ecovillage with meeting halls, gardens, kitchens, showers, compost toilets, etc. sprang up overnight. Thanks to its good press connections and proximity to Central London, it received lavish publicity, and held out for five months before it was evicted.

What made Pure Genius different was that it wasn't about anything other than itself. The purpose of the occupation was the occupation. Yes, the people involved opposed the supermarket and the penthouse flats, and the gentrification of London generally. But the principal demand was for access to land, for homes, for workspace, for communities and it articulated this demand by taking the land and creating these things. The medium was the message.

The key event for me there turned out to be a small meeting held round a campfire on the site, bringing together a few people who wanted to tackle rural planning policy and make it more amenable to low impact developments. Out of this meeting emerged a group that called itself the Rural Planning Group of The Land Is Ours, which was expanded in 1999 to a membership organisation with a mission to campaign for 'access to land for all households through environmentally sound planning'. This was a paraphrase from chapter 7 of Agenda 21, the international agreement that the UK had signed up to at the Rio Earth Summit in 1992, so I called the new group Chapter 7.

I also moved my office into what had formerly been the potato store at Flaxdrayton Farm, a couple of miles' bike ride from

Tinker's Bubble. This 500-acre estate had once been a model of Victorian high farming, employing some twenty people in 1911, and equipped with an impressive range of infrastructure, including a steam engine large enough to require a factory chimney, powering farmyard machines through underground line shafting. But in the agricultural slump of the mid-twentieth century most of the land had been rented out on a three generation lease, and later the stately home that the land had supported was demolished, and replaced by a trailer park. Since the farmyard was no longer functional the council had given permission for it to be turned into business units.

The first issue of the new organisation's newsletter *Chapter 7 News* was published in spring 1999. Technologically it was only one step up from the duplicated publications of the 1960s and covered, amongst other things: the granting of planning consent for ninety turf-roofed eco-buildings in Sutton later to materialise as the BedZED development; an alternative scheme for the area around Brighton station advanced by a group opposing a Sainsbury's supermarket; and the use in the US of Community Land Trusts (then more or less unheard of in the UK) to buy up and protect small farms threatened by development. The first issue of *Chapter 7 News* went out to a membership of about fifty. By the time of the last issue in 2005, membership had swelled to a still modest four hundred.

Morlands

From 1999 onwards I was helping Chris Black formulate development proposals for a derelict site that he had his eye on, the Morlands factory complex on the main road between Glastonbury and Street. This jumble of stone, brick and concrete buildings of different architectural eras on forty-five acres had been operated as a tannery by Clarks in the days when

Britain made its own shoes, but had remained unused and unoccupied for some fifteen years. The finest of the buildings was a vaulted north light building designed by local architect Jack Hepworth in 1961, a fabulous marriage of space and illumination, and like all north light buildings ideal for posing solar panels on the south-facing roofs.

The consortium who owned the property wanted to build housing on it, but had consistently been blocked by the planning department, because the site was allegedly contaminated, and next to the sewage works. The District Council's development brief prescribed 'demolition and rebuild', requiring serious investment and high returns that could only come from a retail centre that the Town Council and the Chamber of Commerce opposed because they didn't want an out of town shopping centre.

Chris and I, with the support of a number of local residents, drew up a prospectus for developing the site as 'the UK's first sustainable industrial village', in which most of the buildings would be refurbished and rented out for a mixture of uses with an accent on light industry and alternative energy. We suggested a lot could be achieved with affordable repairing leases: we took as a model Gabriel's Wharf, part of the Coin Street development on London's South Bank, which had been given over to makeshift shops, studios and cafés on a stop-gap basis, and that was proving very popular. Today, twenty-one years later, that temporary development has become permanent.

Despite a posh brochure, with an architect's drawings of well-to-do citizens strolling along a tree-lined avenue framed by the reincarnated factory buildings, neither the developers, nor the planners, took much notice of our proposal – there was no money in it. The stalemate continued until in 2001 when Chris and I decided that the best thing to do was to occupy one or more of the buildings with a high-profile squat.

We joined forces with Jim Paton (of Advisory Service for Squatters) and Brendan Boal to plan a large-scale occupation of at least one of the buildings under the banner of TLIO. We cased the joint, and soon a network of potential squatters was awaiting the signal to move onto the mystery location, known only to a select few. A truck was ready to be loaded up with all the kit needed for a successful occupation: tools, paint, catering equipment, provisions, loo rolls and so on. There was every prospect of this occupation matching the success of Pure Genius. Morlands had buildings, whereas the Guinness site was a heap of rubble; and we knew we would get local support, because the place had been an eyesore for fifteen years.

Then, shortly before we were due to move on, disaster struck. The South West of England Regional Development Agency (SWERDA), a government body, announced that it had bought the Morlands site to rescue it from dereliction and oversee its redevelopment. Had they rumbled us or was this just bad luck? Probably the latter. But with SWERDA portrayed in the local press as a white knight, local people, instead of being supportive, would be mystified or angered by our occupation. Chris decided it was best to pull the entire operation. Brendan and Jim were gutted and tried to persuade Chris to go ahead. But Chris was interested in securing the property for future use, whereas Brendan and Jim's main interest was the campaign. Galling though it was, I agreed with Chris – with the change of ownership, parachuting in a load of hippies would not be well received.

The cancellation of the Morlands action was a blow to The Land Is Ours, which was sorely in need of something to revive its spirits. George Monbiot was distancing himself from the movement he started, and others were losing interest. A legacy of £27,000 left to TLIO was mostly given away to other organisations, because nobody could think what to do with it. By about 2010 there was little left of TLIO other than a rump of squabbling males. An attempt to revive it in 2012 came to nothing, and although there are still sporadic actions that adopt the banner of TLIO, it exists mainly as a website, albeit quite a good one. The land may not be ours, but a little corner of cyberspace is.

Despite the decline of TLIO, the saga of Morlands was to continue. In 2009, SWERDA announced that it was going to demolish a rambling range of north light brick buildings at the southern end of the site, because they were 'unsafe'. Now was the time for a squat: seven years of SWERDA's inertia, relieved only by outbursts of architectural vandalism, had turned the town against them. Chris Black together with other local activists occupied the building, and the RDA agreed to suspend demolition pending a rescue plan. An ad hoc local group managed to raise £440,000 to buy the building, and has restored it as a now thriving cultural centre, with café, bar, workshops and dance floor.

In 2012 all the Regional Development Agencies in the country were abolished, in one of the few sensible moves of Cameron's coalition government. SWERDA sold off its assets, mostly to its pals. The 'Bauhaus building', a three-storey glass and concrete warehouse, went to a local developer, reputedly for one pound, who made a tidy profit selling it to Chris Black for a six figure sum, the last of his money. Chris rechristened it the Zig Zag building, offered a home to waifs and strays in return for helping to repair all 2,400 window panes, and has turned it into a cross between an art gallery and a scrap yard.

The southern end of the Morlands site is now an enclave for Glastonbury's thriving alternative community, with an 'off-grid living zone', a community shop, a proposed energy farm and a 20-foot-high rope suspension bridge linking the Zig Zag building with the Red Brick building. The more conventional consumers of Glastonbury need not feel aggrieved: the rest of the Morlands site is given over to the big sheds of Mammon.

The Battle of the Roundhouse

During this time Chapter 7 continued to function as 'the planning arm' of The Land Is Ours, campaigning for planning policies that encouraged low impact developments, and providing planning advice for people who were struggling to obtain permission, or facing enforcement. We had funding for three years from a private individual well known in the world of permaculture, so we acted as advocates in a number of appeals, several of which we won. Our most cherished achievement was winning permission for two residential double-decker buses in an Area of Outstanding Natural Beauty in Sussex, after a high-flying planning barrister had backed out of the case on the grounds that it was unwinnable.

In early 2003, I and James Shorten, a planning consultant sympathetic to low impact development (LID), were invited to give a talk at the annual beano of planning appeal inspectors held at Warwick University. Normally you only see one planning inspector on their own, and if you bump into them during the lunch break during an appeal, you are not allowed to talk to them. When I arrived at the student bar the evening before my presentation, there were about three hundred of them all gabbling away, in different stages of intoxication. I felt like David Attenborough stumbling upon a freak gathering of rare and normally solitary animals.

I learnt a lot about the mentality of planning inspectors that evening. They were often of a liberal persuasion, and I suspected were frequently people who had made some headway in public life, but who sought a retreat from the fray and corruption, while still exercising an influence. Both James' and my presentations on low impact development were well received by an audience of more than one hundred that comprised a high proportion of the younger inspectors. The most notable audience response was the warm ripple of agreement when James stated that Welsh planning policy was far more visionary than the English. Wales at the time was way ahead of England in respect of its policies on sustainability, and it still is. After the talk one inspector came up to me and jabbed me with his finger saying, 'Give us the ammunition for sustainable development, and we can deliver.'

This was encouraging. In the years that followed, although English planning policy remained unhelpful to LIDs, the majority of inspectors were well disposed towards them. Appeals against local authority refusals of planning permission for LIDs had a success rate of approximately 75 per cent, about twice as high as the average for all appeals. Eventually local planning officers began to grasp that a refusal of permission for a competent smallholding or low impact development had a high chance of being overturned at planning appeal, at considerable expense to the local authority.

Welsh planning policy had begun to diverge from the English model after devolution in 1998. *Planning Policy Wales*, the central document, laid down nine principles for sustainable development and eighteen objectives, including addressing climate change, renewable energy and the proximity principle. Moreover James Shorten and colleagues had been commissioned by the Countryside Council for Wales and the Welsh Assembly to carry out a survey examining and evaluating low impact development. The resulting 180-page document, published in 2003, recommended that *Planning Policy Wales* and local development plans should include a policy for LIDs. Early next year Pembrokeshire National Park, who had a disproportionate number of hippies and smallholders within their bounds, commissioned their own report that recommended that the Park should introduce a low impact development policy, with appropriate tests and criteria into their development plan.

Meanwhile conflict over LID was coming to a head through a prolonged planning battle over a roundhouse built by Tony Wrench and Jane Faith at the Brithdir Mawr community, that was in Pembrokeshire National Park. With its roundwood walls and reciprocal roof covered in turf, the house viewed from a distance was indistinguishable from the surrounding vegetation, but the Park's planners had discovered it when their helicopter had spotted the glint of a solar panel. A failed planning application was followed in turn by an enforcement notice, an appeal resulting in a temporary stay of execution, a second failed planning application, a second appeal that was dismissed and an enforcement notice.

By 2003, the Park's chief planning officer, Cathy Milner, was expressing her determination to carry out enforcement and see the house demolished. She even, at our invitation, wrote an article for *Chapter 7 News* explaining why: 'This seems to be the belief that runs through the whole of Chapter 7: "Because we are doing something different and laudable, planning policies should not apply in the same way to us as they do to the rest of the population." That is not a basis on which a democratic and civilised society can survive.'

She was partly correct: we did indeed believe that 'laudable' low impact developments should be allowed in places where less laudable developments were normally prohibited. But clearly, planning policies allowing people to create laudable developments would apply to the entire population – why would they not? The real insult to democracy, we maintained, was a planning system that imposed stringent financial and functional tests on anybody who wanted to build a home in the countryside, but not on the elite who could afford to buy an existing house.

The roundhouse was becoming well known, not least because Tony Wrench had published a book in 2001 explaining how to build your own for not very much money. The battle over its existence reached a climax in spring 2004 when Tony, worn out by the struggle, and bruised by a £1,000 fine for failing to comply with the enforcement notice, announced that he would demolish his house over the Easter weekend and arranged for a posse of friends to come and help him. At Chapter 7 we decided that this should not be allowed to happen and that the best way to prevent it was to squat in the house over the weekend, so that, with the best will in the world, Tony and his gang could not carry out the demolition.

We let it be known, through our network, that we were organising an 'Easter Parade' protest against demolition of the roundhouse, though we didn't divulge our stratagem. Shortly before Brendan Boal and I were due to visit the National Park to reconnoitre, I received a phone call from the Chief of Police for the area around the Park, whom I will call Robert Evans. Could he have a chat with us about the impending protest? He wanted to ensure that there would be no 'trouble'. We made an appointment to meet him in Newport, the nearest village to Brithdir Mawr.

Brendan and I met up with him as planned. Robert was congenial, more bobby than bouncer. He apparently didn't want anyone to hear what was going on since he took us down to the sea at low tide and we walked out onto the rocks. There he explained: 'I won't say whether or not I support your protest, that's not my business. My job is to see that there is no trouble. This is a quiet, friendly community and I want to keep it that way. Can you give me your word that you will keep it peaceful?'

We promised that we would do our best, and we left shaking hands, as he said, 'If you co-operate with me, I will co-operate with you.'

On Maundy Thursday, about twenty protesters arrived at Glaneirw, a large, once prestigious farmhouse just outside the

Park to prepare for the action. By all accounts Glaneirw had once been amongst the most together of hippie communes, achieving high levels of self-sufficiency, including arable production, a cheese and dairy unit, and a commercial pottery. Now it was in a sorry state, with the main house unlived in and the grounds strewn with all the detritus of untrammelled hippiedom. According to the three people who still lived there, the rubbish had been even worse, and they had already carted quite a bit to the tip. They apparently had seen off an aggressive take-over by a co-op member who had tried to drive everyone else out. It was a sobering reminder what can happen to a community if problem people are let in, standards drop, old timers leave in despair, and a vicious circle of decay sets in. Nonetheless, the residents of Glaneirw gave us a warm welcome, and use of a large room in which to paint banners, prepare our line of attack and stay for the night.

Early on Good Friday we converged from different directions on the Iron Age fort at Castell Henllys, within the park, and took possession of it. The main building there was a replica Iron Age roundhouse that, so we were told, had been built by a rogue archaeologist some ten years before. His problem had been that he didn't have planning permission for it, and the Park's planning department had required its removal. During negotiations the owner died – some said of stress caused by the planning saga – whereupon the Park purchased the site, and gave itself planning permission to operate the roundhouse as a tourist attraction and to build another two roundhouses.

It seemed an appropriate place to commandeer as a base of operations. And it wasn't the only example of the Park's double standards that we drew attention to. They had also, only recently, given permission to the Bluestone holiday village comprising 340 cabins, a 'Celtic-style village', a Waterworld and a Snowdome.

We stuck up a huge banner, visible from across the valley saying 'Roundhouses Aren't History'. There were soon about fifty of us and the site's manager arrived in a state of panic, followed by the police, led by Robert. He came up to me shaking his head. 'Simon, I'm disappointed in you,' he said. 'Very disappointed.' But I fancied I could detect something of a smile beneath his outwardly stern expression. We reassured him that we would be utterly peaceful, would look after the property and leave it on Tuesday.

The Park announced that the Iron Age village would be shut for the duration of the Easter holiday, but we, being the occupiers, declared it open. In Jim Paton's words: 'At the entrance visitors were met by both National Park bods telling them the place was closed and they would be trespassing if they went any further and by protesters with leaflets who warmly encouraged a bit of bank holiday trespassing. So those visitors undeterred by petty authority got to see the Iron Age roundhouses, without paying £2.80 and were equally fascinated by the twenty-first-century yurts and tipis. Oh and the tea was free, which the National Park's insipid brew ain't.'

More people joined us, and on Saturday about one hundred people marched to Brithdir Mawr, to be met by Tony at the gate. There he defended his property with pantomime oratory before giving way to the sheer force of numbers. We swarmed down to the house and occupied it in the most respectful manner while Tony hammed up the rhetoric of dispossession outside, and his demolition gang lay around in a tipi drinking tea.

We therefore had two squats going, so we thought we'd do a third for good measure. On Easter Sunday we took over a layby on the A487 close to Castell Henllys, and constructed an exhibition of low impact dwellings including a straw bale house and a structure with a reciprocal roof. Passing motorists stopped to examine or lend their support, and Robert turned up again, apparently happy with what we were doing.

On Tuesday the planning officers were back at work and so we could enact the final part of our show. About 150 people, led by bagpipes, marched through Haverfordwest to the Park's office, where we congregated in the forecourt, demanding to talk to Cathy Milner about the roundhouse. She refused to appear.

Our next step was to erect a yurt in the forecourt and post a Section 6 notice declaring it to be a squat that could not be removed without a court order. We also told the planning authority that we wanted to put in a planning application for the yurt and gathered £220 for the fee by passing a hat around. By this time poor Cathy must have been seething. She had wanted to avoid the media, but her refusal to talk and our continued occupation were what attracted them. Reporters and television presenters came and filmed us in the yurt and we were the top story on Welsh TV news and in the Welsh daily press.

About twenty of us dug in for the night, and the negotiations continued into the next day. In the end we agreed to leave on the condition that Cathy would address a public meeting about the roundhouse. It never took place because the planning committee refused to allow her to attend. But the press publicity was what we had been aiming for, together with a show of force sufficient to make the Park think twice about bringing in the bulldozers.

Not long after, Tony and Faith were summoned to court for the second time and the case was referred to Crown Court in Swansea. There Tony's evidence included a video of the Easter Parade and seven pages of comments about the case taken from the Park's own guest book on their website. The judge stated that he sympathised with much of what they said, and imposed a modest fine for a second offence of £150 each, some of which was paid for out of our collection at the Haverfordwest protest. The council then threatened to bring an injunction against the roundhouse, but in the end they backed out of this, since it was apparent that they were not going to get much support from the judiciary, and because the Park had an emerging policy for LIDs. The case staggered on until 2008 when the roundhouse was finally given permission under the new policy. A few years later an adapted version of the policy was extended to the whole of Wales under the title 'One Planet Development'.

Of all the various protests and actions I was ever involved in, the Easter Parade was my favourite: it went according to plan, it achieved its aims, it was good humoured and it was fun. Some of the credit must go to the exemplary policing of Robert Evans.

Exit from Tinker's Bubble

While I was spending time helping other people getting planning permission, I was also enjoying the fruits of our own success at Tinker's Bubble. On the May Day weekend after our victory we held a party to celebrate, with music provided by, amongst others, Seize the Day, who were based at the bender community at King's Hill, which was still fighting for permission. Early that evening, I was on car park duty in the woods when a blue Dodge truck rocked up and a couple who I hadn't met before got out. He was tall and had poise, she was tiny and Indian looking; he did the driving, she did the talking, with an American accent. She was Jyoti Fernandes, her husband was Dai Saltmarsh, and they were living at an unofficial bender site near Glastonbury called Dragon Hill.

Not long after the party they moved to the Bubble, along with their young daughter Ele. Jyoti, who is a born campaigner, began to work with me in the Chapter 7 office. Other people followed, attracted by the potential and the security that our planning permission offered. Rebecca Laughton who had previously been living at Ben Law's well known forestry holding joined us; Olly and Kerry arrived separately but soon became a devoted couple. They all moved into our settlement in the woods, building themselves houses of timber and canvas, and enhancing the social atmosphere.

These were all people I liked, they were competent and they brought with them fresh energy and enthusiasm. Like the rest of us, they joined the community on the understanding that the people who lived there aimed to make a livelihood from the land. We now had much of the communal infrastructure in place – roundhouse and kitchen, bathroom, compost toilets, stable, polytunnels, sawmill, cider house, piped water, fencing, wind power and solar panels. Mary and I were building a house together, and I was helping her to school Joe, who had reacted strongly against the primary school in Norton. With a core of about ten residents, and security for five years the community looked set to thrive.

One element of the farm holding that had yet to fulfil its potential was the twelve acres of grass in the orchards, pasture and meadow. Samson needed only a fraction of it, our neighbour Lee grazed some with his sheep until they discovered how tasty apple tree bark is, and we made hay with scythes on a couple of acres. But the most productive use of grassland is dairy farming, and our efforts to produce milk in the first five years had been less than satisfactory.

In the first year we bought a Dexter cow called Notary, but she didn't last very long. Some well-meaning soul brought us a pile of highly poisonous yew cuttings as a gift and dumped them in her field, and that was the end of Notary. We did have her long enough for me to decide not to get a Dexter next time. After Notary, people tried keeping goats, again without much success. Since they eat apple trees and are difficult to fence, goats and orchards are not a happy combination. Tethering them was often the only option, and in the British climate that is a maddening business, because with the merest hint of rain goats start bleating pathetically to be taken indoors. After one died of ketosis, a second succumbed to bracken poisoning and a third hung itself by jumping out of a trailer to which it had been tied, we gave up keeping them.

The solution was Jersey cows. They don't bark trees, they respect fences, they are (mostly) of a friendly disposition and they give gallons rather than pints of rich creamy milk. After looking for the right animal for some time, and being warned more than once that we shouldn't buy from a dealer, we bought a heifer in calf called Millie from a dealer. She was everything you could want from a house cow: she calved without problem and almost overnight was supplying a sizable proportion of the community's protein requirement. Mary had learnt how to make Tomme on a trip to France and soon wheels of cheese were maturing on a shelf beneath the ceiling in the smoky kitchen. After a year or so we bought a second cow, Fern, and started selling cheese in our stall at the farmers' market, along with pork from pigs fed mostly on the whey and on food waste. The cows also turned the hay from our meadows into a mountain of manure in their winter quarters, conveniently situated next to the communal garden. I came to see them as the hub around which the cycle of farming activity revolved. And it did not escape my notice that if you don't use machinery, it is quicker and easier to produce high-quality protein and fat from milking cows than it is by cultivating a garden.

My other main focus was working with Samson. Pulling the logs out of the woodland down to the sawmill was his most important job, and one that he enjoyed, particularly if you let him go at a trot using the momentum of the logs behind him. The bit he wasn't keen on was going back up the hill for the next log. Like most logging horses he wasn't too clever at ploughing; he wanted to go too fast, thinking that he could build up momentum with the plough in the same way he could with a log. He did all the heavy carting around the holding with a nifty little chariot made out of two windswept butts of Douglas fir, the shape of hockey sticks, mounted onto a boat trailer axle. With its low centre of gravity you could take it anywhere through the steep and bumpy woods, and the curved body prevented the load, or when empty the driver, from sliding off.

His favourite job of all was pulling out the stumps of the old Cox apple trees that had never been much good. Once we had dug out round the trunk a bit, and severed the roots nearest the surface, he could pull the whole thing out like a huge tooth by applying some heavy duty waggling. He soon learnt that he had to lunge in one direction and then another and then a third and fourth to snap all the roots, and would attempt this of his own accord. When it finally popped out he would trot off with it in visible triumph.

At the end of the year 2000, disaster struck. I had to go away to Wales for a few days, and just before leaving I put Samson in the field where the cows had been, failing to notice that he could reach over the fence to a tub of feed that the cows couldn't reach. He managed to knock it over and wolfed huge quantities. By the time I got back from Wales he was already going down with laminitis, a painful and debilitating inflammation of the tissue attaching the hoof to the bone – the equivalent of the quick underneath your fingernail. He was in agony, above all in his front hoofs, which take most of the weight. I consulted two vets who both said shoot him. As a last resort I had some X-rays made and sent them to a specialist laminitis vet in Trowbridge. He wrote back a short note saying, 'There is a ray of hope. That will be £45.' It was the best £45 I ever spent.

Over the next very muddy winter, Mary and I nursed him, putting special circular shoes on his feet that helped relieve the pressure, and dosing him with vast quantities of the painkiller

Bute. If there was any improvement it was negligible. Then after about three months one of his front hooves became infected, and was so painful he could put no weight on it at all. The vet's view was that he must have sustained some injury, and he remained pessimistic about recovery.

We poulticed the hoof and bandaged it day and night, extracting copious amounts of disgusting fluid; after ten days it cleared up and suddenly he was putting his weight on that foot. A day or two later the other front foot did exactly the same thing, and there was another ten days of poultice and bandage before that too cleared up. When it did he was completely cured: the pain subsided and we could take him off the Bute within a week. There was no doubt in our mind that the infection was a way of getting rid of the crap that had accumulated during the course of the ailment. Samson's body had worked out that if it did both feet at the same time, he couldn't stand up, so it did one foot, then the other.

––––––––

After a period of convalescence, Samson was back on the job, but his absence had slowed down our progress. In our planning application we had set ourselves the target of achieving a total net annual income of £18,600 (the equivalent of £33,000 in 2020). This we proposed was to be achieved as follows:

Subsistence produce	*£6,500*
Timber	*£8,000*
Apples	*£2,000*
Livestock	*£600*
Sundries	*£1,500*

In year one we made more than £9,500, more than halfway there, which seemed a reasonable start. In the second year we dropped to £8,300, but that was in part due to want of a horse.

We recovered quite well in year three, and peaked at £13,782 in year four. But in year five, when we had to apply to renew our permission, it fell back down to £9,500 again.

What (if anything) went wrong? How could ten people fail to achieve even such a modest return from such a rich resource?

An auditor perusing the itemised annual accounts (which do exist) would notice immediately that the £8,000 cash income predicted for the timber enterprise never materialised. Despite a willing horse, a hard-won sawmill and limitless supplies of timber, the most cash it ever earned in one year was £1,522, plus producing roughly the same value of timber for building our own dwellings.

The orchards did average out at about £2,000 profit per year as we had forecast. Some of the shortfall occasioned by the failure of the timber enterprise to deliver was made up by vegetable and herb production, minimal in year one but peaking at about £5,000 in year four.

At first sight it might be tempting to attribute Tinker's Bubble's failure to meet its targets to its refusal to use fossil fuels. Obviously the lack of machinery, and especially chainsaws was an economic handicap. A bloke with a chainsaw and a horse could have made a tidy living from the land just from selling sawlogs and firewood.

But there is a problem with blaming our poor economic performance on primitive technology: the one sector where we had enlisted other power sources – namely the steam engine and the horse – was the only one that fell way short of its potential. To an extent this was because of technological issues. Nobody ever managed to operate the sawbench or sharpen its four-foot circular blade as expertly as the fellow who sold it to us, so there were times when it was out of action.

But the main reason was that the timber operation was a joint enterprise that required the co-operation of several people:

to manage the woodland, fell the trees and process them with two-man saws and axes, and operate the steam engine and mill. And we hippies, although we wanted to live in a community, actually weren't too good at working communally. That's not to say that we couldn't. It was more that most of the time most of the people didn't want to. A squad of professional soldiers under orders would have achieved in a few days what took us months or even years to get together.

The problem had been apparent from the outset. We started out with communal work days, but it was often difficult to get some people to join in and after about eighteen months these were dropped. Instead we adopted a system where different people took responsibility for different tasks, but not everyone carried out their roles, and the forestry fell behind. By 1999 when we got planning consent, work was no longer structured around a farm plan. Instead each person was supposed to achieve a land-based income through their own devices, which might include paid work on the collective activities, namely the sawmill and the apples.

The result was a multiplicity of veg patches. More than half the people living there had their own, hand tilled with spade and mattock. We had a communal garden for our subsistence needs, and we had a horse and all the kit for growing row crops on a commercial scale, but nobody was interested; people wanted to do their own thing (some more efficiently than others). Some of the produce was consumed at home, some was sold at farmer's markets, with annual sales peaking at £5,000 – not a lot considering the number of people involved. And while people were concentrating on their private plots, and building their accommodation, it was hard to interest them in management of the wider holding: the woodland, the orchards and the pasture. There is nothing wrong with tilling a veg patch, but you don't need forty acres. A large back garden or an allotment will do.

Meanwhile construction of communal infrastructure almost ground to a halt. A guest house that had been started in the early 2000s took several years to finish. I drew up plans for a barn to replace the temporary sawmill building and all its mattresses but nobody was very interested.

As the failure to meet our targets became more apparent, I began to wonder whether Gummer had been right to class Tinker's Bubble as a 'subsistence' holding in his confirmation of the enforcement notice following our appeal. Subsistence was certainly what we did best. In 2004, residents paid only £19 per week (the equivalent of £29 in 2020) to cover all their food, water, heating and cooking fuel, electricity, waste disposal, insurance, horse transport, accommodation and collective infrastructure, including bathroom and kitchen facilities, furniture, communal tools, and a good deal of their entertainment. Rent/mortgage was an extra £5 a week. That was impressive.

To live at Tinker's Bubble was to live in an alternative economy; it was a bit like living in a developing country in the Global South. The wages we could earn working for the forestry enterprise, or the apples, or indeed growing vegetables for sale were very low, at best about half the official minimum wage; but the cost of living was even lower. The difficulty came when we needed to buy something from the 'rich world' – getting a horse shod for example, where one hour of a farrier's labour might cost six or eight hours of labour at the Bubble. On the other hand if we ventured out and did a bit of work in the rich world, or received income support, or baby cheques, or a pension, then we doubled the value of our money by taking it home and spending it within our local economy. It was like the cash sent home by a migrant worker in an industrialised country, except that we didn't have to cross any borders to earn it; we could, as Norman Tebbit put it, just get on our bike.

This of course was the other reason why people were unenthusiastic to work for the forestry enterprise. They could earn more in the outside world. That doesn't alter the fact that Tinker's Bubble's subsistence economy was (and still is) an achievement. Many hundreds of visitors and volunteers have seen at first hand how, by getting rid of the burden of rent, by building one's dwelling, and by tapping into the abundance of natural resources, anyone can forge for themselves a low impact livelihood where you don't 'have to earn £100 a week before you can even breathe'.

But what about Gummer's ruling in our appeal that subsistence agriculture 'is not a practical pattern of long-term land use'? There is barely one acre of land in Britain for every UK resident, so devoting forty acres to the provision of a subsistence living for a dozen hippies is manifestly unsustainable, especially if they also buy things like gumboots and solar panels. True, but the actual area of land used to provide our subsistence was a fraction of the forty acres. The remainder was available for commercial production, but underexploited for the reasons I have given above.

Had Gummer in his appeal decision instead argued that 'these are a bunch of random hippies and they probably won't get it together to achieve their production targets' he would have been proved correct. But I wouldn't view that as good grounds for refusal. Anything that aspires to establish an alternative to the manic pursuit of economic growth through unbridled consumerism has to be worth trying.

———

As time went on it became plain to me that we weren't achieving what we (or arguably I) set out to do. In 2005 I moved out of the Bubble, and took up permanent lodging in a caravan at Flaxdrayton Farm where Chapter 7 had its offices. I still came back to the Bubble regularly, mostly to work Samson, who was beginning to feel the weight of years. My relations with the people there, which had been strained in my departure, healed. Mary and I split up, then we got back together for a time, but it no longer worked.

One day in 2008, I went to an event in Weston-super-Mare. When I came back I had a message saying that Samson had died that day. I went round to Tinker's Bubble at about 7 pm expecting that, besides the commiserations, I would have to organise the disposal of his body. When I arrived the Bubblers had already finished digging a six-foot-deep hole in the field, big enough to encompass his huge body. I doubt whether Tinker's Bubble has ever rallied its members to do anything so immediate and efficient as the digging of that grave. The next day we were all present for the burial. He got a better send-off from the Bubble than I did.

After the death of Samson, Tinker's Bubble went into decline. The planning permission had been renewed in 2004, but the council's planners had lost all interest (if they ever had any) of monitoring the performance of the community. All the people who had joined shortly after getting permission in 1999 had moved on, four of them, including Jyoti, to start a new project at Fivepenny Farm, near Charmouth in Dorset. For a short time there was another horse on site, but neither it nor its owner were coping with the workload. New people of dubious standing and little commitment were passing through, and little was being achieved. Mary Durling left, eventually to buy land near Fivepenny Farm, and Pete Wright put his energy into Plotgate, the latest of Chris Black's land projects at Barton St David, near Glastonbury. Of the original residents, only Mike Zair remained. Eventually the non-resident shareholders, myself included, who act as a sort of board of governors, stepped in and placed a moratorium on new members until the community found its feet again.

That it did so was largely due to the influence of one person, Pete 'Pedro' Brace. Pedro combines an uncompromising, almost fanatical rejection of fossil fuels with an ability to get things done. He refuses to go more or less anywhere in a car and bicycles dozens of miles to avoid doing so. Without previous experience he acquired a pair of cob horses, which now carry out the log extraction and other jobs. In 2013, ten years behind schedule, seventy soggy mattresses were finally taken back to the same tip from which they had been salvaged and work started on a permanent shed for the sawmill. That was followed by an apple juicing and cider shed that, unlike our first octagonal attempt, meets health and safety standards.

Pedro did a better job than myself, or anybody else, at galvanising the community into productivity. Whether he propelled Tinker's Bubble beyond the level of 'mere subsistence' that Gummer decried, I cannot say. There has been a fast throughput of residents, who typically last only a year or two, while Pedro has remained a perennial surrounded by annuals. But as I write he too is leaving with his girlfriend Charlie, to move onto a holding in Devon. A new era in the community with a fresh group of people is unfolding.

For those who pass through, whether they stay three weeks or three years, Tinker's Bubble offers an experience hard to replicate anywhere else in Britain – a return to the bare necessities of subsistence living, reliant largely on muscle power and the food and energy derived from the land on which one lives. Though its fortunes have waxed and waned, it has been a seedbed for many other initiatives. I can think of a dozen long-term residents who after leaving have gone on to establish successful land-based enterprises elsewhere.

CHAPTER ELEVEN

December Song

A surprising legacy of my time at Tinker's Bubble was that it led me to become a petty capitalist. One element in particular of our fossil-fuel-free lifestyle, I found out more or less by accident, had market appeal.

Every year at Tinker's Bubble we made hay on up to three acres of the grassland, and we had to do it by hand. We advertised for old scythes in the local paper and were donated nearly a dozen of the traditional Anglo-American scythes in various states of disrepair. But at the outset we had no idea how to sharpen or use them effectively, and there was no one around who could teach us. The men who had mown meadows and orchards in the past were all gone. Persuading the blades to cut the grass, rather than bend it flat was a frustrating and exhausting penance. Since haymaking often has to be carried out within a short window of good weather, I argued at meetings that everyone who lived there should help out, but there was often resistance.

Towards the end of the 1990s we came across a couple of secondhand 'Turk' scythes, with 'made in Austria' stamped on them. Someone had been selling them in Britain in the 1960s and 1970s. They were lighter, thinner and easier to sharpen than the old English beasts, and they did actually cut the grass. Then, in 2003, Mike Zair bought me a copy of *The Scythe Book* by David Tresemer, who described exactly the process we had been through – how he was put off using the Anglo-American style of scythe: 'It was awkward, it left me sore, and the grasses laughed at my efforts by bending over and bobbing back up after the blade had passed.' Then, like us, he discovered the Austrian scythe and found it altogether more congenial. But he went further: he travelled to Austria to find out how the tool should be used and kept sharp, came back, applied what he learnt, and wrote a book about it.

The book mentioned that as well as a couple of factories making scythes in Austria, there were scything competitions. Really? I phoned up the Austrian Tourist Office, who put me onto the Austrian Trade Commission. They came back within half an hour to tell me that yes, a scythe competition would be held by the Young Farmers of Steyr in three weeks' time. I contacted, Steve Friend, inviting him for a holiday, and a fortnight later we boarded a bus for Linz.

When we rolled up at the farm where the competition was held, it was a revelation. Young athletes wielding four-foot-long blades mowed one hundred square metres of grass in less than three minutes. They began each stroke with knees bent and body low to extend their reach, then rose to increase the power behind the blade as it sliced through a twelve-foot swathe of grass. We tried our hand at the novices' patches of five by five metres. Later, as beer steins overflowed at the prize-giving ceremony, they fished out a wonky trophy from the back of the farmhouse, declared it the Foreigner's Cup and awarded it to Steve.

The next day we went to the Schröckenfux ('Fux') scythe factory at the village of Rossleithen where the managing director of the factory, who we had met at the competition, gave us a tour, guiding us through the sixteen stages involved in hand-forging a blade. We bought five blades and a couple of snaths (as scythe handles are called) and took them back on the bus to England. Next month, we used them in our haymaking. Everyone liked them and said, 'Can you get any more?' From then on mowing the hay at Tinker's Bubble became a popular activity.

Not long after, I obtained a second edition of *The Scythe Book*, which now included an 'Addendum on the Practical Use of the Scythe', written by one Peter Vido. It provided a lot more practical information, some of which contradicted the advice given by Tresemer. Vido also complained about the ignorant and inadequate service provided by companies selling scythes in the United States. He proposed instead: 'A co-operative network in America and in Europe. It will consist of those who, instead of just selling the scythe, would like to *learn how to use it well* and, by means of workshops, *pass the skill on to others* ... A time of many teachers. Those willing to help with this extended project can contact us by writing to the Vido Family.'

I wrote. He phoned back saying that he was organising 'the First International Scythe Symposium and Festival' in Austria the following year, would I come?

Peter Vido, I discovered, was a remarkable man. He was a *soixante-huitard* from the Eastern Bloc who, at the age of seventeen, escaped by swimming across the Danube after the Russians invaded Prague in 1968. He made his way to Canada where he married and bought a 200-acre run-down farm in New Brunswick with, as he put it, 'baby cheques'. He farmed with horses and subsequently with large working donkeys until his father, on a visit, introduced him to the scythe, with a copy of Tresemer's book. When a storm laid flat an entire field of buckwheat, making it unmowable with horses, Peter tackled it with the scythe, and was hooked. He began to teach himself to mow, and to peen the blade by cold forging the edge with a hammer and a small anvil. Then, like Tresemer, he made the pilgrimage to Rossleithen.

Peter soon acquired the competence to enable him and his family to mow all their hay by hand. But he didn't stop there, for he perceived that the scythe was the epitome of what Ivan Illich in 1973 called a 'convivial' tool: 'Simple tools that allow men to achieve purposes with energy fully under their own control.' The rhythm of mowing grass with a sharp scythe relaxes the mind and attunes the body. As Levin says to his brother, after a day's mowing, in *Anna Karenina*: 'You can't imagine what an effectual remedy it is for every sort of foolishness.'

Peter was now on a mission, not only to proselytise the scythe's virtues, but to 'preserve some genetics of its very unusual craftsmanship'. He was a fastidious perfectionist and on return visits to Rossleithen he came not only to learn, but also to advise Fux how to improve their products, and admonish them if he saw standards slipping. What the good burghers of Rossleithen thought of this wiry Asterix-like figure with his hair in pigtails and his bare feet when he first started handing out advice, we don't know. But although his comments were provocative – he was particularly critical of the snaths that Fux were selling – he was usually right and he gained their confidence. The improved wooden snaths that are now standard in the UK were adapted from a design by Peter Vido.

Peter also foresaw that the way to maintain standards was to increase demand for high-quality scythes in Europe and North America. At first sight, to the factory managers, this was to spit into a wind blowing in the opposite direction. They had seen almost every other scythe factory in Western Europe close as sales declined in the face of competition from mechanical scythes and strimmers, and the bulk of sales were now to farmers in developing countries mostly in the Middle East. But here they faced competition from manufacturers with lower labour costs in places such as Turkey, Kyrgyzstan and China. Peter feared, with good reason, that the tendency would be to drop standards so as to compete on price. To some degree that had already happened.

It was to address this issue that Peter persuaded the Fux managers and others in the Austrian scything community to help organise the 2004 Symposium. The six-day event, funded by the EU, drew perhaps fifty people from nine countries. Aside from Peter himself, I was the only person from an English-speaking nation. In the morning there were sessions on the benefits of the scythe for biodiversity and the climate, on its potential role in affluent regions and in poorer countries, on mowing as a physical therapy, and on how to re-educate the public in its use. In the afternoon there were mowing activities and visits to the Fux factory and to a scythe museum. Most useful of all was an afternoon of scythe tuition; finally I had someone to teach me how to use the tool properly.

I invited Peter to come to Britain the following year, and told him I would arrange a small scythe festival and scythe course. I applied for £3,000 funding from an EU scheme to kick-start what I hoped might be a regular event. My bid was assessed at a public meeting where all the middle-class arty types seemed to think it was a jolly good proposal. But one woman rose and addressed the meeting: 'I'm a farmer and I think this is a ridiculous idea. We stopped using scythes seventy years ago, nobody wants to return to that back-breaking work now.' How wrong can you be?

The First West Country Scythe Festival was held at Five-penny Farm in May 2005. Peter Vido gave a scythe course to a dozen people on the Saturday, and on the Sunday about five hundred people turned up to view a scythe competition – the first to be held in Britain since 1955 – and various musical, theatrical and agricultural entertainments. The following year Peter came for a repeat event, and in 2007 we joined forces with the South Petherton Green Fair to put on the Green Scythe Fair, an event that has since taken place every June until 2020, attracting 5,000 people annually.

I had started importing and selling scythes and giving courses in 2005. At first it was a case of the one-eyed leading the blind, but I improved. Demand increased year by year, with hardly any advertising; scything provided good copy for news-papers and magazines, and footage for TV programmes. Monty Don bought one, panellists on *Gardeners' Question Time* rated them, Prince Charles started using them at Highgrove. Rural landowners bought them to manage the wildflower meadows and orchards that they were planting in pursuit of biodiversity. Conservation bodies such as the National Trust and Wildlife Trusts liked them because volunteers could use them, whereas brushcutter operators needed a qualification.

By 2008 I was already over the VAT threshold. By 2010 I was selling scythes wholesale to other folk who were giving courses, and soon there were more than a dozen scythe tutors around the country who I was supplying rather in the manner of a Tupperware franchise. Some are now importing scythes direct from Austria and Italy. Peter Vido's prediction of a 'time of many teachers' is coming to pass, not only in Britain but in most Western European countries.

Meanwhile Peter's brother, Alex, has been promoting scythes in India, where millions of small farmers painstakingly harvest their crops with sickles. In over-developed nations, people who turn to the scythe are usually downsizing from unnecessary mechanisation; but in countries such as India, peasant farmers are upgrading to a more efficient yet convivial technology.

But to keep things in perspective, I doubt whether thirty thousand scythes have been imported into the UK in the last fifteen years (none have been made here since 1987) yet there are sixty-eight million people in the country. That's one scythe for every 2,200 people. Meanwhile there are ten million members of gyms in Britain, one in seven of the population. If they learnt to scythe, they could harvest all the UK's silage and hay and mow all its lawns in a single day. The 400,000 people who applied to join the London marathon in 2019 could do the same job with the effort put into a few days training. The prize for wasted energy must go to Eddie Izzard who in 2021 ran thirty-two marathons on consecutive days on a treadmill in a London studio, producing absolutely nothing other than a load of carbon emissions. The calories for each marathon could have cut enough grass to produce 1,400 litres of milk – the nutritional equivalent of feeding one adult for well over a year, and the cow for ten weeks.

Izzard's urban capers would make Peter Vido turn in his grave. Sadly Peter died in 2018 before he had time to finish his *Big Book of the Scythe*, but some of this work and other astute observations can be found on his Scythe Connection website. If paradise exists he will be up there, mowing Elysian fields with Ivan Illich and knocking back the occasional shot of vodka.

County Farms

Balham Hill Farm was an eighty-seven-acre dairy holding of top grade land in the village of Chiselborough, a couple of miles from Tinker's Bubble. It ran a farm shop where we sold apple juice and other products and bought provisions. The farmer, Richard Jones, rented it from Somerset County Council who had bought it in 1915 in response to the Liberal Party's 1908 Small Holdings and Allotments Act, which empowered local authorities to buy land to lease to aspiring smallholders and farmers. Since the outlook was grim for dairy farmers of that scale, Richard applied for planning consent to open his shop. The district council refused permission, but he went ahead anyway, and the council didn't bother to enforce. The shop was a great success, providing a service for the village of Chiselborough, whose previous shop had closed more than a decade earlier.

In 2006, the county council announced that they were going to auction off Balham Hill Farm in seven separate lots. It was part of their plan to sell forty-five of their seventy-five farms, on the grounds that they were no longer viable. In fact the rents paid on the estate brought the council an annual profit of £378,000, or about £5,000 per farm. But this they presented in the accounts as an annual loss of £119,000 by factoring in 'capital charges', namely the sum that could have been obtained by renting out the properties at full market value. There was uproar in the village at the news, and still more uproar when the Lib Dem leader of the Council, Cathy Bakewell (now Baroness Bakewell of Hardington Mandeville), told the Parish Council that 'farming is dead' – a statement that was picked up by Radio 4's *Farming Today*.

This looked like a job for TLIO. A couple of us went to talk to Richard Jones. He wasn't worried personally, because he had been offered a farm with a shop on the Duchy Estate, but he was disgusted by the proposed sale. He gave us figures about his production, and told us that the direct sale of beef, pork, eggs, raw milk, fruit and potatoes produced on the farm had been 'unbelievably profitable'. He also let us know the date on which he planned to move out.

On Good Friday, a bunch of us arrived with crowbars and hacksaws, but found that Richard had helpfully left the farm buildings and the shop unlocked. We moved in, stocked up the shop with produce from Tinker's Bubble and other local holdings, and brought pigs, sheep, chickens and Samson onto the property. We couldn't bring the cows because they were organically registered and the Soil Association, rather pathetically, wouldn't give us a derogation. On Easter Sunday, we opened up the farm shop to the public with an egg hunt. Over the course of the next week we had more than five hundred visitors.

Amongst them was the county council's legal officer. It took him more than a month to turf us out, during which we received plenty of press attention and managed to get the farm withdrawn from auction. That gave us an opportunity to attend the council meeting scheduled for the day after the auction.

We set about lobbying county councillors by telephone and found that several were sympathetic. But suddenly they all stopped talking to us. The council's legal officer, we learnt, had emailed out a gagging order on the grounds that we were facing court proceedings, as if the matter were *sub judice*. There was no legal basis for this; it was a political order dressed up as a legal one. Balham Hill Farm was sold by sealed tender the following month with the house, farmyard and seventeen acres bought by a speculator who did nothing with it. A year later it was put up for auction again and sold at a profit rumoured to be more than £100,000. Now it is a horseyculture holding.

The most infuriating aspect of the sale of county smallholdings, not just in Somerset but nationwide, is that it has occurred in an economic climate where demand for smallholdings is soaring. As commercial farms are forced by stagnant commodity prices to become larger by swallowing up less successful neighbours, it has become hard to make medium-sized farms of about a hundred acres pay, and impossible if you have to borrow the million pounds or more that it costs to buy one.

On the other hand a smallholding producing high-quality organic food for direct sale to local consumers is a potentially viable proposition for the growing number of people seeking a fulfilling outdoor livelihood. It also requires less capital investment in the land, but even so with land selling at close to £10,000 an acre and rural housing commanding prices well beyond the reach of people making a living from farming, establishing a smallholding is a considerable challenge for anyone who does not have savings running a long way into six figures. Renting agricultural land is cheaper than buying it, but the Farm Business Tenancies introduced in 1995 offer no security. County councils are empowered by law to provide for this demand, and could have done so in some cases by subdividing non-economic farms; but instead too many cash-strapped local governments have opted to asset-strip their farm estate.

A year later another Somerset County farm near Glastonbury came up for auction. Chris Black was interested in acquiring one of the lots, comprising three fields situated between a horseshoe factory and a scrap yard adjacent to the village of Barton St David. It was called Plotgate because, long before the 1908 Small Holdings and Allotments Act, the land had been divided into allotment strips. Chris thought it looked like a suitable site for a development of low impact, affordable, live–work dwellings with access to some agricultural land. I agreed, but I also thought it proper to register a protest against its sale. The other slight problem was that Chris no longer had any money left to speak of, having sunk all his cash into a watermill that he had bought cheap at an auction, only to find out that a much larger sum was required for repairs.

On the morning of the auction, Chris picked me up, and over lunch we visited a couple of his friends who he wanted to persuade to invest some money in Plotgate. His tactic was to uncork a bottle of wine in the hope of loosening their purse strings, but the larger portion of the bottle was consumed by him, and no pledges were forthcoming. By the time we got to the hotel where the auction was to be held that afternoon, Chris was quite squiffy, but that did not stop him downing another pint or two at the bar.

The auctioneer tapped his gavel to begin the sale. I strode up to the front and launched into a rant lambasting the council's policy of selling farms and the auction house's complicity in the process. The auctioneer tried to silence me, so I assured him that I would only be a few minutes. 'I'll call the police!' he warned. 'Go ahead,' I responded and continued. The auctioneer summoned assistance from a reluctant member of the hotel staff who made a half-hearted attempt to bodily remove me.

Undeterred I finished my tirade, and returned to my seat next to Chris, to a scatter of applause.

The bidding began on the lot that Chris was after. The auctioneer was perhaps surprised to see the fellow I was sitting next to raising his hand. As the bids escalated, another group of Glastonbury hippies whom we knew entered the fray. Chris shouted across the room: 'Marco, don't bid against me, I'll cut you in.' That sort of collusion is strictly against the rules, but the auctioneer was in no mood for more rumpus and let it pass. Marco stopped bidding and the hammer came down on Chris's bid at a price slightly under £100,000.

It must help to be plastered to buy a plot of land for a hundred grand when you have hardly a penny to your name. I was beginning to worry about Chris's sanity, but within a week he had secured a loan from Triodos Bank. Several years passed while the hoped-for affordable housing development failed to materialise. Nobody was willing to take on the challenge of co-ordinating a random selection of prospective residents and steering the scheme through the planning permission labyrinth.

The agricultural land on the other hand was soon taken up by smallholders – a community supported farm that now supplies vegetables locally through a box scheme; and a quarter acre greenhouse erected by Pete Wright, late of Tinker's Bubble. Chris found other people to take over payment of the loan. His gamble had turned out to be more effective than my protest action at ensuring that the land continued to provide plots for landless farmers. Since local authorities were failing in their duty to provide land, perhaps some other body needed to be taking the job on?

At about the same time Alex Lawrie moved into the unit next to my own at Flaxdrayton Farm. With his clipped accent and well-groomed appearance he could have passed as an aspiring Tory MP – but the last time I had seen him he had his arm D-locked into a hole in the road at the MII eviction. Alex ran an enterprise that specialised in setting up co-operative ventures, then bailing out and letting others get on with it.

That meshed well with what Chapter 7 was doing. We hatched a plan for an organisation that would buy land and then sell or lease 'oven-ready' smallholdings. In other words we would raise some loan capital, buy a suitable plot of land at agricultural prices, obtain approval for some farm buildings, subdivide the land into say three holdings, apply for residential planning permission on each of them and sell or lease them at a price much lower than a normal residential property.

For the purpose we founded a not-for-profit business in 2007 called The Ecological Land Co-op (ELC), which eventually managed to scrape together enough loanstock to buy about twenty acres, the minimum area feasible for a group of three holdings. We examined three or four sites before we settled for land at a place called Greenham Reach not far from Wellington, Somerset. The ELC then engaged Zoe Wangler to negotiate with the local planning authority, who viewed the project as a very strange fish. They required Zoe to select applicants for each of the three plots who had to draw up business plans for their holdings, even though those particular people might not be the eventual occupiers of the plots. A planning application for temporary permission was lodged in 2012, rejected by the committee despite the recommendation of the planning officer and allowed at a Public Inquiry in 2013. It had taken six years from the founding of the co-op to winning planning permission. I contributed little to the co-op after the first two years, and it was largely due to Zoe's persistence and expertise that the planning application succeeded.

That planning victory demonstrated that the model could work and ELC began to acquire a track record that attracted more funding. A second site was acquired in Sussex, which again had to overcome planning resistance, and by 2020 the organisation had five sites in England and Wales in different stages of development. Why a fledgling independent organisation has had to take this on when it could be done so much more quickly and efficiently by local authorities is a mystery, but that's Thatcherism for you.

The other boost to the fortunes of the UK's growing smallholder movement has been the founding, in 2013, of the Landworkers' Alliance. Initially proposed by Jyoti Fernandes, the LWA is a union representing small-scale farmers and forestry workers. It advocates agro-ecology, food sovereignty and access to land for small farmers and is affiliated to Via Campesina, the confederation of 182 unions representing some 200 million small farmers around the world. By 2021 the LWA had grown to 1,600 members – still a lot less than the 10,000 adherents of the Confédération Paysanne, a similar union launched in France in 1987 to 'represent peasants opposed to productivist agriculture'. But then the *néoruraux* in France tend to be ahead of the back-to-the-landers in the UK.

Flaxdrayton

Three options present themselves in the course of adult life: living on your own, living with one other adult, or living with lots of them. All are challenging, and it takes some people years to find out for themselves which is the preferable, or least objectionable, of the three.

From 2006 to 2010 I lived on my own in my office and caravan at Flaxdrayton Farm. I'd never spent anywhere near that long alone before. It was OK, a bit lonely sometimes, but uncomplicated and it gave me plenty of time, which I filled mostly by writing and promoting scythes – too much of the former really because I started to get tubby. Being without a car and reliant on a push bike and trailer didn't seem to keep me slim. Giving up smoking made things worse.

Chapter 7 was still functioning, but after Jyoti moved to Fivepenny Farm I was running it single handed. I stopped doing planning consultancy and acting for people in appeals. There were now other planning consultants who were familiar with the issues faced by smallholders and low impact builders. But I still faced a flow of phone calls and email enquiries from people seeking advice, mostly about residential permission. Some were smallholders who, if they ran a competent enterprise, had a good chance of success, though often at appeal. Some were people who had been living unlawfully in a barn, a cabin, a caravan or a yurt in the woods, usually because they didn't have anywhere else to go. They had a chance of obtaining a certificate of lawful use if they had been resident on site long enough to become immune from enforcement.

But about half the people seeking advice were neither of these – they were best described as 'lifestylers' or 'downsizers'. They didn't aim to earn their living from agriculture – they wanted to build themselves an affordable ecohome in a rural situation, perhaps with a workshop or studio on site, or with access to a small amount of agricultural land – enough for a large garden and some chickens or a pig. There was and still is a huge demand for this sort of self-build development and it would be such a simple matter to draw up planning policies to allow them on the edge of villages, where they would help to support local schools and services. I have spent a lot of effort arguing for such policies in both English and Welsh planning circles and got nowhere. It was disappointing that the architects of One Planet Development in Wales ignored the needs of these people and focused solely on the tiny number of people who wanted to achieve self-sufficiency in the middle of the open countryside (or at least thought that was what they wanted).

Meanwhile The Land Is Ours was now a shadow of its former self, and no one was keen on maintaining its newsletter, so we took over its mailing list, and combined it with Chapter 7's to produce a new magazine. The first issue of *The Land* appeared in 2006, edited by Jyoti and myself, and with a format designed by Lilia Patterson. It introduced itself as a magazine 'written by and for people who believe that the roots of justice, freedom, social security and democracy lie not so much in access to money, or to the ballot box, as in access to land and its resources'.

The last paragraph of its manifesto read: 'Rome fell; the Soviet Empire collapsed; the stars and stripes are fading in the west. Nothing is forever in history, except geography. Capitalism is a confidence trick, a dazzling edifice built on paper promises. It may stand longer than some of us anticipate, but when it crumbles, the land will remain.'

Fifteen years later *The Land* magazine has lasted rather longer than some of us anticipated. It is edited, published and distributed by a small team of part-time workers; Gill Barron, Mike Hannis from King's Hill and I have all been working on it for more than ten years, and Gill works tirelessly on the distribution. Special issues have focused on matters such as The Enclosure of the Commons, The Luddites, Land Grabs, Human Population, Rewilding, Livestock, Water, and Fire. In respect of illustrations, the magazine has remained resolutely black and white, which means that we shun photographs with poor contrast, and seek out line-drawings, woodcuts and engravings. While a good photo can capture a moment in time, hand-drawn prints with high contrast are visually striking and a more effective vehicle than photos for conveying detailed information.

Many people who have never worked on a magazine don't realise how much work goes into producing seventy-two pages of ephemera. After each issue goes to bed, my feeling is 'never again'. We only sell about 2,500 copies and there are 68 million people in Britain, so it's tempting to wonder what is the point? But then, how can we disappoint the people who re-subscribe saying things like '*The Land* is a ray of light, keep up the good work'?

My other pre-occupation during my solitary spell at Flax-drayton was writing a book. Another one! This one was about the environmental impact of meat. I started to research it because the vegetarian diet that was the rule at Tinker's Bubble while I lived there seemed perverse. We were producing pork and beef as a by-product of the dairy cows, yet declining to eat them, and instead importing vegetable oil, soya products, nuts and various other kinds of fat and protein from the other side of the globe – a curious anomaly for a so-called self-sufficient community. On the other hand, some vegan arguments about the unsustainability of meat and dairy production were ostensibly strong ones.

In this dispute I occupied the middle ground between vegans and intensive livestock farmers, a refreshing change from being at a far end of the political spectrum. After lengthy research, I concluded that some meat has a negligible environmental impact because it is a by-product of an agricultural ecology primarily focused on producing grains and vegetables. I called this 'default meat'. On the other hand, growing grains specifically to feed to livestock is inefficient and ecologically unsustainable in an overpopulated world. It was an unremarkable conclusion but one that both vegans and factory farmers find hard to swallow.

Monkton Wyld

I nearly abandoned the meat book in 2008, when Jyoti proposed that I should apply for the position of land manager at Monkton Wyld Court, a rural community between Lyme Regis and Axminster. I had known of Monkton Wyld for many years without ever going there. It was one of those places that made an income by hosting alternative events – straw bale building courses, yoga retreats, gay shamanic drumming and so on – not quite my cup of tea. It seemed to have a high turnover of members. More than once a bunch of fresh faces had turned up at

Tinker's Bubble saying, 'Hi, we are the new people at Monkton Wyld, pleased to meet you.'

By 2008, the place had become so run-down that the trustees who owned the house and grounds had thrown everybody out and were looking for a new team. I paid a visit, passing quickly over the neo-gothic pile that was the main house and making a beeline for the farmyard, a group of single-storey masonry buildings arranged around three sides of a courtyard overlooking a south-facing hillside pasture. It was just the sort of yard that a chap of my persuasion dreams of. There were three Guernsey cows and I doubt if there was half a bucket of milk a day between all of them. Jyoti mentioned that there were moves to convert the yard into holiday cottages: she knew I would covet it, and want to save it.

Some days later I attended a trustees' meeting and outlined a hesitant proposal for taking over the management of the farm and dairy. One of the trustees vetoed my proposal and instead they engaged a well-known permacultural designer to manage the land. I went back to my book.

Two years later, when the finished book was at the publishers, the post became vacant again. I was by now desperate to get out of the office. Taking over a farmyard with five acres of grass and a 'market' for the milk on site looked like a good opportunity. I drew up a more detailed proposal, which was provisionally accepted, and went for a trial week at the community.

It was a cold snap just before Christmas 2009. The temperature was well below freezing, and they put me in a room with no heater and a window that wouldn't shut. It was indeed a trial, but I survived. I liked the way the place was now organised. Everyone living there had a role in the operation of the place as a business; people couldn't join simply because they 'wanted to live in a community'. There were also obligatory five minute meetings every morning at 8.30. This was a much tighter ship than Tinker's Bubble, and I wasn't the skipper. I was accepted and moved there in March 2010.

The history of Monkton Wyld Court, I soon found out, was chequered. In the early 1840s, Elizabeth Hodson, an extremely rich widow, sought a sinecure for her son-in-law, the Reverend Robert Hutchings, possibly to prevent him taking her daughter with him to his native India. She persuaded the Bishop of Salisbury to create the new parish of Monkton Wyld (population 350) by hiving off land from two existing parishes. She then commissioned a prominent disciple of Pugin, Richard Carpenter, to design a church of disproportionate magnificence for so tiny a parish, and a twenty-five roomed rectory to match, not to mention an eight-roomed stable block. The humble farmyard that I occupied predated all this.

Such a spread would normally require a home farm, or else an endowment for its maintenance, and Mrs Hodgson did leave an endowment of £1,000 for this purpose. However this was deemed insufficient to deal with the maintenance cost by the end of the century, so the church sold the rectory in 1901, and presumably pocketed anything that remained of the endowment.

In 1940, Carl and Eleanor Urban opened Monkton Wyld as a progressive school, on similar lines to A.S. Neill's Summerhill. By all accounts – pupils' and teachers' – it functioned very well at least until the death of its founders in the early 1960s. But in the climate of the 1970s it became too libertarian for its own good. Pupils were regularly caught shoplifting, and the school gained a reputation amongst the local youth as a place to score dope. In 1971 the Dorset Drug Squad conducted a raid and after reading the diary of a 14-year-old girl, unlawfully interviewed 26 of the girl pupils, asking them whether they had ever had sexual intercourse. There is a charming TV documentary about the school made in 1972, which begins with a girl pupil insisting that the school's reputation as a 'shag-shop' was unjustified. But the school's overdraft kept doubling in size throughout the 1970s, and in 1981 there was a damning report from the Chief Inspector of Schools. In the following year seven out of nine teachers voted to close it down.

At this point some of the teachers contrived to change the charitable status of Monkton Wyld from a school to an 'education centre' run by a resident community. That (with some adjustment) has been its official status for the last four decades. How to interpret the term 'education' is open to debate, not least by the Charity Commission. In the eleven years that I have lived there we have held courses on matters as diverse as tantric therapy, singing, cob-building and cheese-making; we have run kindergarten classes, forest schools, toddler groups and lessons for home-educated kids; we have hosted school visits, from local primary schools and private boarding schools, and we take in apprentices and volunteers. All in the name of 'education'.

Unfortunately education doesn't pay the bills, at least not those required for the maintenance of a 170-year-old mansion and the salaries of those who maintain it. The only thing we have found that will do that is 'bums in beds'. We have forty beds in a dozen rooms in the house, and the charity has its commercial arm whose purpose is to fill them by whatever means possible: conferences, courses, weddings, private parties, B&B guests, and school reunions. We also have a pub in a garden shed that helps to mitigate the Victorian atmosphere of the architecture. Pursuing this strategy improved finances from the rather perilous state they were in when I arrived in 2010, to the point where we can carry out necessary repairs on the house and pay everyone who lives and works here the equivalent of a living wage (or at least could do until the COVID pandemic closed us down).

That's not a bad achievement. I can't think of any other residential community that provides a living for all its members and their children without any exterior funding. Admittedly

I'd rather live in a community that made its living from agriculture and forestry, than from one that made its living from 'hospitality'. Catering for other people means having to meet their standards rather than your own. We are part of the service economy, successors to the servants that once ministered to the needs of the rector and his family. But land work is underpaid by society, and on balance I prefer living in a community that succeeds in making its living from hospitality, to one that fails to do so from land work.

It is a commonly held view that communities are reliant on one strong personality to hold them together. That is not the case at Monkton Wyld where there is no dominant figure; each person is responsible for their own field of activity, but is answerable to the community for their performance. Consensus decision-making works fairly well on that basis. If it did break down then the trustees would step in.

Another common view is that successful communities are held together by a collective philosophy, religious belief or ideology. In the case of Monkton Wyld, our collective purpose is to keep this potentially dysfunctional Victorian pile in working order. Personal animosities between residents, which of course always exist, are not allowed to interfere with the pursuit of this objective, and so are less likely to balloon out of control. Nothing bodes worse, in my view, than 'feelings meetings' called to resolve interpersonal problems or plumb the depths of the communal psyche – all they usually do is focus disproportionate attention on conflicts that are frankly tedious, and usually blow over or settle down if ignored. Occasionally we get visitors, or prospective members who want to promote this kind of collective narcissism and I'm glad to say they get pretty short shrift from most of our members. 'Least said, soonest mended' is not a solution for all ills, but it is the policy to be preferred in the first instance.

This is not to suggest that Monkton Wyld has achieved a state of benign stability. As I write it is going through a post-lockdown crisis and for all I know, by the time you read this it might have gone tits up. Communities are volatile and can move from safe to sorry pretty quickly; and they are fragile because, as Chris Smaje puts it, 'the costs of walking away are too low'. In 2015, Monkton Wyld was subject to an aggressive takeover bid by a rogue trustee who, amongst other gambits, commissioned a report from consultants Driver Jonas on the feasibility and economics of selling the entire property. He had been, we discovered, a trustee of no less than sixteen other charities, one of which had sold off a hostel for homeless people in London for £11 million. Fortunately he was seen off, largely thanks to Jyoti Fernandes, who was still on the board of trustees.

The most common focus of disputes in communities these days is the war between vegans and meat eaters – with lacto-vegetarians in the middle. At Monkton we have navigated this problem in this manner: the main kitchen is vegetarian and serves vegan meals and dishes on request, while the outdoor kitchen under an open-sided roof in the garden is available for cooking meat, which is a free by-product of our farming system. It is used perhaps once a week, with the result that meat-eating is a special and festive event. The other advantage for us carnivores is that the waste food from the vegetarian kitchen and dining room can be fed to the pigs without risk, thus amplifying the supply of sausages.

Communities as a movement appear to have absorbed a few lessons on maintaining harmony over the 150 years. Left-wing proto-hippie communities in the nineteenth century were prone to collapsing within a few years of their establishment. John Ruskin's project, St George's Farm, founded in 1877 in Derbyshire, lasted just two years. Julius Wayland's 'co-operative commonwealth' called the Ruskin Colony established on 1,000 acres in Tennessee in 1894 had a meteoric rise and fall. By 1897 it boasted 250 members, a printing press and a canning factory. In 1899 it was dissolved as a result of internal legal disputes.

By contrast a decent proportion of the rural communes established in the UK between 1970 and 1985, typically in former stately homes that nobody else wanted at the time, are still in existence: for example, Beech Hill, Birchwood Hall, Canon Frome Court, Crabapple, Laurieston Hall, Monkton Wyld, Redfield, Old Hall. I doubt whether anyone has made a statistical comparison, but it is possible that rural communities are more stable than nuclear families in the UK, 42 per cent of which end in divorce and have an average lifespan of twelve years.

The family, as a social unit, has become nucleated and fragile. It is also notoriously inefficient. Communities offer economies of scale, both ecological and financial, over a wide spectrum of activities: transport, heating, cooking, housing, laundry, packaging, childcare, entertainments and so on. If governments deigned to look at social solutions to the environmental crisis as well as technical ones, then support for so-called intentional communities and co-housing ought to be high on their list.

Cows

Unlike a nuclear family, a community provides an economic foundation for a viable farming operation at a scale appropriate to its size. Monkton Wyld with its quota of visitors and volunteers is well-suited to a small herd of three cows, and indeed has supported just such a herd since 1982, apart from the two years prior to my arrival. In fact a functioning micro dairy goes back to 1941 when the school began. It may well be the oldest dairy enterprise of its size in Britain.

When I arrived most of the infrastructure for providing this was still in place: a milking parlour with stalls for six cows, cowsheds and a small dairy. Not so long ago there were thousands of such steadings around the country, supporting up to a dozen cows. Every stately home possessed one and so did countless humble smallholdings; the cash flow of family farms was guaranteed by regular payments from the Milk Marketing Board for a few churns left out for collection every morning. But by 2010 virtually all had either been left to go derelict, or else been converted into holiday cottages.

Monkton Wyld's dairy farm was on the way to a similar fate. There were all the symptoms of a hippie commune in decline. The milking parlour and cowsheds were full of plastic guttering, unused beehives, broken tools, old timber and bags of rubbish. One room was stuffed with detritus from courses in which children were taught to manufacture hideous contraptions out of yoghurt pots, toilet rolls, plastic bags and all the other effluvia of capitalist culture. A tile was missing from the roof above the beehives: instead of replacing the tile – a ten minute job – someone had placed corrugated iron inside to divert the dripping water away from the beehives onto a tie beam, which as a result had rotted away.

The state of the land was similar. The pasture, which hadn't been grazed or mown for two years, was thick with yellowing tussocks, while briar and bracken patches were invading from all sides. A half-acre orchard was completely engulfed in six foot high brambles and bracken. The fencing was in total disrepair. Even today, if you dig into the earth through decades of top soil, you are likely to uncover hippie archaeology – rotting carpets, plastic sheeting, or woven 'tarpaulins' that disintegrate into thousands of polypropylene strands – indicating that the ground had once been 'mulched' or was the site of an old sweat lodge.

All of this decay could be remedied. It was not a priority for the community, which had more pressing matters to address on the main house. But the rent I was paying Monkton Wyld for accommodation for the scythe business covered the cost of installing fencing and carrying out repairs. My old friend Gill Barron, now a well-known painter, came to visit, decided to stay, and helped me get set up. Eleven years later, I'm glad to say, she is still here. Within a few months we had bought one Jersey cow, and borrowed another. Within a few years we had rented a further three acres and milked three Jerseys.

Now, a decade later, the dairy is still functioning, usually with three cows, though we went down to two during the pandemic. Our oldest, Folly, has been with us ten years and is still in top form. After my half-cocked attempts at agriculture in previous years, it is good to have tumbled on something that works.

The reason it works is because the cows, the land and the community are in near-perfect symbiosis. The cows benefit because we provide them with the winter feed they cannot harvest for themselves in the form of hay, with medical care, and with a more painless death than nature can offer. In return they each give us about four thousand litres of rich creamy milk a year, containing enough fat, protein and calories to feed four people indefinitely. They produce this by grazing Britain's most abundant, easily grown and biodiverse crop, grass, keeping bracken and brambles at bay, and letting the sunlight in to allow meadow plants to flourish, along with butterflies and other insects. Moreover about 85 per cent of the nutrients that a cow ingests come out the rear end. She harvests biomass, chips and shreds it, bioactivates and digests it, transports it, and extrudes it as the manure that is vital for our acre of vegetable garden, all without using a gram of fossil fuel. Meanwhile the whey from our cheese, along with vegetable and food waste, goes to feed our pigs.

Our cows are the backbone of a traditional mixed farming system that enables us to provide thirty people a day with healthy home-produced food, and to do so with zero packaging and zero food miles. Perhaps, given today's nucleated social structure, this cannot be widely replicated, but it can be scaled up. There is no reason why schools, hospitals and prisons couldn't run their own dairy farm providing, in the case of school children, the free milk that Thatcher took away – a nourishing and educational alternative to sugary carbonated beverages. That was precisely what Monkton Wyld did when it was a school feeding seventy pupils and staff from the milk of six cows.

And what if villages reclaimed some ownership of their land, and members of the community supported the agriculture that flourished around them? That's what real Community Supported Agriculture should look like – not just green hippie types driving miles to pick up their ethically sound vegetables, but every rural settlement with its farm shop and its milk dispensing machine selling all the fresh dairy produce, meat, bread, fruit and vegetables that its farmers can sensibly produce. This must surely be the direction rural people should be taking if we are to eliminate fossil fuels and plastic packaging, while safeguarding the complex relationship we have forged with the natural world through traditional agriculture. The alternative looks increasingly likely to be a diet of hydroponic and lab-grown junk food, courtesy of a hydrogen-powered urban bio-technocracy.

A revival of micro dairies would also bridge the gulf between the majority of citizens, especially children, and the farm animals and plants that provide their nourishment; this rupture is a direct result of the centralisation of livestock production. Visitors to Monkton Wyld come to gawp at us at milking time and bring their children to view the spectacle as if it was an educational rite of passage, when once it was as banal an activity as changing a baby's nappy. A generation of urban youth is subjected to propaganda about what goes on in intensive dairy farms, some of it accurate but most of it exaggerated, and comes away with an erroneous interpretation of the bond between cows and humans. Yes that relationship is open to abuse – as is the bond between married couples, or parent and child – but that doesn't prevent it being basically a benign one.

Like all farm animals, over the course of several thousand years, cows have adapted to domestication. Literally, that means acceptance into the household (though in the case of cows, not the sitting room). For the most part, cows and oxen are pretty chilled creatures, more so than horses, pigs, sheep, chickens or dogs, all of which are prone at times to over-excitement or panic. Whether grazing, giving suck or chewing the cud, their presence soothes the human spirit. The act of ruminating has become a metaphor for composed contemplation. Even vegans like domesticated cows, and those that visit our farm are hard put to find anything to object to.

Hindsight

There is one little matter that takes the shine off our farming enterprise – close to a quarter of people who come to Monkton Wyld, as residents, volunteers or guests, won't consume milk or dairy products. We produce nearly all the dairy products we need from the grass that grows around us, but to feed these dissidents we have to buy in expensive and often imported substitutes – oat and soya drink, plant-based yoghurt, margarine, tofu, nuts and so on.

There are two main reasons why people won't drink the milk. One is the prevalence of veganism, and dairy scepticism amongst the urban young, who are currently bombarded with anti-dairy propaganda. Oatly, suppliers of an oat-based drink that costs nearly twice as much as cows' milk in Tesco, but has only half the nutrients, deploys much of its massive profits in a high-profile, anti-dairy campaign specifically targeting adolescents. The mainstream dairy industry operating on tiny margins cannot afford this scale of publicity. Gone are the days when the Milk Marketing Board could plaster billboards with the slogan 'Drinka Pinta Milka Day'. Happily, some of these discerning consumers come round to drinking our milk once they see that the way our cows are treated bears no resemblance to that portrayed by the vegan lobby.

The other objectors are those who are or claim to be lactose intolerant. It is impossible to know how many people are amongst the 5 per cent of Europeans estimated to be genuinely intolerant, and how many just like to think they are. We have the same problem with the growing number of people who say they are gluten intolerant: a few will be coeliac, some may have other reactions to gluten or to wheat, some may think they do, and some may simply be following a fashion. Most of the time we have no way of knowing, so we cater for dietary idiosyncrasies in all their variety, at considerable extra effort and expense. But then there are some who like playing silly buggers: the vegan who has insisted on dairy-free meals all week and then decides that our home-made ice cream is an exception; the man who demands a gluten-free diet but is happy to down three pints of beer.

It's a growing issue nationwide, but we attract an unusually high proportion of these fussy eaters, and they tend to be clustered in events of a certain kind, notably yoga retreats. Courses on practical matters such as building or farming tend to have few or none at all. So what's going on?

In addressing these questions my father's book comes to mind. Refusing food is a favourite ploy of the spoilt child, of the infant throwing a tantrum against parental authority. Hunger strike is the last resort of the disempowered, the Pyrrhic revenge of the unjustly imprisoned. To what extent is dietary dissidence (from vegetarianism and macrobiotics to raw foodism or the Paleo regime) the preoccupation of those intent on controlling what goes inside their body, because they feel powerless to affect what happens outside?

It may help to view this phenomenon within a wider context. At Monkton Wyld we are a practical bunch – we have to be to keep the house, the grounds, the room service and the kitchen functioning. We try to put on courses that teach useful skills, and events that address social and environmental problems. But our bread and butter mostly come from hiring out our facilities to groups whose concern is their inner self. Yoga retreats dominate, and there are the customary assortment of shamanic rituals, primal therapies and voyages of tantric self-discovery. The programme for one group included events such as these:

> *Shamanic Journeying: Journey to the beat of my drum to meet your spirit guide or spirit animal for a particular intention.*
> *Circle Time: In this circle we will lovingly include all of ourselves and each other ... I will be bringing my whole self, including my personal practices and my Shadow Work facilitation experience.*
> *Mindfulness in Nature Walk: Spacious time in nature to slow down and connect sensorially and sensually to ourselves and all of life, nourished by mother earth and father sky.*
> *Cacao and Sacred Song: Open your voice and heart with ceremonial Guatemalan cacao and allow the vibrations of the voice to support a deeper dropping into Being.*

It is this persistent streak of quasi-religious narcissism within the hippie movement that lends force to my father's Spoiled Child thesis. I wouldn't want to deny people their personal heaven and there is nothing inherently wrong with finding enlightenment in a mug of cocoa. What is dangerous is when enthusiasts delude themselves that such activities bring benefits to the public estate or to the natural world.

For a few years, we hired our hall once a week out to a group who practised what they called Dances of Universal Peace. They arrived from who-knows-where in their motor cars to spend a couple of hours circle dancing. Again, there is nothing egregious about holding hands and prancing about to the exhalations of an accordion; I've done plenty of that myself. But to consider that this might have the slightest impact upon the scale of global conflict is a narcissistic delusion. Possibly if they conducted regular dances on the steps of the US Embassy, or beneath the wall that separates Israel from Gaza, they might eventually have some influence on warring factions, though even that is questionable.

But it is not as though the hippie movement has a monopoly on narcissism; nowadays we see it everywhere. We live in the era of the selfie, where people accumulate 'likes' on social media. We adulate elite athletes who perform feats of physical prowess for no purpose other than to prove they are better at it than anyone else. Some aspects of the identity politics that is prevalent within left wing circles today are curiously solipsistic. If my father's book on *The Spoiled Child of the Western World* has any distinction it is that it grasped something of the coming narcissism of the times – though Henry never uses the word, which at the time mainly signified a psychological condition defined by Sigmund Freud. It was Christopher Lasch in his 1979 book *The Culture of Narcissism* who popularised the term and gave it a broader meaning.

However hippie culture was to influence human development in one other important way that both my father and I failed to anticipate. I am writing this book on a Macintosh computer made by a company that was both pioneered and revived by someone who in the 1970s had long hair, took LSD, dropped out of college, travelled to India, studied Zen Buddhism and lived on a commune in Oregon. Steve Jobs, in his own words, was 'clearly a hippie and all the people I worked with were clearly in that category too'.

Jobs and his colleagues weren't essential to the development of computers: joyless nerds such as Bill Gates were capable of bringing on the technology. But in the early years the freaks were ahead of the game. When I first encountered friends with computers, in 1990, they waxed lyrical about Apple Mac, who, I was told, refused to allow their products to be used for nuclear weapons, while IBM were the computer of choice for the military industrial complex. At *The Ecologist* in 1992, we used Macs with the 'graphic user interface system' of icons activated by mice – while our IBM computer, kept for administrative purposes, struggled on with MS DOS, which required typing painful formulae to execute any command. At the time it looked like the triumph of the hippies over the nerds.

But IBM and Microsoft simply pirated Mac's graphic system with their Windows 95. Then along came the internet, and Google, and smartphones, and Facebook. Within thirty years, the nerds have created the cyber universe that we know today (owned by a handful of corporations that are individually richer than many countries) that is now killing off libraries, post offices, high streets, auctions and half of the institutions we grew up with. The idea of there being anything benignly alternative about computers is losing credibility. Yes, for the hippie geeks there are still open-source systems, such as Linux, but frankly, who except the geeks cares? What exactly are the advantages of making financial transactions within the time-span of a nanosecond or expending more energy than it takes to power a country so that speculators can collect Bitcoins? The computing power that enables scientists to unravel genetic codes and create intelligent robots lays the human race open to greater existential evil than it ever could provide in the way of benefits. With all due respect to the hippie credentials of

Messrs Jobs and Brand, that's not the alternative society I signed up for.

Happily what I did sign up for is still alive and kicking, even if, with the onset of age and the demands of the farm, I am sometimes less able to participate. The Climate Camps held from 2006 to 2009 adopted the well-tried occupation tactics to highlight the threat of global warming. In 2011 the Occupy movement outside St Paul's Cathedral placed a welcome focus on economic issues and might have prompted a few youngsters to look up Karl Marx. Protest camps, along with some helpful earthquakes, have prevented fracking from happening on any scale in Britain. The current campaign against the HS2 high-speed rail link between London and Birmingham has revived the tactics of the road protests, notably with its protest camp and tunnels at Euston station.

But it was the Easter 2019 Extinction Rebellion that lifted the art of the hippie protest camp to new heights. Four sites in London were occupied for ten days. A pink boat sailed into Oxford Circus; Waterloo Bridge was captured and converted into a public park with forty-five trees, a skateboard ramp, a speaker's podium, theatre, music, yoga and all manner of inventive props. It was a triumph of anarchist organisation. Though it disrupted the flow of London traffic, the public was surprisingly sanguine, and the press was almost supportive – even the police behaved quite well. Along with the extraordinary Greta Thunberg, the rebellion really did manage to trigger a change in consciousness. A week later, Labour leader Jeremy Corbyn proposed a motion in parliament that a 'climate emergency' should be declared, and the Tory government accepted the motion without a vote, though as I write it has yet to do anything very convincing to address this emergency. That will be the focus of the next battle.

By way of comparison, there is no way that during the Road Protests of the early 1990s we could have occupied four strategic areas of London such as Waterloo Bridge and held them for nearly a week, especially with such sympathetic press coverage. We could not have mustered and maintained those numbers for an environmental cause and, even if we could have, we would have been swept away by the police in a matter of hours, as indeed we were at the poll tax protest.

Meanwhile an evolving post-industrial peasantry continues the centuries-old struggle for access to land against forces of enclosure. The engrossers of land, keen to deploy robots, precision technologies and gene editing to replace those pesky labourers, now farm such huge haciendas that, funnily enough, there are not very many of these landowners left. The Oxford Real Farming Conference, first staged with a hundred or so people in a church crypt in 2010, is now held in Oxford Town Hall and attracts more people than the mainstream Oxford Farming Conference down the road. The Landworkers' Alliance may one day be bigger than the National Farmers' Union. Via Campesina, to which the LWA is affiliated, is the largest federation of unions representing a single trade in the world – 200 million people fighting for (in Chris Smaje's words) a 'Small Farm Future'. At Monkton Wyld, as at any other small organic farm, we are visited by waves of youngsters from the UK and abroad, seeking a more fulfilling alternative to the opportunities offered them by mainstream capitalism. They represent an enquiring minority of their generation, not the majority. Aside from their smart-phones, they are not a lot different from how I and my friends were at that age. But now they do not have to strike off into the unknown and found a community at the age of twenty-three; they can visit or join an existing one and learn from our mistakes.

When you are young, and swept up in a revolutionary moment it's easy to believe there is everything to win. When you look back towards the end of a full life you realise you have just been treading water – one of many fighting a rearguard action for justice and ecological modesty against the forces of corporate greed and technological rapacity, who have wealth and power on their side. We can never win, because if ever we accede to power, power corrupts. But we can keep a check on these idiots, and limit or delay their excesses.

The weary trooper can at least take some credit for having played a role in this Manichaean confrontation, along with millions who have gone before. I am not just thinking of the celebrities – John Ball, Robert Kett, Gerrard Winstanley, William Cobbett, Feargus O'Connor, Henry Thoreau, Peter Kropotkin, Ralph Borsodi, Mohandas Gandhi and others; more of those whose names are forgotten, or recorded only in some historical footnote. The women and men who rose against the feudal pyramid in medieval peasant revolts, who questioned God, Monarch and the universe in the English Revolution, who tore down the fences of enclosing landlords, who defended handlooms by burning down cotton mills, who set up alternative communities in the New World, who deserted the colonial service or merchant navy to 'go native', who fought for the Paris Commune, or for anarchist collectives against the forces of Franco. The roll call of history is long, and our little *bobo* revolution at the end of the 1960s is trivial by comparison, but that was the part we were given to play.

Christmas Eve

According to certain mediaeval almanacs the human lifespan can be divided into months of the year with each month representing six years of life – from the day of your birth until your sixth birthday you are in January, then February covers from six till twelve, etc. On the 30 June you are 36, and the 31 December is your 72nd birthday. By that reckoning I am now, at the time of writing, on the very eve of Christmas, when it is traditionally time to take stock and enjoy the fruits of your labours.

One of the fruits of my labours is that I still have labours to perform. Let me be clear: I'm not one of those bronzed and wiry septuagenarians who take on challenges like rowing across the Atlantic. I'm pink and fat, and I avoid having to bend down to tie up my shoelaces. Yet despite this corporeal decadence, I can still milk the cows, muck out the yard and mow quarter of an acre of hay in a morning, and I intend to keep it up. I expect to die in bed with my boots on, having been too knackered and drunk to take them off.

The convenient fact is that small-scale dairying requires just the right amount of energy expenditure, and takes up just the right amount of time, for a reasonably fit person in their seventies or possibly their eighties. In Carl Larsson's pictorial documentation of a Swedish family farm, it is an older woman who peers out from behind the rump of the cow she is milking, or is tugged away to the pasture by her charge as she tries to converse with the artist at his easel. In India and in some countries in East Africa, widows are awarded dairy cows as an appropriate activity for single women. If we had real land-based communities in Britain instead of dormitory villages, then looking after a couple of dairy cows would be a viable and rewarding part-time option for fit senior citizens.

As I toddle up the hill with my bucket and my churns of milk, young men bare their torsos in the sunshine; nubile lasses swing mattocks. 'That is no country for old men,' wrote a sour W.B. Yeats in his early sixties. 'The young in one another's arms, birds in the trees.' He settles for sailing to Byzantium 'into the artifice of eternity'. But the farm where I hang out is a country that welcomes old men. I hope to stay there, with luck till February or March by the medieval almanac – long enough to see another spring come round, and the seeds of revolution burst into life once again.

Acknowledgements

My thanks are due to all those who helped me with this book, especially Charlotte Fairlie, Emma O'Grady, Carol Ann Highfield, Jane Barry, Andrew Sanger (whose contribution was reluctantly cut), Pius Wetzel, Moira Hirst, Chris Black, Mary Durling, Jyoti Fernandes, Tony Wrench, Alex Lawrie, Marion Rose and Camilo Liarte.

I would like to thank, in advance, anyone mentioned in this book for their forbearance if my memory of events differs from theirs. I also wish to thank my editor Brianne Goodspeed, for her enthusiasm and the work she put into it.

Most of all I must thank my unofficial editor and long-suffering companion, Gill Barron, to whom this book is lovingly dedicated.

About the Author

Simon Fairlie worked for twenty years variously as an agricultural labourer, vineworker, shepherd, fisherman, builder and stonemason before being ensnared by the computer in 1990. He was a co-editor of *The Ecologist* magazine for four years, until he joined a farming community in 1994 where he managed the cows, pigs and a working horse for ten years. He now runs a micro dairy at Monkton Wyld Court, a charity and co-operative in rural Dorset. Simon is a founding editor of *The Land* magazine, and he earns a living by selling scythes. He is the author of *Low Impact Development: Planning and People in a Sustainable Countryside* (1996) and *Meat: A Benign Extravagance* (2010).